Design for Aging Review **11**

AIA Design for Aging Knowledge Community

Design for Aging Review

AIA Design for Aging Knowledge Community

 THE AMERICAN INSTITUTE OF ARCHITECTS

Published in Australia in 2012 by
The Images Publishing Group Pty Ltd
ABN 89 059 734 431
6 Bastow Place, Mulgrave, Victoria 3170, Australia
Tel: +61 3 9561 5544 Fax: +61 3 9561 4860
books@imagespublishing.com
www.imagespublishing.com

National Library of Australia Cataloguing-in-Publication entry:

Author:	American Institute of Architects Design for Aging Center
Title:	Design for aging review / American Institute of Architects
Edition:	11th ed.
ISBN:	9781864704983 (hbk.)
Notes:	Previous ed. 2011
Subjects:	Older people—Dwellings—United States—Design and construction.
	Old age homes—United States—Design and construction.
	Barrier-free design for older people—United States.
	Architecture—Awards—United States.

Dewey Number: 725.56022273

Executive editor: Virginia Ebbert
Edited by Debbie Fry

Designed by The Graphic Image Studio Pty Ltd, Mulgrave, Australia
www.tgis.com.au

Pre-publishing services by United Graphic Pte Ltd, Singapore
Printed by Everbest Printing Co. Ltd in Hong Kong/China on 140 gsm GoldEast Matt Art

Contents

M Merit recipient
S Special Recognition recipient

AIA Foreword

According to legend, upon hearing Plato's definition of "man" as a "featherless biped," the cynic Diogenes burst into the room holding a plucked chicken. "Behold," he said, "your man!"

Defining what is unique to us as a species has never been easy. However, there is at least one trait that separates us from most of our fellow warm-blooded creatures – the way in which we age.

Americans who celebrate their 40th birthday this year can expect to live another 37.6 years on average. That's more than most animals, but the difference doesn't stop there. Long after most of us have stopped reproducing, we enjoy decades during which we can continue to learn and make positive contributions to our families and communities: this is evolution's way of giving our species the time to pass vital information on to future generations.

It's true that we can't move with as much agility, our inventory of wrinkles grows far more quickly than our bank balance, and body fat accumulates in unwanted places. However, barring serious illness, our cognitive skills show no dramatic deterioration right through middle age and often

beyond. This certainly has implications for how society prepares for the increasing number of men and women who live past 70, 80, and even 90 years of age. This is an important issue, and a relatively new one.

A hundred years ago, those who lived past middle age typically lived in the homes in which they were born, or with their children as part of an extended family. Surrounded by and interacting with different generations, their brains and bodies were constantly stimulated. Unless gravely ill, they helped mind the grandchildren, provided counsel to their own children, and carried out a host of chores. Even when they became ill, they were tended by relatives who fully expected to receive the same care when they were themselves weak or incapacitated.

In most industrialized countries the pattern has changed, and it has changed precisely at a time when the elderly are among the most rapidly growing segment of the population.

Global in its implications, the challenge of how best to provide for the aging demands a global response. This means developing a national, if not

an international policy that invites, among others, the participation not only of design professionals, but also business, industry, scientists, health-care providers, and elected leaders. As this latest edition of the *Design for Aging Review* shows, architects and other design professionals are engaging with this challenge in creative, caring ways that have earned their professions the right and the responsibility to take a leadership role in the conversation about aging.

However, such a conversation must not be framed as a matter, to put it crudely, of where and how to store the elderly. Nor can we take a single-minded approach that focuses primarily on affordability, sustainability, or aesthetics, although these are all important. Rather, we must be guided by a commitment to ensure the elderly will be housed and cared for in such a way that they can continue to be a contributing part of society, if not for their sake, then surely for ours. Because in the end, what we do for the elderly we do for ourselves, as we inevitably take their place in the cycle of life. For us, as well as for them, we must ensure that unlike Diogenes' man, they – and we – do not go uncared for or marginalized into that good night.

Jeffery Potter, FAIA
2012 AIA President

LeadingAge Foreword

In the early 1960s, John Cumming and Elaine Cumming wrote a classic book that helped revolutionize the treatment of mentally ill patients in state hospitals. The book is called *Ego & Milieu: Theory and Practice of Environmental Therapy*.

Cumming and Cumming discuss the "therapeutic power of the total environment." They argue that "environment itself should be the primary treatment as well as supporting or complementing other treatment." The importance of "normal" and "life-like environments" and the "creation of neighborhoods" are paramount.

This argument can equally be applied to senior care. Environments dictate what we believe about seniors, the people who care for them, and those who visit them. So, how do we challenge ourselves to create therapeutic environments? The goal is to create environments that have purpose in mind with respect to the quality of life of those who live and work in them.

I perused last year's edition of *Design for Aging Review* through the Cumming and Cumming lens.

It is chock-full of illustrations of their principles. New Bridge on the Charles wants to signal "abundant choice in living." Atlanta's Lenbrook has the intent of a "holistic sense of wellness." Porter Hills in Michigan wanted to reinforce "teamwork" among staff, so vital to quality care.

Last year I visited the Masonic Home of Kentucky. They brought the beauty of nature into the nursing home through creative photography. In fact, I toured their nursing home and could not tell I had been in a nursing home.

The Design for Aging Review continues to push all of us to challenge our beliefs about aging and reminds us of our responsibility to create health-fostering therapeutic environments that assure the aging experience is a fulfilling one.

The environment is a major determinant in whether or not we are successful in assuring quality of life for seniors. The DFAR process and award recipients serve as an inspiration for the next generation of senior living.

William L. (Larry) Minnix, Jr.
President and Chief Executive Officer
LeadingAge

Jury Statement

August 2011 marked the unveiling of the Martin Luther King Jr. National Memorial in Washington, DC. *The Design for Aging Review 11* (DFAR 11) jury joined many sightseers one spectacular evening to witness the new attraction and were reminded of Dr. King's unwavering commitment to compassionate change. As we gathered together to evaluate many diverse architectural submissions, we quickly realized that the panel of six providers and architects also shared a commitment to ongoing change. We were seeking architectural solutions that challenged our preconceptions of environments that promote quality of life and care for older adults.

This comprehensive review of architectural design trends for the aging serves as a snapshot of today's innovative solutions, and we hope that it will become a reference for providers, developers, users, advocates, architects, and interior, landscape, and other design professionals.

If it were possible to capture the theme of this year's deliberations, it would be "engagement." Award-winning projects addressed this concept in different ways. These were not artificial connections, but rather authentic relationships sending a clear message that neighborhood is important, whether the neighbors reside on-campus or within the greater community that the building or campus serves. This commitment was represented by projects that included, or were sited adjacent to, coffee shops, art galleries, retail, recreation centers, neighborhood parks, and convenient connections to public transportation.

Nowhere was this idea of engagement more evident than in the student competition, which appeared for the first time in DFAR 11. Student submissions from around the world emphasized the physical and social relationships between the buildings they designed and the cities that were enhanced by these designs. The jury commented that some of these submissions were among the most innovative of the entire process. Perhaps this perceived outcome is a result of student projects not being subjected to the functional and financial rigors of real-world initiatives. Or, could the students' visions stress a purpose and craft not diluted by past project stereotypes? Either way, we all hope that the next *Design for Aging Review* cycle will continue to connect the future of our trade to this most important building type.

Occupied projects and conceptual designs were not treated as equal. It is important to remember that those designs already constructed were envisioned two, three, four, or more years ago. Therefore, the jury held "paper architecture" to a much higher standard, with the understanding that these proposed solutions have benefitted from our own processes of lifelong learning and the progression of thought that informs senior living and care environments. LeadingAge currently highlights this priority on their website, with the phrase "Expanding the World of Possibilities for Aging." We think that this says it all!

As a review of design trends, we searched for projects that incorporated fresh ideas and those that challenged our own notions of purposeful living and care environments. Several well-executed, stand-alone CCRC campus submissions were appreciated by the panel of jurors for their skillful execution, but were not represented among the award winners because they echoed tested strategies of the past. DFAR 11 beckons submissions that exhibit conscientious solutions and research that advances environments for aging.

It is important to identify consistencies that the jury noticed during the evaluation process. We found it difficult to say whether these observations represent current fads, future trends, or if they are merely a product of the process of submitting a project for consideration and the related information that is requested. Noteworthy observations include:

- **Increased value on community engagement.** This was evidenced by the walkable and intergenerational locations, by the communal assets transparently located on the first floor of many buildings, adjacency to public transportation, and by the deliberate inventory of greater community destinations noted within walking distance of building sites.

- **Households and private rooms.** The household concept has been popular for several years. Only those considered exceptional and incorporating unique care strategies caught the attention of the panel. Very few healthcare submissions included semi-private rooms.

- **Affordable housing.** These submissions were architecturally among the most exciting projects reviewed. The perceived priority of affordable housing could be the result of the challenging economy that this country is currently enduring, or might reflect changing public priorities towards this building type that is in such high demand.

- **Inviting outdoor spaces.** The jury was most impressed with projects that included outdoor spaces that received equal design attention to their interior counterparts. These projects seemed to beckon residents, visitors, and the community to enjoy the entire site. Outdoor enrichment might be viewed from a favorite window or through active engagement in appropriately purposed outdoor spaces and pathways.

- **Repositioning.** Several submissions centered on repositioning older buildings and campuses originally constructed in the 60s, 70s, and 80s. As these organizations transform themselves into community centers for successful aging, many of the spaces and forms that functioned in the past have become obsolete in today's market. One such project was consistently recognized by the jury as a place that they would want to live. Well done!

- **Hospice.** Many alluring submissions were dedicated to hospice care. These projects were often rural and provided residents and families with options for private gathering and personalized choices of social engagement. Outdoor spaces enhanced these submissions offering intimate, contemplative garden spaces and scenic walking paths.

- **Dining choices.** Providers are trading their large dining rooms for varied spaces offering choices of dining style, menu, and atmosphere. Residents of all care levels are provided tasteful dining spaces reflecting quality consistent with independent living venues. One recognized project lured residents to an inviting outdoor venue of choice that included an event chef and preparation station.

- **Wellness.** Few campus submissions or independent living projects were reviewed that did not include a central wellness initiative. Whether it is mind, body, or spirit, a wellness focus dominated repositioning and other whole campus efforts designed to attract residents searching for places of meaning and personal growth.

- **Going green.** Sustainable efforts continued to increase, although not at the pace anticipated. As green technologies offer more aggressive financial pay-backs, we expect the related environmental strategies to be more common.

The jurors often asked themselves and each other "would I choose to live there?" This might be the ultimate barometer in a market where consumers have choice. I am happy to report that the answer to this question was often, YES! We have all witnessed the evolution in environments for aging, and most of us would not have responded positively to this question a generation ago.

An organization represented by one of our jurors uses the term "repriorment," which is defined as "discovering the joy of new directions and rethinking your shelved but not forgotten priorities, passions, and dreams." What a wonderful word. This is the principle that binds us together in the quest to create environments that elevate the care, position, and choices afforded to elders in our society and community. As we return to our daily responsibilities with renewed passion, we hope that the exceptional body of work contained within this volume elevates the expectations of providers and architects alike. It is this commitment for compassionate change that energizes all of us who collaborate to shape future senior living and care environments.

On behalf of the DFAR 11 Jury,
Dodd M. Kattman, AIA, LEED AP
Jury Chair

The Jury

Dodd Kattman, AIA

Dodd Kattman, AIA, is a founding partner of Morrison Kattman Menze, Inc., an architecture, planning, and interior design firm offering over 20 years of senior living and care project experience. Through his role as Senior Living Managing Partner, he dedicates time to design, research, publish and present topics that elevate the expectations of supportive environments that promote the process of aging with dignity.

Linda L. Lateana

Linda L. Lateana is Executive Director of Goodwin House Bailey's Crossroads, a continuing care retirement community in Falls Church, Virginia. She is a licensed Nursing Home Administrator and Preceptor with over 30 years of experience working with seniors in long-term care and community-based settings. She is a former member of the AAHSA House of Delegates and former Vice-Chair of the Board of Directors of the Virginia Association of Non-Profit Homes for the Aging. She has been a CCAC evaluator and has served on community boards. She recently guided her community through a $240 million expansion and renovation, completed in 2010.

Vicki Nelson, AIA

Vicki Nelson, AIA, is a Senior Partner with Diekema Hamann Architecture and Engineering based in Kalamazoo, Michigan. She is a member of the AIA's Design for Aging Knowledge Community and has been certified by the American College of Healthcare Architects. The better part of her 30-year career has been focused on the design of healing environments with an emphasis on environments for end of life care.

Betsie Sassen

Betsie Sassen currently serves as Assistant Vice-President, Community Initiatives for Mather LifeWays in Evanston, Illinois. In her role, she oversees the operations of three 'Mather's – More Than a Café' locations in Chicago. She also consults with other organizations, nationally and internationally, who are interested in replicating the Café Plus model. She is a published author with articles in *Nursing Homes/Long Term Care Management*, *Generations*, and *Seniors Housing and Care Journal*. She has been interviewed and quoted in various publications including *The New York Times*, *The Washington Post*, and *AARP Bulletin*. She is regarded as a thought leader in the field of aging, and has provided aging expertise through consulting, national task forces, and on radio shows.

Jack Carman, FASLA

Jack Carman, FASLA, president of Design for Generations LLC, is a Landscape Architect with over 20 years of experience in the analysis, planning, design, and management of outdoor spaces. As a design consultant, Jack has specialized in creating therapeutic exterior environments for senior communities and healthcare facilities. Jack is co-editor and contributing writer to the recently published book *Re-creating Neighborhoods for Successful Aging*. He is an adjunct faculty member at Temple University teaching "Healing Garden Design" and "Introduction to Horticultural Therapy." He is also an instructor at the Chicago Botanic Garden School of Healthcare, Garden Design Certificate Program.

Chris Keysor

Chris Keysor is responsible for the fiscal operations of Lenbrook Square in Atlanta, Georgia. In this capacity he is responsible for the accounting, financial management, and reimbursement for Lenbrook, as well as reporting this information to the various internal and external stakeholders. Prior to joining Lenbrook, Chris had been involved in over $2 billion of healthcare and senior living projects since 1989 in various financial capacities including as a CPA, Financial Planner, Financial Development Consultant and Investment Banker.

Design For Aging Review 11
AIA Juried Projects

Affordable
Building
Planning/Concept Design

David Baker + Partners Architects

Armstrong Place Senior Housing

San Francisco, California // BRIDGE Housing

Facility type: Independent Living, Onsite Social Service Office Space to Support Formerly Homeless Residents (Occupants of 23 Units)
Target market: Low Income/Subsidized
Site location: Urban; Brownfield site
Project site area (square feet): 35,000
Gross square footage of the new construction involved in the project: 131,800

Number of parking spaces added by the project: 31
The site is within 1000 feet of public transportation and everyday shopping and/or medical services. The project offers transport to nearby shopping, medical, and/or cultural services/amenities.
Provider type: Non Sectarian Non-Profit
Completion date: October 2010

Below: Third Street with retail, residential entry, and metro tracks
Photography: Brian Rose

Opposite: Armstrong Place Senior and Family Housing helps keep families together in San Francisco
Photography: Steve Proehl

Overall Project Description

This affordable senior rental apartment building is part of a complex development that fills a formerly industrial city block with a housing mix: affordable urban townhouses to keep growing families in the city and senior apartments to prevent seniors from living in isolation.

Leading a trend of transit-oriented development along the district's main business corridor, the development lies just a block from a new light-rail line, a park, a health center, and a public pool.

With 116 affordable rental units over five levels, the senior building serves as an anchor for the development, housing neighborhood-serving retail space and services, together with an iconic tower at the corner that signals a sense of place.

The building features apartments designed for independent living for residents 65 years and older, and 23 of the units are set aside for formerly homeless seniors participating in San Francisco's

Direct Access to Housing Program. These residents are eligible for intensive on-site social services that will assist them through the transition from homelessness to independent living.

One of the main goals is to serve local, extremely low-income seniors (individuals at or below 30 percent of Area Median Income). The current residents pay rent ranging from $0 to $635 per month, depending on income.

To reflect the historically African-American population of the neighborhood, design details are drawn from traditional African textiles and symbols. Textile-inspired paint and window arrangements combine to wrap the public face of the building in an interlocking quilt of color and pattern.

The building is LEED NC Gold Certified. It features many complementary green strategies, including stormwater management, solar arrays that heat domestic water and light the common spaces, and healthy interiors and materials.

The senior apartments overlook the park, the courtyard, or a landscaped mews that runs between the building and the family townhouse development. The mews – an extension of the city street grid – provides direct access to the surrounding neighborhood and serves as a walking path away from the main arterial roadway.

The adjacent townhouses flank a large central courtyard that features vegetable gardens, outdoor seating, and a picnic and play structure. The courtyard serves as both refuge and mid-block passage and is available to the population of the senior housing building.

This senior housing building is the second phase of a complex urban development planned and undertaken by the same developer, redevelopment agency, and design team. It shares a redeveloped urban infill brownfield site occupied by a vacant manufacturing facility on a large city block in the Bayview Hunters Point District.

With high-density residential units and ground floor retail, this senior development is setting the stage for revitalization of the area. A significant new residential mixed-use presence is alive along the city's newest transit rail line.

Project Goals

What three project goals had the greatest impact on the project?

Promoting a sense of community; providing green/sustainable design; and responding to local conditions.

The project provides a supportive opportunity for independent living for a diverse range of low-income seniors, and to engender a feeling of home. Outside of their secure private apartments, seniors are afforded a wide range of small social opportunities in keeping with their needs, energy levels, and mobility. Wide corridors allow walkers and wheelchairs to pass without creating a disturbance. Corridors, stair towers, and landings all feature furnishings where seniors can gather, sit comfortably, and socialize. This allows for social interaction outside of the units and also affords opportunities for rest. An abundance of natural light and views in the units, corridors, and stair towers facilitate connection to the outdoors. Every level features a landing-living room near the elevator, as well as a laundry and lounge that can double as a television room or meeting place. The adjacent family housing has a semi-private courtyard and garden open to the senior residents. Ground-level retail spaces are slated to serve seniors with a senior support center, juice bar, and other retail opportunities. Secure bike parking and car-share pods preserve seniors' independent mobility. Units feature doorbells to emphasize ownership and a sense of home and also feature custom display shelves outside the door.

This low-income residential rental project provides a comfortable living environment where senior residents can benefit from sustainable building design and construction methods. From initial project design through to construction, sustainable building strategies – such as

appropriate solar orientation, day-lighting, and efficient building planning – were incorporated to achieve LEED NC Gold Certification. The project remediated a brownfield site and reused much of the previous building's foundation materials.

Energy conservation strategies and systems include:

- A 52 kilowatt photovoltaic array on roof (289 modules)
- A cool roof
- Daylight controls and occupancy sensors in all corridors
- Operable windows for daylighting, ventilation, and views
- EnergyStar-rated refrigerators
- The interior of the garage is painted white, reducing lighting needs
- Solar hot water (36 collectors) that preheats domestic hot water (raised Title 24 compliance by 10 percent)
- The project has energy savings exceeding California's Title 24 by 23.5 percent.

Water conservation strategies include:

- Drought-tolerant and native adaptive landscaping reduces water use by 50 percent
- A site-wide stormwater management system, in which more than 75 percent of rainfall is captured and retained to prevent runoff from overwhelming the city system. Roof and podium drains capture and then filter water into two vegetated bioswales to enter the sewer system gradually.

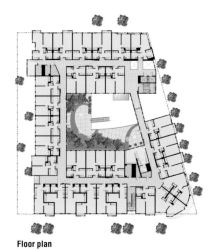

Floor plan

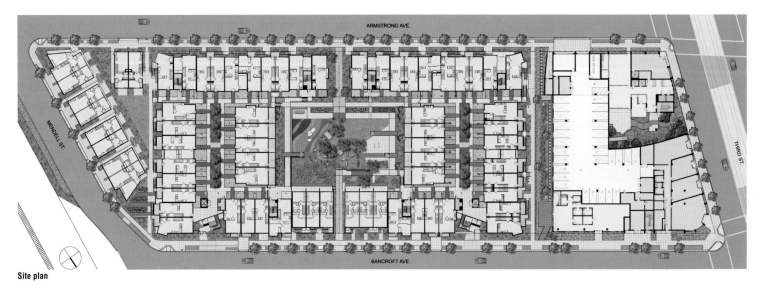

Site plan

- Dual-flush toilets, where allowable, created a 20 percent reduction in water use
- Low-flow fixtures in baths and kitchens.

Materials choices include:

- The team exceeded 75 percent recycling of construction waste
- The design includes separate recycling and trash chutes for residents
- Recycling bins are built into site furniture
- Use of durable and rapidly renewable woods where possible
- Plyboo railing caps, mailbox surrounds, and interior benches
- Ipe (a rapidly renewable hardwood) rain screens and exterior siding at the building base
- Materials include 20 percent post-consumer and pre-consumer content.

Indoor air quality and daylighting initiatives include:

- Roof-top photovoltaic panels create power for common spaces
- Automated lighting in common spaces
- High-efficiency fluorescent lighting throughout
- Thermally efficient and operable windows
- Tight building envelope
- Individual thermostats
- Zero CFC mechanical refrigerants
- Low-emitting materials for healthy interiors
- 90 percent of spaces have views.

Below: South elevation with sunshades, vegetated bioswales and ipe siding
Photography: Brian Rose

The project responded to local conditions, such as the site opportunities and cultural expectations.

• Site opportunities: the goal was to create an iconic tower at the entry to the neighborhood and add an inviting arcade along the base of the building. This would incorporate neighborhood-serving retail opportunities across from a light-rail stop and maintain

Above left: Pop-out bays with seating overlook the two-tier courtyard and allow rest stops for seniors.
Above right: View of courtyard toward entry with the rain garden and circulation bridge
Photography: Brian Rose

a lively streetscape. Additionally, a publicly accessible landscaped mews runs between the senior building and the adjacent family townhouses. An extension of the city street grid, the mews brings connectivity to the surrounding neighborhood and serves as a sheltered walking path away from the main arterial roadway. The building additionally maximizes views to the city park across the street and the surrounding San Francisco hills.

• Cultural expectations: to reflect the historically African-American population of the neighborhood, design details were drawn

from traditional African textiles and symbols. Textile-inspired paint and fenestration combine to wrap the public face of the building in an interlocking quilt of color and pattern. The courtyard is ringed by a wall inset with symbols representing security, wisdom, power, love, unity, and hope.

Challenges: What were the greatest design challenges faced by the project?

One of the greatest design challenges was to create a building that is both inviting and secure, and striking the appropriate balance between the two. A population of seniors, including formerly homeless seniors, in an intense urban setting requires an environment that is both safe and safe-feeling. The goal was to create a building that maintains a connection with the larger community and provides easy visual and physical access to the outside world.

The building has a controlled entry door set into a heavy perforated gate that allows passersby to view the landscape and colors of the courtyard within. The gate entry is well-lit and sheltered from the elements. The management office and front desk are set in a centrally located glass office in view of the entry, lobby, courtyard, mailbox area, public restroom, garage entry, and community room.

Another challenge faced by this project was that it was designed at the same time that the city was overhauling its stormwater system and plan. The architect teamed with the city to maximize the onsite management of stormwater, diverting as much as possible from the city system and also controlling the release of water into the system. The urban site required a complex system to accommodate this, and the design team had to work closely with consultants to right-size and install the appropriate components. The building system features roof drains, catchment pipes, permeable pavement, and vegetated bioswales with appropriate plantings and grading.

A third challenge was obtaining commitments for financing to allow the developer/owner to target the seniors most in need of quality housing while making the project financially feasible. The key funding source was the US Department of Housing and Urban Development (HUD). Each year the developer met with community leaders and the Redevelopment Agency to weigh funding options, and each time the group overwhelmingly supported the decision to apply for HUD funding rather than

pursue other sources. Through perseverance from the developer, the City of San Francisco, and the Bayview Hunters Point community, the new affordable apartment homes were completed in August 2010.

Innovations: What innovations/unique features were incorporated into the design of the project?

A nested unit design allows for units to have a functional layout without complicating construction. In this instance, studio units are designed with a separate sleeping alcove, which allows for a discrete living space for residents to share with guests. The sleeping alcoves of pairs of adjacent units are nested together, and the resultant duo of units has a standard rectangular footprint.

Another feature is the adjacent nature of the senior building and the family townhouse development. The two distinct projects were developed by the same developer and designed by the same design team; however, they target different communities and have different management services. The landscape design includes both developments, creating a consistent, inclusive identity for the neighborhood. Also, the courtyard of the family townhouse development is available to the senior population.

An innovation reveals the commitment to creating small opportunities for social connection throughout the building. Outside the official common spaces of the community room and courtyard, this building has a wide array of small social spaces scattered throughout. These include living-room-style landings near elevators and stair towers; laundry lounges on every level; pop-out bays in the stair towers and corridors on every level, which are furnished with tables or benches for rest or conversation; and wide corridors that allow for walkers or wheelchairs to pass or accommodate conversation without compromising traffic flow.

Features/Services/Amenities: What are the most important features/services/amenities that were incorporated into the project specifically to attract the targeted market?

- 100 percent accessible or adaptable affordable units for independent senior living, including 23 units reserved for formerly homeless seniors and office space for support services.

- Secure, ample, flexible common spaces that can accommodate resident needs easily and safely.

- Adjacent positioning to transit and retail preserves seniors' independence; adjacent positioning to family townhomes prevents seniors' isolation.

Green/Sustainable Features: What are the green/sustainable features that had the greatest impact on the project's design?

Conscientious choice of materials, site design considerations, and water efficiency.

What are the primary motivations for including green/sustainable design features in the project?

Making a contribution to the greater community, supporting the mission and values of the client/provider, and supporting the mission and values of the design team.

What challenges have you faced when trying to incorporate green/sustainable design features?

Actual first cost premium.

Aesthetic: Identify which aesthetic your project embraces, why it was chosen and how it was achieved.

The architect chosen for the firm's bold, colorful, modern designs achieves affordable housing budgets through creative use of color and materials and innovative approaches to maximizing usable space.

Creating a home-like environment often misses the mark for many residents, who come from

various backgrounds and cultures, especially in a diverse city like San Francisco. Clean modern lines and materials create a blank canvas for residents to place their own imprint on the space.

Dynamic common spaces and restful, efficient private spaces help residents strike a balance between seclusion and inclusion based on their needs.

The bright palette and dynamic patterning of the building create a sense of place and iconic identity for the new community. The building is recognizable and actively asserts itself within the surrounding neighborhood.

For the residential component, what was critical to the success of the project?

Improving common spaces and amenities.

Households: Describe the role households had in the project.

This is a predominantly residential project – 116 independent living rental units for seniors in one five-story building, with common areas and service and retail spaces.

Common Spaces: What common spaces are included in the project?

A large multipurpose room, secure bicycle storage room, and laundry lounges.

For a typical household wing/facility, describe the common spaces.

Courtyard – the building features a landscaped 4600-square foot, bi-level courtyard with a rain garden, bench seating, and barbecue grill.

Community room – the 1650-square foot common room features a kitchen and media center/television lounge.

"Living room" landings – breakout seating areas on each floor near the elevator landings featuring sofas, armchairs, and coffee tables.

Laundry lounges – three floors feature a 447-square foot laundry lounge with two sets of laundry machines, a laundry sink, a restroom, couches and televisions. The fourth floor has a 250-square foot laundry room with two sets of laundry machines, a laundry sink, and a restroom.

Gathering nooks – small pop-out bays at periodic intervals along circulation corridors and in stair towers feature windows and bench seating or chair and table seating to create resting spots for senior residents between building uses, or small gathering opportunities outside of apartments, scaled for card games or conversation.

Describe the largest interior common space in the project (excluding dining).

Community room: The 1650-square feet common room features a kitchen and media center/television lounge. It has an upright piano and is generally set up with eight, four-person tables and comfortable chairs. The community room walls open entirely to the lobby and the lobby walls open entirely to the lower level of the courtyard, creating one expandable/contractible space that can accommodate gatherings of different sizes and types. When closed, the community room is 24 by 34 feet (816 square feet). With the addition of the lobby, the indoor community space is 24 by 60 feet (1440 square feet). With the addition of the lower courtyard, the indoor/outdoor community space is 24 by 88 feet (2112 square feet). Expanded, the common room can accommodate the entire population of the building. Additionally, the walls dividing these rooms are clear glass, adding visual porosity and activity to the common areas.

Design Process: Who did the design team work with to gather information that could be applied to the design of the project?

Affiliated yet independent agencies, city planners/code officials, contractor/construction team, design consultants, neighbors/members of the greater community, and non-profit affordable housing developer.

Which techniques were used with non-design team members to gather information that could be applied to the design of the project?

Charrette/working session, focus group/interview, meetings with neighborhood design review committee and local PAC (project area committee), and presentation to a review board.

In addition to the client and designers, who had a key decision-making role?

City planners/code officials.

Off-site Outreach Services: What off-site outreach services are offered to the greater community?

The building is slated to include a Senior Services Office with support for seniors in the building and from the larger community.

Opposite: The main courtyard at the adjacent family townhouse development is open to seniors.
Photography: Brian Rose

David Baker + Partners Architects

Mabuhay Court Senior Housing and Northside Community Center

San Jose, California // BRIDGE Housing

Facility type: Independent Living, Senior Community Center
Target market: Low Income/Subsidized
Site location: Urban; Brownfield site
Project site area (square feet): 74,389
Gross square footage of the new construction involved in the project: 110,726

Number of parking spaces added by the project: 77
The site is within 1000 feet of public transportation and everyday shopping and/or medical services. The project offers transport to nearby shopping, medical, and/or cultural services/amenities.
Provider type: Non sectarian non-profit
Completion date: 2002

Below: Western elevation and Community Center entry along 6th Street

Photography: Cesar Rubio

Opposite: Mabuhay Court and Northside Community Center aerial view

Illustration: David Baker + Partners

from the development. Parking is in surface lots, and in a half-level depressed concrete garage. All units are adaptable for full accessibility.

Project Goals

What three project goals had the greatest impact on the project?

Serving the community, filling a need; integrating with the surrounding neighborhood/greater community, and collaboration during design development to achieve the best possible design result for the client.

The key goal was to use the site to its potential to accommodate the needs of low-income seniors capable of living independently, and to prolong their independence through a safe, comfortable home environment, sense of home-ownership, diverse community, access to nature, opportunities for socializing and engagement, and wellness support. This goal is fundamentally met by the creative approach taken in treating the two sites as one and sharing resources to support the overall goals of the design. By annexing the air rights over the community center for housing and concentrating the parking beneath the community center, the team was able to create a much larger, interactive community center along with 96 units of senior housing in a low-profile structure that reflects and enhances the existing built context.

To be a good neighbor, fitting into the neighborhood as it stands but also bringing positive effects and opportunities to the community at large was another main goal. Creating housing and a community center that communicate with each other, as well as integrating the public park on the corner, enhances the look and feel of the resources available to the community. Additionally, creating individual stoop entries to the housing echoes the houses in the neighborhood and

Overall Project Description

This project is a mixed-use public/private partnership combining two separate uses: 96 low- and extremely low-income Senior Housing Units, and a brand new Intergenerational Community Center that provides services to senior residents and local residents, including children. The community center also provides a commercial kitchen, a 6000-square foot auditorium, full-time staff, and three classrooms.

The integration of the two allows seniors the opportunity to easily access services to enhance both their physical and mental wellbeing. Seniors living in the housing have access to daily cooked meals, programs on nutrition and health, classes on financial management, social activities, and a large intergenerational social network.

The development replaces a municipal maintenance yard and small, outdated community building. The community building, located in a historic neighborhood just north of downtown San Jose, was a vital social center for seniors and had outgrown the original 3250-square foot structure. The architect worked in conjunction with a senior community organization, the long-term operator of the existing community center, in the design of both the new 15,415-square foot center and the housing development.

The design team proposed integrating the separate elements of the housing and community center by expanding the housing site into the air rights over an addition to the existing senior center. Utilizing air rights allows the housing to be accommodated in a three, rather than four, story structure, which blends with the existing neighborhood. Shared parking is underneath the community center.

The Senior Housing Complex has a mix of studio, one-, and two-bedroom units. Apartments have private balconies and porches linked to walk-up stoops, reflecting the homes across the street

Far left: Main residential entrance for
   senior housing
Left: The feng shui-inspired courtyard
   provides a green gathering space
   for senior residents.
Below left: Rain chain sculpture
   and water management in the
   Community Center courtyard
Below right: Entrance to the adjacent
   public park

Photography: Cesar Rubio

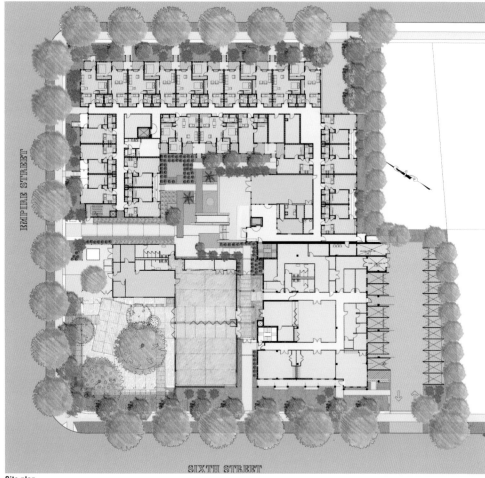

Site plan

further enhances the independence of the resident seniors and enriches the neighborhood through diversity and activity.

The community center was designed to have both capacity and flexibility. It is now an intergenerational center, serving the senior and child populations of the area and providing a large space for community events, such as weddings and concerts.

Collaboration during design development was vital in assisting the goal of creating a design for the client. The design firm's expertise ensures both sustainable, affordable development and that the city and existing communities' needs and desires are met. The project team worked closely with a local senior community organization, the long-term operator of the existing community center, the city of San Jose, and the Parks & Recreation Department to create a place that met or exceeded the needs and wants of the stakeholders.

Challenges: What were the greatest design challenges faced by the project?

A main challenge was fitting all the desired housing and amenities on the site within zoning parameters, and in keeping with the low-scale

neighborhood profile. An innovative public/private partnership between the non-profit housing developer and the city of San Jose resulted in the development of a new 15,418-square foot community center (replacing the outgrown and outdated previous center), plus 96 new housing units for low-income seniors above the center and on an adjacent site.

As a result of this collaboration between the city, the developer, and the architect, the design team was able to treat the two sites as one. The housing annexes the air rights above the community center, a design move that enabled construction of a three-story rather than four-story structure without compromising the number of new homes.

By taking a holistic approach to the shared site of the community center and the adjacent senior housing, it was possible to maximize the site to the benefit of both projects. The private residences now have a thoughtful relationship to both the surrounding streets and the adjacent community center, which joins a corner public park and meditation garden in creating an open and welcoming gathering place for the neighborhood.

The creative combination of the housing and community center into one development provides the following benefits:

- more integrated and cohesive design
- greater synergy between the two uses
- cost savings through more efficient design and construction process.

The new center serves the previous and new residents, and the new residences bring life and diversity to the neighborhood and are well integrated into the area fabric.

A second challenge was the design and development teams' shared goal of sustainable building for this project. The development

exceeded Title 24 by 20 percent, and met Energy Star Home standards. Highlights include the 50 percent construction waste diversion. Other green measures include:

Infill sites

- re-use of underutilized city corporation yard
- pedestrian access to many neighborhood services
- proximity to public transit
- higher density mixed-use development.

Energy savings

- radiant barriers to reduce summer heat gain and winter heat loss
- light timers and motion sensors in common areas
- sunshades along façades with sun exposure
- efficient fluorescent lights and LED exit signs
- operable, thermally efficient windows with low-E glass where appropriate
- insulation with high R values
- tight building envelope
- individually metered thermostats in every unit.

Building materials

- onsite recycling for residents
- use of long-term/long lasting building materials including concrete and stucco
- recycled wood for common area furnishing
- use of renewable resources such as bamboo in the building finishes
- recycled content carpet; carpet tiles to allow for small replacements as needed
- concrete flooring.

Left: Stoops along the eastern elevation allow direct access to the street.
Opposite left: One-bedroom "nested" unit with private deck
Opposite right: Mabuhay Court lobby lounge

Photography: Cesar Rubio

Indoor air quality

- well ventilated units (operable windows, bath fans)
- chemical and pollutant source control at entries
- maximized daylighting and exterior views
- stovetop hoods vented to exteriors.

Water efficiency

- high-efficiency showerheads and faucets
- native, drought-tolerant landscaping
- water-efficient irrigation for landscaping
- front loading, coin-operated laundry machines.

Social gathering places

- outdoor courtyard and private outdoor stoops and spaces to encourage connection to outdoors
- common rooms
- furnished corridors
- game tables.

A third challenge was that at five times the size of the outmoded center it replaced, the new community building would improve a vital existing social center for seniors in this San Jose neighborhood. In order to maximize all the potential afforded by a new design, the project team worked closely with a senior community organization and the long-term operator of the existing community center to create a place that amply serves the senior residents from the adjacent senior housing, as well as being an asset for the surrounding area.

Innovations: What innovations/unique features were incorporated into the design of the project?

The project team designed the affordable housing and community center to be integrated into the surrounding single-family homes in the neighborhood. Each of the residential apartments has a private balcony and porch linked up to a walk-up stoop, echoing neighborhood homes, and all share a large common courtyard. For its density, the development has a large amount of open green space.

Among the design elements in the new center are higher ceilings in the auditorium for performances, a pre-function area for the many senior-oriented social events, and the effective use of wood to evoke traditional Asian architecture. The public art component – a stained glass installation and a large steel sculpture – is developed in response to the presence of a significant Filipino-American community.

The housing is also an example of a smart growth, urban infill development. Prior to the construction of the housing, the site was an underutilized corporation yard in a residential area. The project replaces this use with one that is more appropriate for its surroundings and an asset to the overall neighborhood. The location of the community center also minimizes car use, as seniors from the adjacent housing and the greater community can easily access the center from their homes or by public transportation.

Features/Services/Amenities: What are the most important features/services/amenities that were incorporated into the project specifically to attract the targeted market?

- Safe and secure low- and very-low income housing dedicated to an independent living senior population
- Integrates a well-programmed Intergenerational Community Center
- Connection to outdoors and high percentage of open space given unit density.

Top: Entry plaza for Northside Community Center
Above: Northside Community Center multipurpose room

Photography: Cesar Rubio

Opposite: Section sketch showing the housing using the air rights over the community center

Illustration: David Baker + Partners

Green/Sustainable Features: What are the green/sustainable features that had the greatest impact on the project's design?

Energy efficiency, maximized daylighting, and site design considerations.

What are the primary motivations for including green/sustainable design features in the project?

To make a contribution to the greater community, support the mission and values of the client/provider, and support the mission and values of the design team.

What challenges have you faced when trying to incorporate green/sustainable design features?

Perceived first cost premium.

Aesthetic: Identify which aesthetic your project embraces, why it was chosen and how it was achieved.

This design features a warm minimalism, combining clean contemporary lines with traditional detailing that takes its cues from the scale and style of the neighborhood. Materials include polished concrete floors and fixtures, rough-hewn wood stoops and trellises, and homely tile roofs that create a sense of place that both fits in and stands out in its neighborhood.

For the residential component, what was critical to the success of the project?

Improving common spaces and amenities.

Households: Describe the role households had in the project.

Housing is the predominant reason for the use of the building. The senior rental apartment complex consists of one building with 96 units of housing ranging from studio to two-bedroom units. The organization of the units is undifferentiated by use (that is, there are not discrete sections reserved for particular types of residents).

residential   community

Common Spaces: What common spaces are included in the project?

Dedicated classroom/learning space, dedicated conference/meeting space, a large multipurpose room, and an outdoor courtyard.

For a typical household wing/facility, describe the common spaces.

The housing building contains a 960-square foot common room with a kitchen; a 250-square foot laundry room; a 400-square foot activity room available for arts and crafts, games, or television viewing; and a 6000-square foot outdoor terraced courtyard. The adjacent community center features 15,418 square feet dedicated to neighborhood-serving senior and childcare services.

Describe the largest interior common space in the project (excluding dining).

The project's largest interior space is a 6000-square foot auditorium that offers a location for lunch, exercise classes, educational workshops, and entertainment offerings for residents and the greater community.

Describe each dining venue incorporated in the project.

The adjacent community center, built by the same project team, provides high quality, cost-efficient, nutritious meals to seniors and promotes the role of nutrition in preventative health and long-term care. The meal plans are approved and monitored by a registered dietitian.

Design Process: Who did the design team work with to gather information that could be applied to the design of the project?

City planners/code officials, contractor/construction team, design consultants, neighbors/members of the greater community, and a non-profit affordable housing developer.

Which techniques were used with non-design team members to gather information that could be applied to the design of the project?

Charrette/working session, in situ observations, and a presentation to a review board.

In addition to the client and designers, who had a key decision-making role?

Affiliated yet independent agencies, for example non-senior living provider partners, and city planners/code officials.

Off-site Outreach Services: What off-site outreach services are offered to the greater community?

The city-run community center provides a range of services for seniors including access to daily cooked meals, programs on nutrition and health, classes on financial management, social activities, and a large intergenerational social network.

The seniors living in the adjacent housing and those in the greater San Jose community take advantage of the center's shared commercial kitchen, a 6000-square foot auditorium, full-time staff, and three classrooms. The center is open Sunday – Thursday from 9.00am – 5.00pm. It is a neighborhood gathering place serving over 100 people each day.

The integration of the senior housing and the community center makes it easier for seniors to access services that encourage self-sufficiency. The community center is four times larger than the previous center on the site. It provides a senior nutrition program and senior activities such as classes and workshops for line dancing, karaoke, tai chi, yoga, conversational English, Chinese calligraphy, Red Cross Disaster Preparedness, and American Legion meetings.

Many of the seniors living in the housing use the services at the center to improve their health and take advantage of the social services, as well as socializing with seniors and others from the greater community.

GGLO

Atria Tamalpais Creek

Novato, California // Atria Senior Living Group

Facility type: Assisted Living, Assisted Living Dementia/
Memory Support
Target market: Upper
Site location: Urban
Project site area (square feet): 155,509
Gross square footage of the addition(s) involved in the project: 771

**Gross square footage of the renovation(s)/
modernization(s) involved in the project:** 81,181
Purpose of the renovation/modernization: Repositioning
Number of parking spaces added by the project: 0
The site is within 1000 feet of public transportation.
The project offers transport to nearby shopping,
medical, and/or cultural services/amenities.

Provider type: For profit
Completion date: December 2010

Opposite: Entry procession with new building
    E main entry beyond
Left: New outdoor terrace adjacent to main
    lounge at building E

Photography: Derek Reeves

Overall Project Description

The property owner/operator elected to do a full renovation of this existing late-1970s building to reposition the property to appeal to a broad range of local residents. The existing building located in Novato, California had many underutilized interior and exterior spaces. The renovation prioritized opportunities to repurpose underutilized common areas, creating new and enhanced amenity spaces in support of the owner's mission to address goals for sustainability.

The design concept for the redevelopment of this in-city senior living facility draws on the local context of vineyards and rolling hills. A pattern language develops with the careful selection of refined materials and agricultural details. The extensive terraces, rich gardens, and generous trellised roofs are reminiscent of a vineyard estate. There is special emphasis given to creating strong indoor–outdoor connections for the common spaces. An overriding goal is to create a sense of place and permanence for the residents. The design is welcoming, accessible and safe, and the details are rich with herbal scents, colors, and textures.

A new addition to the main entry allows for the extension of the new axial entry from the main parking through the procession gardens to an enlarged reception hall with a tall cupola and generous entry roof overhang. It also includes the addition of a much-needed enlargement and remodel of the main lounge, including the main lounge terrace overlooking the procession gardens.

The renovation includes the enhancement of shared common spaces, extensive refinishing and minor remodeling of the apartments to increase their accessibility and upgrade the quality of the interiors. All aspects of the renovation focus on choices that are appropriate for sustainability and for providing a healthy environment for the residents. Low-emitting materials are selected for all new interior finishes and all new appliances and light fixtures are selected with energy efficiency in mind. The new interior plumbing fixtures and landscape upgrades focus on water efficiency. Landscaping includes the use of drought-tolerant planting with drip irrigation.

Project Goals

What three project goals had the greatest impact on the project?

Offering daily choice through extensive amenities; providing a hospitality/resort feel; and repositioning to appeal to a broader market.

- The primary goal for the renovation is repositioning to appeal to a broader market. The owner/operator recognized that the property needed a renovation to appeal to the existing and future residents. To attract and retain these residents, the renovation focuses on enhancing the quality of design, creating more amenities, and integrating sustainability.

A vineyard estate design concept is created to respond to the existing buildings and landscape, the greater context of the site in Novato, California, and the existing culture among the residents of the buildings. With an emphasis on enhancing the quality of design, this entire-property renovation left no finish untouched: every floor, wall, ceiling, chair, sink, light fixture, tree, path, and fence was considered.

The additions of the bistro, fitness room, massage room, theater, cognitive fitness computer room, and resident gardening spaces bring more options for daily amenities to the

Building C (Life guidance wing)

Building D

Building E

First floor plan
- Studio
- Large Studio
- One Bedroom
- One Bedroom/Corner
- Studio Deluxe/Den
- Two Bedroom
- Life Guidance Unit
- [A] Accessible Unit

Building A

Building B

residents. The enhancements of other spaces, such as the activity room, salon/spa, and outdoor terraces, also help to support the goal of creating amenities.

Because existing and future residents are savvy to the benefits of earth-friendly choices, sustainability goals inform the design process. With an emphasis on water conservation,

energy efficiency and construction waste reduction, LEED points are carefully tracked from design through to the end of construction. Tenant education is an ongoing component of the sustainability goals, with a comprehensive signage program to educate the occupants and visitors to the benefits of green buildings.

- Another important goal is to provide a hospitality/resort feel. The renovation adapts a newer residential model infused with amenities and services borrowed from hospitality, retail, and resorts. The focus on hospitality carries throughout the design with amenity-rich spaces, such as informal living and lounge areas, a salon with spa services, and a diverse range of dining

Left: New outdoor terrace adjacent to main lounge at building E

Photography: Derek Reeves

library shelves, computer stations, grand fireplace, and French doors to the main lounge terrace all enhance the comfort and usability of this space.

The addition of the cognitive fitness room with two computer stations allows residents to test their brain activity and work on improving their brain function.

The remodeled activity room provides a functional and adaptable space for various smaller group activities of up to 32 people.

Also the addition of the fitness room gives residents a new single-purpose room designed for exercise, flexibility, and balance.

Challenges: What were the greatest design challenges faced by the project?

The greatest design challenge was to ensure that this total building renovation allowed for a comfortable transition in the existing residents' living environment. To help the residents feel involved in the renovation process, the owner/ operator assisted the design team in creating image and materials boards to be posted before the construction began. These boards featured design renderings with written descriptions of the new spaces that were being created for the residents. The materials included on the boards allowed the tenants to see the selected carpets, tiles, and stone finishes. The design team also focused on creating environments specially suited to the food-enthusiast culture of this community. The main dining room's enhancement with four-star, restaurant quality finishes, and the introduction of a casual dining option at the new bistro, brought even more options.

choices with longer hours of operation and extensive menu choices. This hospitality-oriented residential environment enhances the quality of life for the residents by fostering independence, choice, dignity, and privacy.

- An important goal for the community is to enhance the quality of resident living by offering enhanced choices of extensive amenities. The addition of the bistro and outdoor bistro terrace create dining options – residents now have the option to choose an informal meal at the bistro or formal dining in the main dining room.

A larger spa/salon creates space for more patrons to receive salon services each day. The two new pedicure chairs in the salon enhance the spa experience for the residents. The

addition of the massage room allows residents to get therapeutic massage without having to leave the campus.

The new theater room provides the residents with another amenity to use at any time of day. The space with seating for 16 can be used to watch television, DVDs, or home movies.

The addition of raised planting beds gives residents another option for their daily activities, while also fostering a sense of pride and ownership.

The renovation and addition to the main lounge have reinvigorated this gathering area in the community. This space is akin to the living room of a home, and the new vaulted ceilings,

Another challenge for this project was integrating a new Memory Care wing into the renovation design. One of the most difficult aspects of this unique program is to successfully incorporate security for the Memory Care residents. The Life Guidance wing is a discrete household that provides 11 different private and semi-private rooms. This secure wing has its own kitchen, dining, lounge, library, and medications room. The enclosed outdoor deck and gardens allow the residents access to outdoor spaces while still providing safety within tall perimeter fencing. Although the emphasis is on a secure space, careful planning of the finish selections creates a welcoming environment for the residents and guests.

Another challenge this project faced was the coordination of two contractors. Because this was an entire-building renovation the owner/operator elected to have one contractor focus on the common area renovations, and a second contractor focus on the residential renovations. Delineating the scope of work for each contractor was critical. Equally critical was the construction credit tracking for LEED. The owner/operator communicated with both contracts throughout construction.

Innovations: What innovations/unique features were incorporated into the design of the project?

A comprehensive tree survey was conducted by a certified arborist at the outset of the design process. Each tree was assessed for its suitability for preservation based on its age, health, structural condition, and ability to coexist in the redeveloped environment. A densely planted site when originally constructed in 1978, a balanced approach was required – including management, thinning, and replacement – to restore the health of the existing tree canopy, with the goal of positioning the site for the next 50 years.

During design, new circulation, planting, irrigation, utilities, and grading were designed around the existing trees to preserve as much of the historic tree canopy as feasible. Over 109 trees were identified for preservation and protection, while trees in poor health were identified for removal, and other specimen trees were identified to be transplanted and incorporated into the project renovation. New plantings were designed to complement and enhance the remaining existing trees.

During construction, trees were protected using protection-zone signage, fencing, and organic mulch. Machine excavation and other digging were not allowed within the drip-line. Hand excavation was utilized as necessary for implementation of the design. Drainage of water and construction materials were directed away from the zone of protected trees.

Features/Services/Amenities: What are the most important features/services/amenities that were incorporated into the project specifically to attract the targeted market?

Life Guidance wing, bistro and outdoor bistro terrace, spa/salon, and massage room.

Green/Sustainable Features: What are the green/sustainable features that had the greatest impact on the project's design?

Energy efficiency, site design considerations, and water efficiency.

What are the primary motivations for including green/sustainable design features in the project?

Lower operational costs, to stay competitive against other similar/local facilities, and to support the mission and values of the client/provider.

What challenges have you faced when trying to incorporate green/sustainable design features?

Applying LEED Certification standards to an existing residential building that is fully occupied while undergoing a major renovation.

Aesthetic: Identify which aesthetic your project embraces, why it was chosen and how it was achieved.

The vineyard estate design concept for this renovation was inspired both by the existing residents' love of fine cuisine and fine wine, and by the native landscape of Novato, California with its rolling hills and vineyards. The site and building renovation focused on creating a welcoming identity with an enhanced arrival sequence. The new formalized gardens, with an abundance of color, texture, and scents, are the focus of the entry procession and create endless opportunity for views from within the buildings. The central building's new formal entry is designed with refined natural materials, defining the pattern language of stone, wood, and stucco echoed throughout the project.

The building renovation included many large-scale gestures with simplified forms to enhance the estate scale of the buildings. Both the interior and exterior were designed with nature-based patterns and agricultural details. The site design emphasizes the creation of outdoor terraces that are bounded by low stone walls, which create a perceived boundary and sense of security for the residents while still allowing visual access to the lush gardens of grape, lavender, and cypress beyond. The introduction of these terrace "rooms" creates a seamless extension of the interior spaces.

This renovation sought to create a sense of place for the residents while also enhancing the connection to the natural environment. The vineyard estate concept allows for an elegant display of natural materials, textures, colors, and fragrances in the building design, the landscape design, and the interior design.

For the residential component, what was critical to the success of the project?

Improving common spaces/amenities.

Households: Describe the role households had in the project.

The existing property had four, two-story wings radiating from a central single-story common area building. Each of the four wings creates a neighborhood on each floor. One emphasis of this total building renovation was to create more meaningful gathering spaces in the neighborhoods by repurposing the underutilized common spaces to provide enhanced amenity areas.

Common Spaces: What common spaces are included in the project?

Bistro/casual dining, dedicated fitness equipment room, large multipurpose room, massage/aromatherapy room, a cognitive fitness room, the bistro terrace – a partially covered terrace with outdoor kitchen and seating adjacent to the bistro, resident gardening space with raised planter beds, exterior entry procession gardens with seating areas, water feature, and a bus waiting shelter, main lounge terrace – partially covered terrace with casual seating adjacent to the main lounge area, salon, and a small-scale cinema/media room.

Opposite top left: New Memory Care library
  Photography: Derek Reeves
Opposite top right: New main dining at building E
  Photography: Dean Lavenson
Left: New bistro at building A
  Photography: Derek Reeves

For a typical household wing/facility, describe the common spaces.

A Wing Level 1 – bistro/outdoor bistro terrace. The bistro space has a wine display, island bar seating, and decorative lighting. The high-quality kitchens allow for informal gathering to watch the chef prepare lighter-fare meals at both the indoor and outdoor kitchens. The adjacent bistro terrace features casual seating overlooking the procession gardens and fountain.

- 727 square feet of indoor area with seating for 24.
- 645 square feet of outdoor area (418 square feet is covered area) with seating for 16.

A Wing Level 2 – corridor lounge. This enlarged area of the corridor is out of the circulation path but is situated near the elevator and stairs. It comprises subtle carpet color transitions and comfortable seating for two with a small side table to encourage residents to sit for a while to rest or visit with neighbors.

- 133 square feet with seating for two.

B Wing Level 1 – fitness. This new modern fitness center with senior-friendly equipment also connects to a new private outdoor terrace. The fitness room is outfitted with elliptical trainers, treadmill, exercise bike, and a stretching and balancing area with a ballet bar.

- 380 square feet of indoor area with an eight person capacity.
- 659 square feet of outdoor area.

B Wing Level 1 – spa/salon and massage. The existing residents love their new salon with its pedicure, manicure, and hair styling stations. The soothing palette of calming colors and natural materials create an inviting atmosphere for the patrons. The massage room provides another new amenity to the residents.

- 412 square feet in spa/salon with seating for 10 patrons.
- 115 square feet in massage room with massage table for one patron.

B Wing Level 1 – corridor lounge. This node in the corridor is adjacent to the new spa/salon, new fitness room, and new public restrooms. A feature wall with mosaic tile is an elegant backdrop to this small lounge area.

- 59 square feet with seating for two.

B Wing Level 2 – theater. The theater room is a gathering space with wide comfortable seating and a rich color palette for a group to enjoy TV shows and movies.

- 568 square feet with seating for 16.

B Wing Level 2 – corridor lounge. This space in the corridor is adjacent to the new theater room and the new public restrooms. This informal lounge is for residents to use before a movie or to rest in while traveling through the corridor.

- 105 square feet with seating for three.

C Wing Level 1 – Life Guidance dining and kitchen, lounge, and lounge terrace. The Life Guidance (Memory Care) wing is designed as an entirely independent household wing for the security of its residents. The Life Guidance dining is informal with a familiar, residential scale kitchen accessible to the residents. Open to the dining is the lounge, where soft seating is around a living room setting with a television. The dining and lounge spaces are used throughout the day and are a hub of activity, where residents have daily interaction with support staff.

- Dining room and kitchen – 680 square feet with seating for 20.
- Lounge – 487 square feet with seating for 10.

- Lounge terrace – 447 square feet with seating for eight.

C Wing Level 1 – Life Guidance library. This smaller scale library incorporates bookshelves and comfortable seating for residents and guests of the new Life Guidance wing.

- 123 square feet with seating for two.

C Wing Level 1 – Life Guidance garden and outdoor deck. This new secured deck and garden space provides the Life Guidance residents with safe access to a pleasantly landscaped area. The residents can walk through this garden on a predictable circular path with over 200 linear feet of travel distance. The garden also features a generous terrace with a pergola structure to create an outdoor "room" where residents can sit and enjoy the weather. Another notable feature of the garden is the plant selections, chosen for their familiar fragrances, and the enjoyment and safety of the residents.

- 6221 square feet with seating for six.

D Wing Level 1 and Level 2– corridor benches. Along the corridor are two benches with soft seating to encourage residents to rest for a while or linger chatting with a neighbor. Carpet color transitions and ceiling soffit relief in these areas further enhance their function as a respite space along the corridors.

- 81 square feet at each bench (two per floor) with seating for two.

Describe the largest interior common space in the project (excluding dining).

Main lounge/main lounge terrace – this 1090-square foot room with exposed wood trusses and a vaulted ceiling functions as the main casual gathering area and library. The soft, living room-style furnishings accommodate as many as 16 people and encourage the residents to stay a

while with intimate seating groupings. There are library shelves and a desk area featuring computers with free wireless internet service. A focal point is the new fireplace clad in stone reminiscent of native quarry stone. The room opens onto a partially covered 818-square foot terrace through two sets of French doors. The terrace features an outdoor fireplace clad in the same stone as the interior fireplace, and a tranquil water feature. It is surrounded by low, seat-height stone walls and has comfortable teak tables and chairs with seating for 16. The low walls around the terrace create a sense of security and comfort for the residents who want to enjoy this outdoor room. Residents seeking respite at the main lounge terrace enjoy a view of the main entry arrival beyond, and procession gardens with lush four-season planting.

Describe each dining venue incorporated in the project.

Bistro for casual dining with indoor seating for 24; outdoor bistro terrace adjacent to bistro that has casual outdoor dining and outdoor kitchen with outdoor seating for 16; the main dining room that has formal dining with seating for 100; private dining room that has formal dining with seating for 10; and Life Guidance dining room that has informal dining for Memory Care residents with seating for 20.

Design Process: Who did the design team work with to gather information that could be applied to the design of the project?

City planners/code officials, contractor/ construction team, design consultants, and provider administrators.

Which techniques were used with non-design team members to gather information that could be applied to the design of the project?

Full-scale mock-up, in situ observations, and presentation to a review board.

In addition to the client and designers, who had a key decision-making role?

Contractor/construction team, provider administrators, and provider board of directors.

Top left: New pedicure stations at spa in building B
Top right: New Memory Care garden
Above: New theater

Photography: Derek Reeves

DiMella Shaffer

Leonard Florence Center for Living:
New 100-bed Skilled Nursing Green House®

Chelsea, Massachusetts // Chelsea Jewish Foundation

Facility type: Hospice, Long-term Skilled Nursing, Short-term Rehabilitation
Target market: Mixed Income, Long-term Care for the Frail Elderly and Residents with Amyotrophic Lateral Sclerosis (ALS) and Multiple Sclerosis (MS); Short-term Rehabilitation.
Site location: Urban

Project site area (square feet): 82,877
Gross square footage of the new construction involved in the project: 94,442
Number of parking spaces added by the project: 25
The site is within 1000 feet of public transportation.
Provider type: Faith-based non-profit
Completion date: February 2010

Below: Reception area

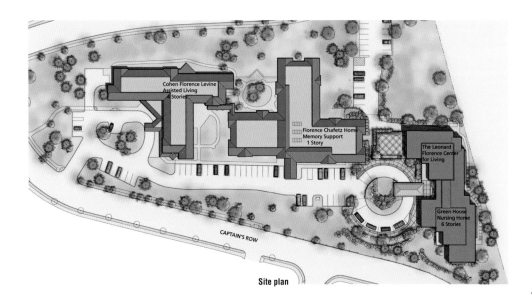

Site plan

Labels on site plan:
- Cohen Florence Levine Assisted Living 4 Stories
- Florence Chafetz Home Memory Support 1 Story
- The Leonard Florence Center for Living
- Green House Nursing Home 6 Stories
- CAPTAIN'S ROW

Overall Project Description

Located in Chelsea, Massachusetts, the Leonard Florence Center for Living is a supportive community modeled on an urban apartment house, which provides Skilled Nursing Care for 100 residents in independently managed houses of 10 residents each. The project is the country's first "Green House®" community to be constructed within an urban setting. Ten independent houses focus on enhancing the quality of life of each resident by providing nursing care within the comfort, privacy and familiar surroundings of "home."

Continuing the mission of the sponsoring organization, the Chelsea Jewish Nursing Home Foundation, The Leonard Florence Center for Living completes the senior housing campus on Admirals Hill, which comprises 69 units of affordable Assisted Living at the Cohen Florence Levine Estates and 36 studio apartments at the Florence and Chafetz Home for Specialized Care. The new resident-centered nursing houses serve frail elders of all economic backgrounds from the local Jewish and broader community, as well as residents with

Amyotrophic Lateral Sclerosis (ALS) and Multiple Sclerosis (MS), offer three houses for short-term rehabilitation, and provide hospice care.

Project Goals

What three project goals had the greatest impact on the project?

Creating a home-like environment; offering choice through a diversity of housing options; and responding to local conditions.

- Offering choice through a diversity of housing options – the project sponsor sought to extend the continuum of care on their existing Assisted Living and Memory Support Campus by creating a new nursing home to replace a 30-year-old nursing home they owned on a remote site. The envisioned home was a place where the Skilled Nursing Care would be provided in a non-institutional environment for 100 residents.

Using the guidelines of the Green House® project within the small available site area indicated that the residential houses could

be stacked vertically on five floors, similar to apartment housing common in the urban community where the project is located.

The individual houses of 10 residents provide the comforts and privacy of "home." Two of the houses offer advanced assistive technology for individuals with ALS and MS.

Additionally, the multi-level arrangement of the houses allows for semi-public common and administrative spaces on the first-floor entry level. A bakery-café, deli, chapel, and spa offer residents social opportunities outside of their private houses, and the ability to interact with friends, family and the broader community.

- Creating a home-like environment – the organization of the building plan is conceived as an apartment building, in which the hierarchy of spaces lead from the public street to the semi-private common areas and elevator lobby, moving through the front door of the individual apartments into the privacy of the home.

The houses are configured without corridors: spaces flow from one to another and are arranged in distinct rooms of a residential scale for living, dining, meal preparation, and sleeping. Each living area is carefully configured to allow for windows to provide daylight, and a screened balcony offers a direct connection to the outdoors in each house.

Spaces within the houses are designed to be used as they would be in a home. Residents may visit the living room for socializing with friends and family members next to the fireplace, or the dining room that accommodates residents, staff, and family at meal times, or the den, which has a fold-out couch for overnight visitors.

Prominent in each house is a fully functional kitchen where all meals are cooked to meet the needs and requests of each individual living in

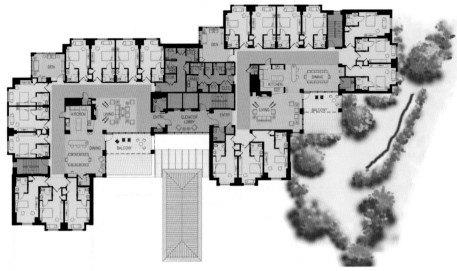

Second floor plan

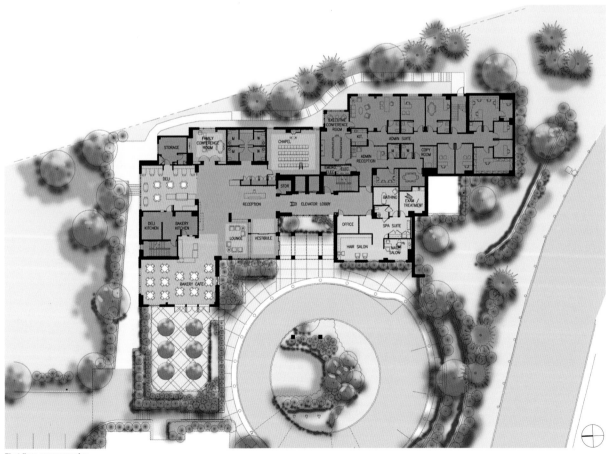

First floor commons plan

on breaking the traditional model. Features central to the Green House® concept, such as a living room with a fireplace, a residential kitchen open to a family dining room, and no corridors or central nursing station, do not comply with Massachusetts' state codes for nursing homes. Ongoing discussions with regulating authorities resulted in proposed compliance alternatives including upgrading fire protection systems and separations throughout the residential floors, and incorporating fire shutters at the open kitchens. Necessary waivers and variances were ultimately granted, allowing the design to proceed uncompromised.

A second challenge was creating residential spaces with abundant natural light and connection to the outdoors. Because portions of the building are buried in the hillside, priority was given to dedicating the maximum available window area to resident use. The building footprint was configured to maximize available window area, providing natural daylight in every living and community space. Each house has an outdoor balcony that provides fresh air and sunlight within the privacy of the household. In addition, the first-floor Peace Garden adjacent to the bakery-café provides a secure outdoor enviornment for all residents and guests.

A third challenge was integration of the new building into the existing campus site. The available buildable area on the site was limited to a small, narrow parcel of open land, comprising a steeply sloping section – with a 49-foot drop in grade across the length – and a low-lying flat portion restricted by wetlands.

The design solution was to develop a compact building footprint of approximately 14,200 square feet that preserves the wetland area. The 36-foot grade change across the length of the building

the home. Residents participate in the familiar and meaningful activities of family life, such as enjoying the aromas and activities of meal preparation.

Bedrooms are private and include bathrooms with showers and overhead lifts for assisted movement between the bed and bathroom. Service and support spaces required for Skilled Nursing Care are provided in each house, discrete from and secondary to the main living spaces. The state requirement for a nursing station is met by a built-in desk with upper cabinets situated in the family dining room.

- Responding to local conditions – the project is located on Admirals Hill, the former site of a historic 19th-century naval hospital. The original red-brick hospital buildings currently house residential condominiums and provide the context for recent development in the area, including the Admirals Hill senior living. The new building utilizes similar building materials, trim colors, and scaling elements, as do the adjacent Cohen Florence Assisted Living and Florence and Chafetz Home for Specialized Care buildings, and the neighboring community. The new building is also designed to be of similar size, massing, and scale to neighboring residential buildings in order to maintain a cohesive architectural expression within the neighborhood.

Challenges: What were the greatest design challenges faced by the project?

Maintaining critical design elements of a "home" in the face of regulatory hurdles. Existing state nursing and building code regulations presented a challenge to the design of a multi-story nursing home intent

Right: Private bedrooms feature large windows, bathroom with shower and an overhead lift
Opposite: Residentially scaled living spaces promote meaningful engagement in familiar surroundings

partially buries the first floor and basement levels below grade. Ten nursing households are arranged vertically on five floors, each floor containing two houses of 10 beds for a total of 20 beds per floor.

The sloping site ultimately worked to the advantage of the project, offering direct access to the outdoors on multiple building levels and affording opportunities for garden terraces on the main entry/ commons level and the first residential level above, while allowing the service entrance to be located at the lowest level, separated from public spaces.

Innovations: What innovations/unique features were incorporated into the design of the project?

Two houses are dedicated to the care of individuals with ALS and MS. These "smart houses" offer renewed independence and quality of life to residents at all stages of disability. Residents have access to advanced assistive technologies, ventilator support, lifts, and personalized mobile command centers that, with eye-gaze computer technology, allow residents to open and close doors, turn lights on or off, adjust temperature settings, surf the intenet, or navigate television channels. Through his or her command center, the resident is able to take the elevator to the chapel or deli, venture outdoors to the terrace or the garden, or order from the lobby café via email, all without assistance.

Features/Services/Amenities: What are the most important features/services/amenities that were incorporated into the project specifically to attract the targeted market?

As a Jewish-sponsored organization, a primary project objective was to provide for the spiritual and cultural needs of future Jewish residents

while offering an open and accepting environment to people of all faiths. Distinctive common areas were developed to bring people together and to celebrate the Jewish culture. The chapel provides a peaceful space for all to worship, where multi-denominational services are held throughout the week.

Green/Sustainable Features: What are the green/sustainable features that had the greatest impact on the project's design?

Energy efficiency, to maximize daylight into the home, and site design considerations.

What are the primary motivations for including green/sustainable design features in the project?

Lower operational costs, to support the mission and values of the client/provider, and to support the mission and values of the design team.

What challenges have you faced when trying to incorporate green/sustainable design features?

Actual first cost premium.

Aesthetic: Identify which aesthetic your project embraces, why it was chosen and how it was achieved.

The project exemplifies a contemporary style that reflects the era in which it was created. The client and design team embraced the aesthetic of a modern home with the understanding that the warmth and character of a residential space has less to do with the style of its furnishings than with the scale and flow of its spaces; the quality of materials, finishes, and lighting; and the functional relationships of the rooms that afford opportunities for both social interaction and privacy, connection to outdoor spaces, and abundant natural daylight.

The project employs the comfortable and familiar elements of home. The open household kitchen combines a mix of commercial- and residential-grade equipment with stone counter tops and wood cabinetry, which has been carefully designed and detailed to meet the stringent requirements of health and life safety codes while maintaining the feel of a custom residential kitchen.

Furnishings are both contemporary and elderly friendly. Upholstered furniture is firm with arms to assist in sitting and standing. Table lamps provide light at eye level. Residential-scaled living rooms feature electric fireplaces, built-in millwork, and large windows with soft fabric draperies. The use of natural cherry on walls, contemporary-style paneled wood doors, carpeting, and contrasting color accent walls offer warmth, orientation cues, and visual interest to the home.

For the residential component, what was critical to the success of the project?

Improving units/private spaces.

Households: Describe the role households had in the project.

The project was developed as a multi-story application of the Green House® model, as conceived by Dr. William Thomas. Located in an urban setting, the building contains 10 resident households of approximately 7000 square feet each, configured as a multi-story apartment building, with two apartments (houses) located on each of the five residential floors.

Top: The Bakery Café has direct access to the Garden Terrace
Bottom: Residents enjoy the pleasures of home-cooked meals in the family dining room
Opposite: Small desk and medications room are incorporated directly into the family dining area

Photography: Robert Benson Photography

Common Spaces: What common spaces are included in the project?

Bistro/casual dining, religious/spiritual/meditative space, and a salon.

For a typical household wing/facility, describe the common spaces.

Each private house contains a living room (approximately 450 net square feet); a den (260 net square feet) with a door providing the choice of activity separate from open household areas when desired; a family-style dining room (400 net square feet); an open residential-style kitchen (300 net square feet) where all resident meals are prepared (there is no central kitchen in the facility); and a screened balcony (230 net square feet), a sheltered outdoor space within the privacy of the household.

In addition, the first-floor common areas offer residents opportunities for socializing outside of the private houses. These include a bakery-café (980 net square feet) used for light dining and activities, and also for screening movies; a kosher deli (700 net square feet); a family conference room (360 net square feet) for private gatherings; a chapel (750 net square feet); a spa (800 net square feet) with hair and nail salon, treatment room, and whirlpool bath; and an outdoor garden terrace (1350 square feet) used by all residents and guests.

Describe the largest interior common space in the project (excluding dining).

The chapel serves as a place of worship and is used for other large gatherings (750 net square feet, seats 40–50).

Describe each dining venue incorporated in the project.

Each private household has a dining room with an expandable family-style dining table seating 12–16; the common area casual bakery-café seats 30–40

and serves pastries baked in the adjacent kosher pastry kitchen; an adjacent outdoor garden terrace offers several shaded tables; and the New York-style kosher deli seats 20–25 for casual dining.

Design Process: Who did the design team work with to gather information that could be applied to the design of the project?

Care team staff, city planners/code officials, contractor/construction team, design consultants, neighbors/members of the greater community, non-care team staff, National Green House® Project Administrators, potential/future residents, and provider administrators.

Which techniques were used with non-design team members to gather information that could be applied to the design of the project?

Charrette/working session, focus group/interview, three-dimensional interior and exterior images and three-dimensional walk-through, and presentation to a review board.

In addition to the client and designers, who had a key decision-making role?

City planners/code officials and the Massachusetts Department of Public Health.

Steinberg Architects

Moldaw Family Residences, at the Taube-Koret Campus for Jewish Life

Palo Alto, California // Moldaw Family Residences at the Taube-Koret Campus for Jewish Life

Facility type: Assisted Living, Assisted Living Dementia/Memory Support, Independent Living, New Intergenerational Campus including Community Center, Preschool/Early Childhood Education Center
Target market: Mixed Income – At entry, the majority of residents pay market rate, but 24 units are offered at 13 percent below market rate.

Site location: Urban; Brownfield site
Project site area (square feet): 432,278
Gross square footage of the new construction involved in the project: 432,278
Number of parking spaces added by the project: 0
The site is within 1000 feet of public transportation. The project offers transport to nearby shopping, medical, and/or cultural services/amenities.

Provider type: Faith-based non-profit
Completion date: September 2009

Opposite: Main entrance *porte-cochère*
Left: Midrachov

Photography: Tim Griffith

at every age, engaging with the outside world, transforming a difficult site and traditionally larger-scale social and living environments into more physically, socially and intergenerationally accessible space was a key goal.

Adddressing a campus plan comprising a podium level offset by the placement of "smaller houses" for senior living nested around two landscaped interior courts, the winding pedestrian mall "Midrachov" engages seniors on upper levels and people of all ages "spilling out" below.

Senior residences are vertically organized with balconies and overhead bridges above childcare, a café, meeting rooms, and the Stanford Health Library to integrate living, social, and wellness facilities.

One-stop, dense underground valet parking supports the needs of adults living in the vicinity and their families for parking, and attends to a variety of needs of senior automobile owners.

- Promoting and addressing holistic wellness through supported design detail, for example, compactly organized "small houses" with 6–8 apartments per floor, each with views and entries/exits to campus choices including 130,000 square feet of fitness center and classrooms to encourage physical movement, such as walking, life exercise, and encouraging participatory exercises in others. The Stanford Health Library is open to the public on campus. Memory development programs are offered in the club rooms and through the media classroom.

Overall Project Description

These senior residences are located in the heart of a new, intergenerational village created for Northern Californian families. The entire project was undertaken to fulfill two market research studies on elders' (and their adult children's) needs – analysis was undertaken of over 1000 individuals/families. The analyses covered social, cultural, learning, wellness, and family heritage needs, which were formerly met on scattered sites and required notable travel. In a sense, the campus is designed to make time for meaningful interactions with notable community input to energize a mix of people and age groups, fulfilling individual and family needs, and offering opportunities for mutual discovery. The scope includes, as part of the senior residents contracts, eight homelike Residential Living Apartments with dedicated common areas for Independent Living (IL), Alzheimer's (AL), and Alzheimer's – Memory Care (AL-MC), all layered over and around early childhood education classrooms, 130,000 gross

square feet of fitness, social and educational amenities, and 3470 net square feet of social/cultural meeting and performance arts space. The scope includes construction of a dense parking garage, covered by a landscaped podium and historically inspired "Midrachov" or winding walkway. The project is planned with neighboring affordable housing.

Project Goals

What three project goals had the greatest impact on the project?

Integrating with the surrounding neighborhood/greater community; providing an urban living and community setting to energize generations and optimize physical and social health by addressing market needs and promoting holistic wellness.

- Providing an urban living and community setting to energize generations and optimize physical and social health by addressing market needs including use of meaningful time and energy

Views and easy access to two courts – one a mews, with walking and seating options, the other a "green" for grassy exercise outside, picnics, and programs – inspire participation from those seniors living above the center.

Apartments are detailed to offer open plan, easy-use features, to support physical balance as well as accommodating mobility aides. Readily available health coordination/home care is available to keep people in residential living as long as possible, and wearable support assistance technology encourages seniors to move freely around the campus.

- Integration with surrounding people in greater Northern California. This goal addresses research and incorporates a broad spectrum of community members and agencies through planning, fund-raising, and now-active programs on site. Approximately 1000 non-occupants a week attend wellness/fitness and children's programs, and cultural/performance arts bring an even wider audience. Examples of the amenities include a state-of-the-art community center with gymnasium, three swimming pools, and 130,000 square feet of fitness, yoga, and classes – these facilities draw thousands from all over the greater Palo Alto area. Membership is included in seniors' residency, and the center is designed directly adjacent to the seniors' residences. Other members include families of all ages, and seniors living at home and in the vicinity.

T'enna Preschool and Leslie Family Early Childhood and Family Education Center is directly under the second floor of resident living. Seniors maintain the children's garden/play area that is visible from the apartments above.

The Schultz Cultural Arts Hall is a flexible center for year-round performances, lectures, and events with writers, dancers, artists, actors, and educators. It is both connected to and in view of the residences.

Senior Living in Eight Houses on a Campus of Twelve Distinctive Buildings

"Light, Airy Urban" *apartment living* in buildings D, E and G through M.

Community programs in buildings A, B, C, F and the first levels of D and E as well as the pedestrian facades of G, L and M.

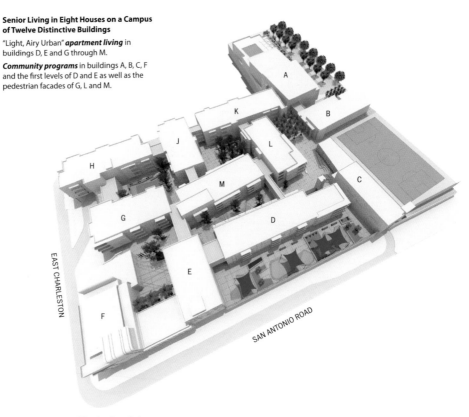

Site visual rendering

Typical large unit floor plan

Typical small unit floor plan

Challenges: What were the greatest design challenges faced by the project?

The greatest design challenges were to balance program desires with the tight site, and the capital/operating budgets and constraints with the commitment to achieve design that inspires and sustains intergenerational collaboration. These were addressed by engaging in visual participatory planning, engaging the design team in understanding capital, soft and operating metrics, designing with each other, and applying outcome data to the design. At one point, senior units were increased without increasing site coverage to meet market and operational needs – this resulted in a stacking of units, which required financing to cover two occupancies (residential/community use) and space calculations.

Working individually and collectively with multiple agencies (such as social, community center, financial, child care and education, senior living, and health care) to understand how people see entry, flow, features, use patterns, and how these transpire through a typical day, was another challenge. This resulted in the location and adjacencies for senior living being placed near the fitness center and the "Midrachov" Mall, providing the option of living near children. The children's programs are uniquely sited to maximize their comfort, use of the outdoors, family access, and security. Independence and relatedness were also taken into consideration, for example, the Cultural Arts and Health Library, both with public uses.

The budget was achieved through meetings, documentation, and searches for alternatives for structural features, parking density, materials, and finishes. The impact of this appears to be a widened base of understanding, commitment, and use.

Innovations: What innovations/unique features were incorporated into the design of the project?

Senior housing is vertically and horizontally integrated with fitness facilities, pools, children's educational/social programs and cultural arts on a small, urban site, yet the organization responds to each agency, sponsor, and use by offering internal and natural connections.

The climate is incorporated in the design, drawing on historic design elements such as the marketplace/"Midrachov," formal palm court, and casual green for different ceremonial, seasonal, and even rental function use.

Aging-in-place is recognized through both onsite services, shorter walking distances, the uses of natural light, and the motivation to maintain activity levels.

The campus is both sustainable (LEED Silver) and intergenerationally sustaining through incorporating design elements from shared heritage in the senior residence façade, such as the use of color.

Above left: Residential lobby
Above right: Typical unit interior

Features/Services/Amenities: What are the most important features/services/amenities that were incorporated into the project specifically to attract the targeted market?

The number and size of apartment units, and their layouts and features to support aging-in-place. The ability to accommodate couples living together with different lifestyles drove unit organization; room sizes were driven by studies of furnishings, groups, and use.

Choices of type and style of community interaction and layout address different age groups, people who are more active, those with reduced energy, and those who maintain regular contact with families on campus.

The decision to incorporate options for smaller-scale, sponsored Dementia and Assisted Living

Dining amenities map at the center

Memory Garden

Small House for memory support.
Individualized Care
Safe and Interesting
Private Suites
    Full Easy-Use Bathroom
    Memorabilia Encouraged
Dignified
Spiritually Supportive

Small, Personalized Staff
Home Style Dining
Personal Routines and Schedule
Memory Gym Programs
Sensorium: Program for Calming

Garden of Memories
Freedom of Movement
Technological and Familiar Security

Supervised Outings

Elder suites

Residences on campus, along with specific Memory Care and Assisted Living programs and dining, was driven by major market studies.

Green/Sustainable Features: What are the green/sustainable features that had the greatest impact on the project's design?

Maximizing daylighting, reducing solar gain/heat island effect sunshades, and planting.

What are the primary motivations for including green/sustainable design features in the project?

Lower operational costs, to support the mission and values of the client/provider, and to support the mission and values of the design team.

Aesthetic: Identify which aesthetic your project embraces, why it was chosen and how it was achieved.

Market research, focus groups, home visits, and designer input all indicated that the prospective occupants represented a broad spectrum in

their definition of home. Residences have open-plan design, wide entries and customizable arrangements, with walls created for fine arts or a display of photos. There is an extension of hospitality in the architectural detailing of the formal dining, the Charleston Room (private dining/terrace), and the cozy fireside lounge. The campus is organized through the findings on color and texture. Natural vistas of the region are visible throughout the campus and its expansive windows. Other attributes of home include apartment patios wide enough for seating, planting, and eating; choices of unit features including kitchen, counters, and lighting; extensive storage; washers and dryers; non-institutional "touchdown" desks for staff; and the use of indirect lighting.

For the residential component, what was critical to the success of the project?

Improving units/private spaces.

Households: Describe the role households had in the project.

The Senior Living Residences applied the small house concepts of scale, outdoor access, and staffing to Residential/Independent living; eight small-scale residences were built and connected to each other. Each provides small group living and ready access to the Californian weather, natural light, and short-cuts, and each has a distinctive name and social amenities. Goals included to reduce scale and increase motivation to engage in activities, including in the intergenerational programs. Households are also designed for Memory Care Assisted Living – 11 with full programs, country kitchens and dining; and two households for those entering into Assisted Living. Of these, 12 are now open and occupied as apartments with distinctive country kitchens, dining, and programs, as well full use of campus destinations and programs.

Opposite: Formal dining at the center
Above: Elder suites, Memory Support units

Common Spaces: What common spaces are included in the project?

Art studio/craft room, bistro/casual dining, coffee shop/grab-and-go, dedicated classroom/ learning space, dedicated conference/meeting space, dedicated exercise classroom, dedicated fitness equipment room, dedicated rehabilitation/ therapy gym, formal dining, large multipurpose room, library/information resource center, massage/aromatherapy room, resident-maintained gardening space, salon, small-scale cinema/ media room, swimming pool/aquatics facility, and others. The Northern Californian location is temperate and many outside social spaces are designed for year-round use.

For a typical household wing/facility, describe the common spaces.

- Greeting lobby (600 square feet – 12 users) – information, socialization, and transportation center.
- Library network (525 square feet – 20 users) – current media, computer, walk-out reading court, wi-fi, and evening table games.
- Three club rooms (350 square feet – 12 users) – all function for meetings, sports, exercise, and arts; each has a butler bar or similar.
- Media/meeting and kitchenette (460 square feet – 26 seats; 16 at tables) – teleconnections, classes, meetings, speakers.
- Three activity studios (200 square feet – 6 seats at tables) – input from residents on uses, including music, writing group, and projects room.

Opposite top left: Midrachov
Opposite top middle: Senior Living: south court "the woods"
Opposite top right: Socializing: Charleston Terrace
Opposite bottom: Senior Living: south court "the green"
Left: Socializing: "palm court"

- Charleston terrace room (576 square feet – 20 seats at tables) – private dining (with catering/chef's kitchen), meetings, learning, family events, meetings, teleconferences. A large terrace provides additional seating/party space and overlooks the Palo Alto skyline and sunset.
- Plaza room (350 square feet – 12 users) – meeting area before or after meals and card/table games.
- Fireside room and al fresco dining (350 square feet – 12 users) – bar, breakfast, provides drinks for al fresco dining.
- Spa (400 square feet – 5 users) – hair care and chat.
- Two residential courtyards (1000-plus-square feet – 50–100 users). North courtyard – mews and court; south courtyard – green quad court and herb garden. Both can provide tai chi, seating, exercise, walking paths, family picnic grounds, movies, concerts, and celebrations. Residents can look down from porches onto events.
- Two bridges – connecting bridges provide seating and views of campus events.
- Two Assisted Living centers (900 square feet) – activities, socializing, music, and exercise.
- Elder suite (Assisted Living Dementia/Memory Support) – dining, club room, quiet, sensory room, and secure court (with gardening groups in shade).

Describe the largest interior common space in the project (excluding dining).

The intergenerational campus includes a cultural hall (3470 square feet) with options for theater seating (360 seats) for cultural events such as lectures and concerts, or it can be set up for formal banquet

Top: Cultural hall theater space
Left: Cultural hall lobby
Opposite: Cultural hall exterior at night

dining and dancing (225 formal dining seats) – this arrangement can also provide a level floor for senior social and holiday events (225).

Describe each dining venue incorporated in the project.

- Formal dining (80 residents per seating) and casual dining (40 residents per seating). Al fresco dining is available for 16 (served off the dining room).

- Private dining and chef's kitchen (second floor) for 20 indoors and 24 outdoors (also used for social hours and receptions).

- One dedicated dining area and country kitchen for the 11 residents in Assisted Living Memory Support, with casual dining for 15 residents plus staff.

- One dedicated dining room, country and resident-use kitchen and club for Assisted Living residents, with casual dining for 24 plus staff.

- The cultural hall, part of the community center that shares the site, is set up for formal dining and dancing for 225 people (kosher and non-kosher food serving options).

- One grab-and-go coffee shop with indoor/outdoor seating for approximately 60 patrons.

- Six flexible alcoves distributed throughout the senior community serve light breakfast and coffee. (Though located on the first floor of the senior residences, they are operated for the full community.)

Design Process: Who did the design team work with to gather information that could be applied to the design of the project?

Affiliated yet independent agencies, care team staff, city planners/code officials, contractor/

construction team, design consultants, family or friends of residents, market analysts, neighbors/members of the greater community, non-care team staff, collaborating agencies from fitness, social services, children's and youth programs, university library (all on campuses), potential/future residents, and provider administrators.

Which techniques were used with non-design team members to gather information that could be applied to the design of the project?

Charrette/working session, focus group/interview, full-scale mock-up, in situ observations, and post-occupancy data on unit features (rooms, furnishings/furnishability, use of valet, walking distances, and staffing "touchdowns" and "stealth services").

In addition to the client and designers, who had a key decision-making role?

Affiliated yet independent agencies, care team staff, city planners/code officials, contractor/construction team, non-care team staff, client/operator (who was key in providing major operational data on IL, AL, aging-in-place, dementia and dining to inform decisions affecting operations, distribution of staff, and economic viability overall), provider administrators, and provider board of directors.

Off-site Outreach Services: What off-site outreach services are offered to the greater community?

Wellness and fitness classes (for approximately 1000 people a month), early childhood education pre-school (for approximately 100 children), and social community outreach (for approximately 500–2000 people).

Top: Wellness at the center: exercise room
Right: Wellness at the center: gymnasium
Opposite top left: Preschool playground
Opposite top right: Preschool interior
Opposite bottom: Wellness at the center: natatorium

Photography: Tim Griffith

Perkins+Will

Willson Hospice House

Albany, Georgia // Phoebe Putney Memorial Hospital/Albany Community Hospice

Facility type: Hospice
Target market: Mixed Income – Willson Hospice cares for terminally ill patients regardless of their income level or ability to pay.
Site location: Rural; Greenfield site
Project site area (square feet): 9,177,207

Gross square footage of the new construction involved in the project: 34,000
Number of parking spaces added by the project: 129
The site is within 1000 feet of everyday shopping and/or medical services.
Provider type: Non sectarian non-profit
Completion date: July 2010

Below: Administrative wing and canopied dropoff
Opposite: View from tranquility garden showing dining terrace outside family living room and typical shared patient porch

Overall Project Description

Willson Hospice is a new 34,000-square foot facility serving terminally ill patients in Albany, Georgia. It includes a 15,000-square foot administrative component for 50 home care staff who travel each day to reach patients in the surrounding 11 counties, as well as providing educational and meeting space for volunteers and community groups. The residential component for 18 inpatients is organized into three households, each arranged around a family living room. Other conversation/assembly areas include a chapel, music room, playroom, family kitchenette, and sunroom. The project contains a full-service kitchen, support services, and shared areas that unite the home care and inpatient care staffs. In addition to patients themselves, Willson cares for family members through a year-long bereavement counseling program, conducting more than 75 annual onsite group programs.

The initial 18-bed project is designed to expand to 24 and then 48 beds. Its 210-acre greenfield site ringed by wetlands has been selectively developed as a demonstration of ecological sustainability. The project included the creation of patient, family, and public gardens; extensive perimeter walking trails linking site features and wildlife habitat; and all necessary parking in separate visitor, staff, family, and service lots.

The project was undertaken to reach hospice patients who could not cope adequately in their own homes, including:

- Patients without a family member able to provide care at home
- Patients with family care givers in need of a restorative respite
- Patients in need of intense care requiring medication adjustment or pain alleviation

- Hospice patients in need of more appropriate care, who had previously been struggling in hospitals or nursing homes where palliative care was not supported by a reassuring setting.

The new building replaces an inadequate 6000-square foot office building that was the former base for the travelling hospice nurses.

Project Goals

What three project goals had the greatest impact on the project?

Connecting to nature; creating a homelike environment; and providing green/sustainable design.

- Connecting to nature – a healthcare building and a wildlife sanctuary. From its inception, the owner intended the hospice not only to serve terminally ill patients, but also to be an ecological oasis for its local community. The project's success is evident in its designation as the only healthcare facility in the world recognized as a Certified Silver Audubon International Signature Sanctuary.

To protect the 210-acre site and its wetlands, the team began by walking the property with a nationally known local ecologist, who identified indigenous species and suggested building placement. Native atamasco lilies, dogwoods, pines, and oaks were preserved. A one-mile walking trail loops the site perimeter, connecting the front courtyard, family gardens, and outdoor chapel with boardwalks and a viewing platform at the bird sanctuary, which is formed by a natural pond. The trail is signed with educational placards describing flora and fauna for bird-watchers and school children.

In order to be responsible stewards of the site the team restricted the building footprint and associated grading, and minimized site

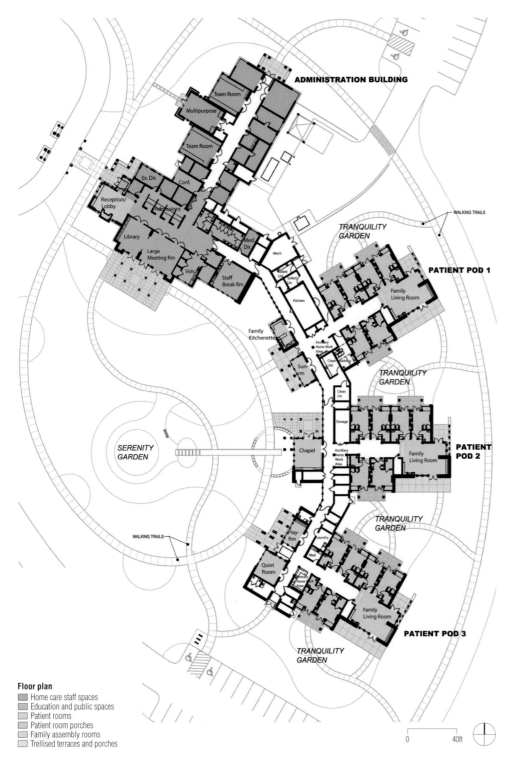

ADMINISTRATION BUILDING

Team Room

Multipurpose

Team Room

Ex. Dir.   Conf.

Reception/ Lobby

Admissions

Med. Dir.

Library

Large Meeting Rm

Vols.

Staff Break Rm

Mech

Soiled Lin

Family Kitchenette

Kitchen

TRANQUILITY GARDEN

WALKING TRAILS

PATIENT POD 1

Family Living Room

Ancillary Nurse Work Area

Sun Rm

Clean Util.

Clean Lin

TRANQUILITY GARDEN

Storage

SERENITY GARDEN

Chapel

Ancillary Nurse Work Area

Family Living Room

PATIENT POD 2

WALKING TRAILS

Play Rm

Laundry

Med

Quiet Room

Nurse Work Area

TRANQUILITY GARDEN

Family Living Room

PATIENT POD 3

TRANQUILITY GARDEN

Floor plan
- Home care staff spaces
- Education and public spaces
- Patient rooms
- Patient room porches
- Family assembly rooms
- Trellised terraces and porches

0   40ft

disturbance to only 14 acres. The Natural Resource Management Plan included measures to prevent erosion and stormwater pollution, to conserve water, and to enhance wildlife habitat. The building is located deep enough into the parcel so that its curving entry drive past oaks hung with Spanish moss emphasizes the spaciousness and peacefulness of the site, in contrast to the busy arterial approach road. The hospice is completely screened from the neighboring community college's light and noise, although the students are appreciative visitors.

- Creating a homelike environment. Patient rooms feature extensive stained wood trim and generous millwork, with space for personal items. Headwalls disguise medical outlets and switches. Overhead ceiling fans and double shades – both screening and blackout – as well as individual room thermostats provide maximum patient control. Reading lights are attached to the beds, not the headwalls, so patients can adjust the bed locations, even taking them out onto shared porches. Beds for family members staying overnight are built into window seats, an arrangement that keeps crucial nursing space around the patient beds clear. Large windows with corner glazing and French doors provide outdoor views and light.

Family living rooms are located immediately outside patient rooms. Each is outfitted with a reading inglenook, millwork for children's games, a dining area, and conversation area. Each living room also has ready access onto two outdoor terraces protected by sunscreens. Other spaces designed particularly for family include a kitchenette with banquette seating, a dedicated children's playroom, a quiet room, a sunroom, and the chapel.

Staff features include bedside charting and pocket pagers to eliminate institutional overhead paging. Nurse servers at each patient

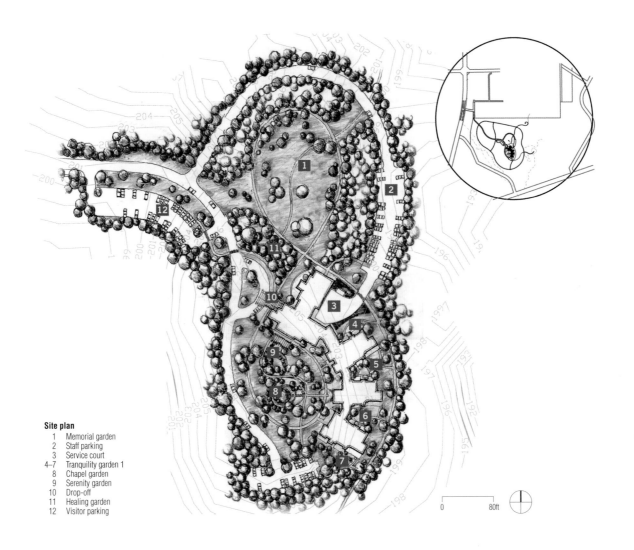

Site plan
1 Memorial garden
2 Staff parking
3 Service court
4–7 Tranquility garden 1
8 Chapel garden
9 Serenity garden
10 Drop-off
11 Healing garden
12 Visitor parking

room allow medical supplies to be stocked at any hour from the corridor side without interrupting patients. Items are kept close to their point of use and are easily accessed directly from the patient room. Two pods are served by small nurse work areas using simple round tables, and the main nurse station in the third pod is finished with stained birch and detailed to be approachable.

- Sustainability. Willson Hospice is both a LEED Silver building and a Certified Silver Audubon International Signature Sanctuary

- Energy use was reduced by 20.8 percent through the incorporation of high-efficiency water source heat pumps, cooling tower, and high-efficiency condensing boilers for heating; roof overhangs, trellises, and other exterior shading devices to minimize heat gain and

control glare; efficient double-pane low-E glazing; and R-21 insulation at walls and R-30 insulation at roofs

- Potable water use was reduced by 21.9 percent by using ultra-low flow water closets, showers, and faucets

- High-glazed walls allow the penetration of natural lighting, reducing electricity use

and dimensioned to conceal outlets, switches, and gases tucked into its sides; staff directed and adjusted their locations. During furniture test fits, the nursing staff realized they preferred a layout reconfigured to provide additional maneuvering space on both sides of the patient bed.

Several patient reading lamps were tested – the successful version attached to the bed, not the headwall, allowing maximum flexibility in bed location. The paired overhead examination lights required careful coordination with the ceiling fan to prevent light strobing; by shortening the fan stem and adjusting all the fixtures' plan locations, the team averted the potential problem. Light levels in the mockup of the patient bathroom were improved by adding an overhead fixture and changing dark wall tiles to a lighter color.

Stained wood veneer panels on ceilings, walls, and doors, and standing/running wood trim of different species were provided by several different subcontractors. The team compared various stains, and used the final mockup samples as color control standards to ensure consistency of appearance. Staff evaluated and adjusted key dimensions of the custom-designed window seat/family bed and nurse server. The latter required particular attention to the code-required double-locking feature for narcotics storage. Cabinet doors from both the patient room side and the corridor were equipped with locks, and staff selected a secure-medicine box bolted into a custom drawer detailed to extend in two directions so it was easily accessible from both sides.

Other distinctive finish details like the bold linoleum pattern were assessed at full scale and finalized. Millwork hardware was evaluated, and pulls chosen instead of touch-latch operators.

- More than 80 percent of spaces are daylit, and more than 92 percent have outdoor views
- The site design leaves 93.5 percent of acreage unspoiled as vegetated space for native fauna and flora
- Heat island effect was reduced by 50 percent
- More than 50 percent of construction waste was diverted from landfills
- More than 13 percent of construction materials contained recycled content
- More than 20 percent of construction materials were harvested or manufactured within 500 miles of the project site
- Rapidly renewable cork, bamboo, and MCT floor finishes are incorporated
- Permanent CO_2 monitoring system verifies performance of the mechanical ventilation system

- Zero-VOC and low-VOC adhesives, sealants, paints, and coatings are used inside the building
- Carpets and pads comply with the Carpet and Rug Institute's Green Label Program
- Urea-formaldehyde products are eliminated.

Challenges: What were the greatest design challenges faced by the project?

A hands-on collaborative mockup. Because free-standing hospices have a short history in America and there are relatively few of them, not many nearby examples were available for staff site visits. This made a full-size patient room mockup critical for hands-on evaluation. Working from early drawings, the contractor first erected simple dry-wall partitions inside a warehouse space. Doors and windows were cut out; millwork was drawn in marker. As design proceeded, the mockup was adjusted and refined with actual millwork, finishes, and fixtures. A unique headwall panel was created

Above: Courtyard view of chapel terrace and family entry
Opposite: Reception lobby

A second design challenge was coordination with local code officials. The owner, design team, and contractor faced several challenges satisfying the local fire marshals. The hospice is a fully sprinklered building that uses wood extensively as structural elements and as interior and exterior finish materials. In designing the drive-through canopy, the architects worked with the state fire marshal to separate it slightly from the building; the local code official required the canopy to be fully sprinklered. The contractor worked with the design team and subcontractors to route the exterior sprinkler lines near the front entry as unobtrusively as possible and conceal them inside wood cladding.

Local officials also elected not to exercise their code-allowed discretion for fully sprinklered buildings, but required a fire-access loop road encircling the entire project. In order to maintain natural views into landscaped areas and minimize paving, the owner decided to create the loop by improving a pedestrian sidewalk to bear heavy-duty traffic and edging it with a swath of stabilized soil to provide the required width. The stabilized soil supports plant growth identical to the adjacent lawn, and its edge is discreetly marked with a series of cedar posts.

A third design challenge was to coordinate trades in order to expose the structural Southern-pine roof planking as the finished ceiling in featured rooms like the lobby, chapel, and three family living rooms. The architects and engineers designed a system that located insulation above the planking, then placed nailable decking on top and used asphalt shingles as the finished upper roof surface. Structural and electrical coordination and careful placement of light fixtures hid conduits above the planking. Sprinkler lines had to be positioned through work sessions with the general contractor, subcontractor, plumbing engineer, and architect. Selected areas of ceilings

in the chapel and family living room were dropped six inches – enough to conceal piping runs but not enough to interrupt the visual rhythm of glulam support rafters.

Innovations: What innovations/unique features were incorporated into the design of the project?

- Transparency. To integrate interior spaces with the site, glazing creates strategic views into the landscape. Of the regularly occupied spaces in the hospice, 92 percent have access to outdoor views. This not only eases way-finding through the building, but it also keeps patients alert and oriented to time of day and season, and encourages them to use gardens as outdoor rooms. Willson Hospice features a series of tall window walls in high-ceilinged major gathering rooms – the lantern-like lobby, family living rooms, chapel, and sunroom glow at dawn and dusk, inviting visitors to join the activity within. Given the quantity of glazing, window selection was particularly important. The project was constructed with direct-set insulated argon-filled low-E glazing units, using 366 tempered/annealed glass with a design pressure rating of DP 35 and custom-designed corner stops.

- Regenerative gardens. Access to outdoor areas of respite is important for every hospice patient, family, and staff member. The east side of Willson's site is a series of private patient/family landscaped settings. The three patient pods are interwoven with accessible tranquility gardens, and each pair of patient rooms shares a porch with double doors, so beds can roll outside. The patient gardens are connected by continuous walkways leading to the outdoor chapel and to longer site trails. Family living rooms open onto trellised terraces.

- A site strategy for privacy. The west side of the site is more public. The four linked buildings (administration and three patient pods) are grouped into a crescent, defining a public courtyard around the specimen oak. This front area greets the public: visitors, volunteers, donors, and board members. The library and large meeting room share a trellised terrace facing into the space. Other significant gathering areas also face the courtyard, including the staff break room, the family kitchenette, the chapel, playroom, and sunroom. This area is the active "front door," the space where the outside community mingles and interacts with our hospice families.

Features/Services/Amenities: What are the most important features/services/amenities that were incorporated into the project specifically to attract the targeted market?

- A design vernacular that refers to local architecture by borrowing its materials, colors, and textures without literally mimicking its forms.

- Interwoven stress-relieving gardens to accommodate the privacy needs of each of the various user groups: patients, families, staff, visitors, and donors.

- A variety of inviting spaces that encourage dramatically increased community interaction. Since opening one year ago, the hospice has hosted a wide range of local groups, among them the Albany Audubon Society (quarterly chapter meeting, annual bird counts documenting 23 species on the site, master gardener lecture); Albany Women's Garden Clubs; American Chestnut Tree planting and lecture; Albany Boy Scout Troop 3 (4 Eagle Scout projects); Albany Rotary Club; Business and Professional Women's Club of Albany; Darton College's track team (cross-country team training on site-perimeter loop); informal runners and walkers; Albany Cancer Support Group; Dougherty County Medical Society; Hospital Authority of Albany-Dougherty County; and Georgia Osteopathic Medical Association (state meeting).

Green/Sustainable Features: What are the green/sustainable features that had the greatest impact on the project's design?

Energy efficiency, maximized daylighting, and site design considerations.

What are the primary motivations for including green/sustainable design features in the project?

To make a contribution to the greater community, to support the mission and values of the client/provider, and to support the mission and values of the design team.

What challenges have you faced when trying to incorporate green/sustainable design features?

Actual first cost premium.

Aesthetic: Identify which aesthetic your project embraces, why it was chosen and how it was achieved.

The challenge of hospice care is to encourage terminally ill patients and their families in their most difficult moments. Willson Hospice's design reflects its unique mission and its connectedness to the south Georgia community it serves. By breaking down the overall building into small households that are welcoming and approachable, its massing creates a sense of refuge. The collection of forms feels like a friendly village, not a formidable treatment center. The simple geometric shapes with sloping gabled roofs and large eaves echo local agrarian buildings. Exterior detailing includes cedar trellises, sunscreens, and canopies, as well as decorative double- and triple-member rafter tails constructed with truss outrigger and joist extensions with paired sisters. The design also incorporates familiar materials like fieldstone, stained cedar, pine, Douglas fir, linoleum, and cork to impart texture and natural color.

The project vernacular is not strictly traditional, however its design emphasizes transparency, incorporating views into the heavily treed woodland landscape wherever possible. Major gathering rooms like the lobby, family living rooms, chapel, sunroom, and multipurpose room feature high, exposed fir plank ceilings, glulam beams, and tall, wood window walls.

Households: Describe the role households had in the project.

Each group of six patient rooms is organized as a household around one of three central family living rooms. The household organization that places the living rooms within earshot of every patient bed is essential – family members who feel audibly and psychologically connected to their loved one use the living rooms extensively. The design team's research has demonstrated that without the direct connection made possible by the household plan, even inviting living rooms remain vacant when they are perceived as being too remote.

Common Spaces: What common spaces are included in the project?

Bistro/casual dining, dedicated conference/meeting space, large multipurpose room, library/information resource center, three family living rooms, sunroom, quiet/music room, family kitchenette, playroom, outdoor chapel, reception/lobby, volunteer activity room, a variety of gardens – including veterans' memorial garden, courtyard serenity garden, chapel garden, and four family tranquility gardens – perimeter walking path with boardwalk and five nature observation decks, religious/spiritual/meditative space, and resident-maintained gardening space.

For a typical household wing/facility, describe the common spaces.

At the heart of each household is a family living room of 805 square feet containing a dining alcove (seating four), reading inglenook (seating four), conversation area (seating six), and play area with game storage (four child seats). Each living room also has direct access to two shaded outdoor terraces of 420 square feet and 140 square feet, with seating for eight and four respectively. The living rooms and their six terraces provide sensitive spaces for conversations, stress-relieving connections to nature, and accommodations for the many extended families who visit.

Top left: Detail of millwork recess disguising utilities at headwall
Top right: Patient room showing view through porch doors into tranquility garden, as well as window-seat bed, headwall mill work, staggered ceiling lights, and fan

More active common rooms are distributed among the three households, located at their western ends where families can join other visitors and enjoy views into the central western courtyard. They include:

- 205-square foot family kitchenette with booth and counter dining for six
- 205-square foot glazed sunroom with seating for six
- 400-square foot chapel that seats 20 for memorial services and opens onto its own terrace and memorial garden
- an enclosed, glazed 195-square foot playroom with toy/book millwork and eight child seats around two tables, located for visual supervision from the primary nurses' work area
- a 340-square foot quiet room with seating for eight that also accommodates small musical concerts.

Describe the largest interior common space in the project (excluding dining).

The 635-square foot large meeting room opens into the adjacent 465-square foot library; sliding, frosted, glazed pocket doors can divide the spaces for separate functions. Both rooms also open to an 1100-square foot trellised exterior patio, and to the wide primary circulation hall leading from the reception/lobby. The meeting rooms and library work independently and/ or together to accommodate executive board meetings, donor receptions, group bereavement counseling sessions, in-house staff training seminars, and community civic meetings and lectures, as well as family, patient and staff education, and research. The rooms are outfitted with audio-visual amenities including projection screen, lectern, and speakers, and digital and analog media storage. Tables and chairs are reconfigurable – the library typically seats 12 around a central conference table and two at research desks, and the large meeting room can be arranged for lecture seating for 48, work sessions for 30, or centralized conferences at a single table for 18.

Describe each dining venue incorporated in the project.

The family kitchenette includes a food preparation area with appliances, as well as counter/bar seating for two, and a built-in booth for four. It provides an informal venue for families. Each of the three family living rooms includes a dining alcove with movable table and seating for four. There are six outdoor, shaded family terraces, each with a table for four. The 18 inpatients generally take meals in their rooms, where they have overbed tables. The staff break room seats 24 and includes a preparation area with kitchen appliances and millwork; this space is important in bringing home care and residential staff together informally during the course of the day.

Design Process: Who did the design team work with to gather information that could be applied to the design of the project?

Care team staff, city planners/code officials, contractor/construction team, family or friends of residents, neighbors/members of the greater community, non-care team staff, local ecologists, Audubon International biologists, LEED commissioning engineers, major donors, program volunteers, program management group, furniture manufacturers and dealers, and provider administrators.

Which techniques were used with non-design team members to gather information that could be applied to the design of the project?

Charrette/working session, full-scale mockup, in situ observations, and a presentation to a review board.

In addition to the client and designers, who had a key decision-making role?

Care-team staff, city planners/code officials, contractor/construction team, non-care team staff, provider administrators, and provider board of directors.

Off-site Outreach Services: What off-site outreach services are offered to the greater community?

- Palliative home care – coordinated care teams of physicians, nurses, aides, social workers, and chaplains provide care to an average of 165 terminally ill patients in their own homes each month through an 11-county area.
- Camp Good Grief – the staff conducts two sessions of Camp Good Grief annually, a free, age-targeted program for children who have lost family members. Between 40 and 50 children attend each session.
- Community speaking/civic programs – staff make 20–25 annual presentations for civic groups.
- Educational programs/training – hospice staff teach pain management techniques to local nursing home and care facility personnel upon request.

Opposite: Family living rooms and terraces
Photography: Jim Roof Creative, Inc.

Perkins Eastman

Air Force Villages

San Antonio, Texas // Air Force Villages

Facility type: Independent Living, Long-term Skilled Nursing, Short-term Rehabilitation
Target market: Middle/Upper Middle
Site location: Suburban; Brownfield site
Project site area (square feet): 1,661,362
Gross square footage of the new construction involved in the project: 139,537

Gross square footage of the renovation(s)/ modernization(s) involved in the project: 29,846
Purpose of the renovation/modernization: Repositioning
Number of parking spaces added by the project: 64
The site is within 1000 feet of public transportation and everyday shopping and/or medical services.

The project offers transport to nearby shopping, medical, and/or cultural services/amenities.
Provider type: Non sectarian non-profit
Completion date: July 2011

Overall Project Description

Air Force Villages required repositioning of its two self-contained campuses, one location offering an urban lifestyle, the other a rural setting. This planning addressed resident preferences at each campus, and did not duplicate options or amenities. The resulting plan integrates the campuses, allowing each to stand as a neighborhood within a larger combined context of the Air Force Villages' community.

While the initial master plan addresses the entire two campuses, this phase of the repositioning did not include the Independent Living apartments, current wellness building, or the main town center at Village I. Village II did not previously include any Independent Living, Dementia Care, or Skilled Care.

Project Goals

What three project goals had the greatest impact on the project?

Offering choice through a diversity of housing options; offering daily choice through extensive amenities; and repositioning to appeal to the market.

- Offering choice through a diversity of housing options, including alternative housing.

  Three new four-story Independent Living Hill Residences have been added to the new entry of Village I, replacing existing, smaller duplex-type homes and apartments. A small house model of nursing care, which includes provisions for short-term rehabilitation, has replaced the existing institutional model. Village II added 75 customized-to-suit, ranch-style Independent Living homes.

- Offering daily choice through extensive amenities. Each campus, previously offering only one large dining venue, gained new dining options. A new bistro and a 16th-floor fine-dining Sky Lounge restaurant and bar were created in the Independent Living high-rise at Village I. At Village II, a grab-and-go style café has revitalized the existing town center.

- Repositioning to appeal to the market. The strategic planning focused on addressing future marketability of housing options, as well as amenities for residents. The first phase of enhancements included complementing the single large dining venue at each campus with additional options.

Challenges: What were the greatest design challenges faced by the project?

A new Skilled Care/Rehabilitation residence. The owner's goal was to create a small house model of care in one large building, providing residential care and scale while maximizing efficiencies of shared support spaces and staffing circulation.

Opposite: Influenced by the vernacular Hill Country architecture, the Hill Residences are clustered together to form neighborhoods.
Above: The rehabilitative therapy services, has its own main drop-off and entry for public outpatient use.

Photography: Casey Dunn

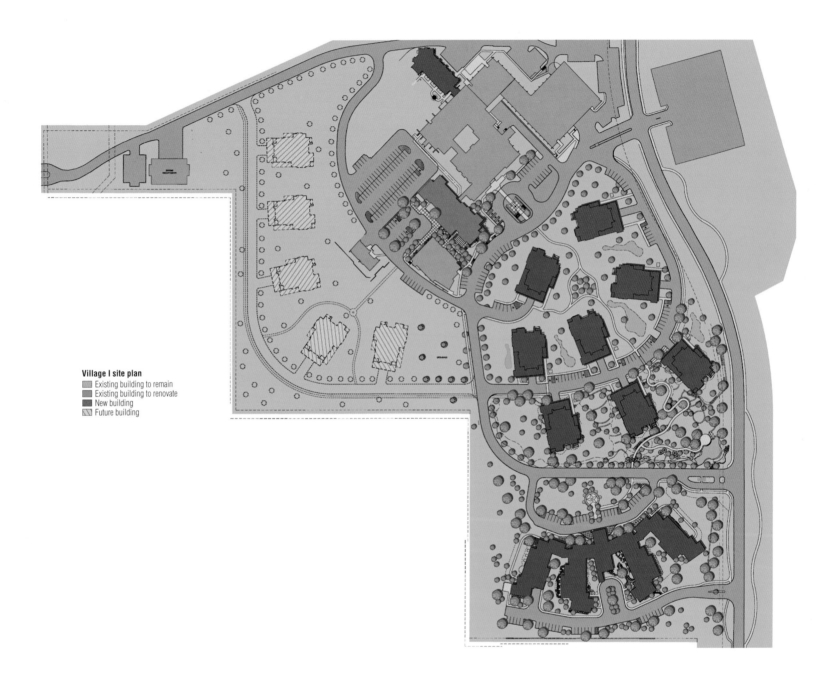

Village I site plan
- Existing building to remain
- Existing building to renovate
- New building
- Future building

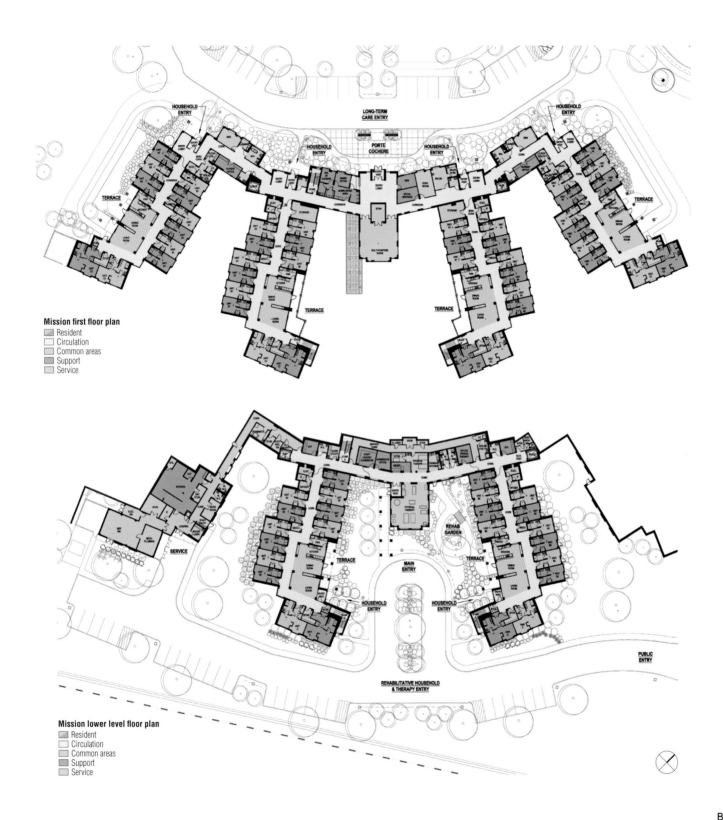

Mission first floor plan
- Resident
- Circulation
- Common areas
- Support
- Service

Mission lower level floor plan
- Resident
- Circulation
- Common areas
- Support
- Service

A hybrid small house model of six connected households was designed. The massing and building elevations are intended to create a unique identity for each household, and to assist in reducing the overall scale of the building.

A second challenge was topography. The site design takes advantage of the challenging, sloping topography and nestles new buildings into the hillside. For the mission, this allows the ability to provide two short-term rehabilitation households on the lower level, with a public entry. The two households also have their own direct entries and private patios off the rooms. The upper level has a main resident and guest entry, each of the four long-term households has its own direct entry, and every two households has a private patio. The Hill Residences maximize the topography slide into the hillside, providing an opportunity to have more ground floor units and enclosed parking.

A third design challenge was adaptive reuse. An underutilized multipurpose room and non-marketable ground floor apartments were transformed into a fine-dining Sky Lounge restaurant and a casual bistro to supplement the one existing dining option on the campus. There was a significant amount of complexity associated with renovating the top floor of the existing high-rise, as well as the ground floor into new dining venues. The renovations included additional floor space, a new kitchen on the ground floor and a finishing kitchen on the 16th floor, as well as a new elevator to supplement the existing slower elevators. The overall design for the Sky Lounge capitalizes on views and provides a private dining venue overlooking the downtown skyline, while the bistro provides a new energy at the base of the building.

Innovations: What innovations/unique features were incorporated into the design of the project?

Unique Feature 1

The master plan addressed two distinct campuses. The plan views each campus as a unique entity, but also as part of a greater neighborhood.

The underutilized multipurpose room atop the high-rise apartment building at Village I offered an opportunity to create a dining destination.

While the new café at Village II and the casual bistro at Village I primarily serve the residents at their respective campus through a shared dining dollar program, they are open to residents of either campus.

Left: Resident rooms offer direct access to the outdoors through private patios. The patios are connected to landscaped courtyards; larger communal terraces provide additional encouragement for residents to spend time outdoors.

Photography: Casey Dunn

Opposite top left: Resident rooms include full private bathrooms with ceiling lifts to assist with transfers from the bed to the toilet and shower.

Photography: Casey Dunn

Opposite top right: Small-scale household living replaces an institutional environment to create a comfortable, intimate lifestyle for long-term care residents.

Photography: Perkins Eastman

Opposite below: The open kitchen and dining rooms allow residents to see, smell, and participate in food preparation. These common, homelike spaces promote resident gatherings and encourage activities.

Photography: Casey Dunn

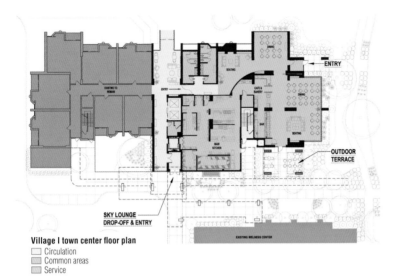

Village I town center floor plan
- ☐ Circulation
- ☐ Common areas
- ☐ Service

Sky Lounge floor plan
- ☐ Circulation
- ☐ Common areas
- ☐ Service

Because Village II has an abundance of land, the ranch homes seemed to fit for this campus – rural, build-to-suit detached homes. At Village I, the compact site lends itself to the multistory Hill Residences. This provides two distinct housing options for prospective residents.

Unique Feature 2

In the small house Skilled Care/Rehabilitation residence, each has a distinct name, entry, front porch, and outdoor space. The selection of a carpet pattern and a rustic modern aesthetic lead to six color palettes, guiding interior themes, materials, furniture, and accessories. This approach created six separate homes.

Unique Feature 3

The existing cottage homes at Village I were less marketable because of their smaller size, outdated amenities, and aesthetic. However, the area of the site did not allow a one-for-one replacement with a similar, modestly larger, updated product. The Hill Residences were developed as a new housing option. All corner units have large balconies and updated amenities, providing an intermediate scale on the campus.

Features/Services/Amenities: What are the most important features/services/amenities that were incorporated into the project specifically to attract the targeted market?

Multiple dining venues, updated Independent Living houses, and a small house model of nursing care, which includes provisions for short-term rehabilitation.

Green/Sustainable Features: What are the green/sustainable features that had the greatest impact on the project's design?

Energy efficiency, maximized daylighting, and site design considerations.

What are the primary motivations for including green/sustainable design features in the project?

Lower operational costs, to support the mission and values of the client/provider, and to support the mission and values of the design team.

What challenges have you faced when trying to incorporate green/sustainable design features?

Actual first cost premium.

Aesthetic: Identify which aesthetic your project embraces, why it was chosen and how it was achieved.

Based on the diversity of the project, the design aesthetic reflects the program, environment, and population being served.

Contemporary Lifestyle – Hospitality Focus

Transformed from an underutilized multipurpose room, the Sky Lounge is a destination dining venue that reflects the aesthetic of a Piano

Opposite top left: The wine tasting room can become a private dining space by closing the draperies, creating an intimate gathering area. This area can also be set up as a dance floor for special occasions.
Opposite top right: The Sky Lounge, a destination restaurant and piano bar, provides spectacular views.
Opposite bottom left: Residents and guests are greeted by a host as they arrive on the 16th floor where choices in dining include a formal restaurant, wine tasting room, and piano bar.

Photography: Casey Dunn

Above: Taking advantage of the sloping topography and maximizing green space provides a more intimately scaled environment.

Photography: Casey Dunn

Common Spaces: What common spaces are included in the project?

Bistro/casual dining, coffee shop/grab-and-go, dedicated classroom/learning space, dedicated conference/meeting space, rehabilitation/therapy gym, formal dining, large multipurpose room, and a salon.

For a typical household wing/facility, describe the common spaces.

Each household includes its own outside entrance. From there, a sitting parlor leads into each household, which includes its own kitchen and great room, providing a dining and living space. On the upper level, a terrace offers space for outdoor dining and activities, while the bottom level has patios. Every two households share a den and a spa.

- Sitting parlor – 150 square feet
- Den – 200 square feet
- Spa – 150 square feet
- Kitchen with breakfast nook – 285 square feet
- Great room – 715 square feet
- Outdoor patios – 385 square feet
- Terrace – 440 square feet.

Describe the largest interior common space in the project (excluding dining).

Other than dining, the largest interior common space is the 1000-square foot multipurpose room in the Skilled Care residence. The room was designed to serve as a chapel, classroom for educational events, celebration space for holidays and special events, and a performing arts space. The room was placed adjacent to the reception area, welcoming both residents and their visitors.

Describe each dining venue incorporated in the project.

The dining venues were structured to provide choice at all levels of care. At Air Force Village I, Cochran's provides a casual bistro dining atmosphere. There is also an outdoor terrace.

Bar and Supper Club. Set in a high-rise, the design offers an opportunity to continue the contemporary lines of the existing high-rise into the space.

Transformed from another underutilized space, Cochran's at Village I is a casual, rustic bistro bar.

The café at Village II recreates an underutilized entry lobby. Various pavilions of space add to the vast lobby to activate the environment. The wood screens define the monumental staircase that descends to an existing dining venue, and color, pattern, and texture help define intimate spaces.

Contemporary Lifestyle – Residential Focus

The Ranch Homes and Hill Residences draw influence from the local Texas Foothill vernacular. Stone, wood, and stucco materials with expanses of glass are designed in a contemporary residential aesthetic for these housing types.

The mission is a series of Skilled Care small homes set in a residential scale. Familiar elements, including massing, materiality, and finishes and furniture, create unique households that are a reflection of home.

For the residential component, what was critical to the success of the project?

Improving common spaces/amenities.

Households: Describe the role households had in the project.

Air Force Villages wanted to deinstitutionalize their long-term care and replace their existing institutional model with a smaller scale, more intimate, residential model. The new Skilled Care/Rehabilitation residence is designed in a small house connected model, and contains six unique households. Each household is unique aesthetically, creating a smaller identity for residents to call home. Each household also has a distinct entry from the outside, breaking down the scale of the building.

The Sky Lounge, located on the 16th floor, is the more formal dining option. What used to be an isolated and underutilized multipurpose room is now a destination restaurant and lounge overlooking the adjacent airfield and downtown San Antonio. The dining room includes the Piano Bar, as well as a private dining room.

At Village II, a coffee shop and deli revitalize a town center. The existing lobby of the town center had become a vast concourse of empty seating. The new coffee shop and deli activate the lobby entry.

Design Process: Who did the design team work with to gather information that could be applied to the design of the project?

Care team staff, current/existing residents, design consultants, market analysts, non-care team staff, potential/future residents, and provider administrators.

Which techniques were used with non-design team members to gather information that could be applied to the design of the project?

Charrette/working session, focus group/interview, full-scale mock-up, and presentation to a review board.

In addition to the client and designers, who had a key decision-making role?

Provider administrators, and provider board of directors.

Opposite top left: Renovations to the entry lobby redefine space and function with an illuminated floor to ceiling wood screen that acts as a natural way-finding element and an artistic piece that reflects changing patterns of sunlight.

Opposite top right: This new town center is the heart of Air Force Village II and features a cafe with grab-and-go items, computer lounge, library, and activity/game areas.

Photography: Casey Dunn

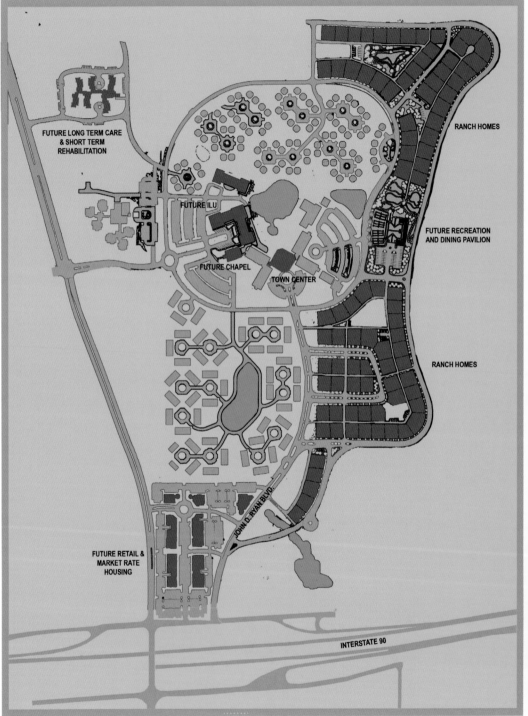

Village II site plan

FUTURE LONG TERM CARE & SHORT TERM REHABILITATION

RANCH HOMES

FUTURE ILU

FUTURE RECREATION AND DINING PAVILION

FUTURE CHAPEL

TOWN CENTER

RANCH HOMES

JOHN D. RYAN BLVD.

FUTURE RETAIL & MARKET RATE HOUSING

INTERSTATE 90

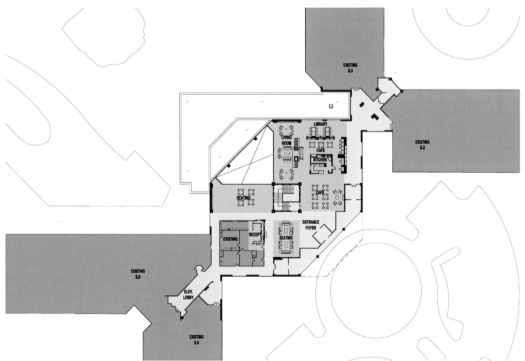

Village II town center floor plan
☐ Circulation
☐ Common areas
☐ Service

RLPS Architects

Foulkeways Community Center

Gwynedd, Pennsylvania // Foulkeways at Gwynedd

Facility type: Senior Community Center
Target market: Mixed Income – Quaker philosophy embraces diversity. This is part of Foulkeways' mission, vision, and values.
Site location: Suburban
Project site area (square feet): 225,640
Gross square footage of the addition(s) involved in the project: 15,540

Gross square footage of the renovation(s)/modernization(s) involved in the project: 21,143
Purpose of the renovation/modernization: Upgrade the environment
Number of parking spaces added by the project: 0
The site is within 1000 feet of public transportation and everyday shopping and/or medical services.

The project offers transport to nearby shopping, medical, and/or cultural services/amenities.
Provider type: Faith-based non-profit
Completion date: May 2012

Overall Project Description

This community center reinvention focused on merging the latest advances in senior living with the center's 350 year old Quaker heritage. The residents of Foulkeways envisaged a vibrant dining, gathering, and activity hub that embodied the Quaker ideals of simplicity, humility, and light while utilizing natural, sustainable materials.

A significant challenge was creating a coherent design image for the building, which had been renovated six times over the past 40 years. After analyzing 16 Quaker meetinghouses in the Historic American Buildings Survey collection – a division of the Library of Congress – the design team identified a consistent pattern of Quaker vernacular, which influenced the final solution.

The building additions create a cohesive façade defined by traditional Quaker design principles, while providing space to expand and update the main dining room, library, lounge, and auditorium on the upper level. On the lower level, a new café/bistro, lounge, and terrace dining area enjoy panoramic meadow views. The previous café location was transformed into an ice cream parlor and marketplace.

Project Goals

What three project goals had the greatest impact on the project?

Connecting to nature; offering daily choice through extensive amenities; and responding to local conditions.

- The primary goal of the project was to offer expanded resident choice through updating community center amenities, focusing primarily on the dining venues. For the formal dining room on the main floor, a new open serving/preparation area was a focal point for expanding the space, which also includes a buffet line. A new fireplace features handcrafted, local Mercer tile. Updated lighting and added glazing significantly improve the natural light and overall ambience. A new bistro replaces the café that was previously located on the lower level, the site of which has been converted into a coffee shop/ice cream parlor and convenience store. The new café/bistro provides a much larger casual dining venue with outdoor seating, as well as varied food stations including salad bar, pizza oven, deli, grille, coffee bar, and grab-and-go options.

- The community center update respected the community's Quaker heritage, and particularly the Quaker values for ensuring that all voices are heard.

- Connection to nature is a campus-wide priority for Foulkeways, and strengthening that connection was an integral part of the

Opposite left: New terrace dining
Opposite right: Main staircase leading to lower level bistro
Above: Former café has been converted to an ice cream parlor/coffee shop.

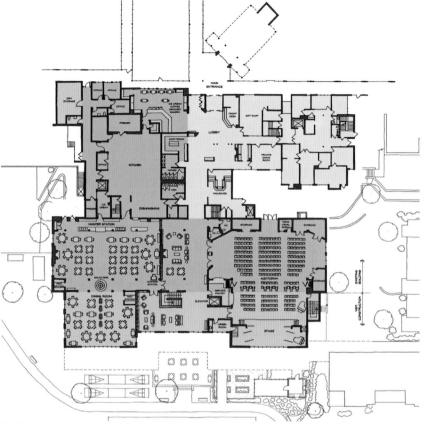

Main level floor plan

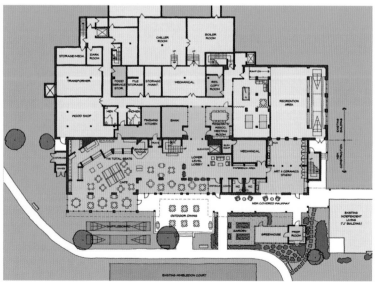

Lower level floor plan

community center update. For the main dining room expansion, this was achieved by simply increasing the size and quantity of windows, while adding a trellis outside to minimize glare. The multipurpose room was oriented to create a unique performing arts space with a window wall behind the stage at the front of the room. Dormer windows bring natural light into the stairway leading down to the new bistro areas, while the bistro itself features clerestory windows along one wall, as well as a patio dining option. The internal coffee shop features a large mirror wall on one side, and windows on the other to maximize light from the adjacent corridor.

Challenges: What were the greatest design challenges faced by the project?

The greatest design challenge for this project was meeting resident expectations for a simple, coherent solution when updating a building that had been renovated and expanded six times over the preceding of 40 years. The design team came up with a simple solution based on a pattern of Quaker design. The design consisted of two simple wings that extend from the existing building and provide additional space for the dining room and a multipurpose room.

Another issue for this project was a debate that ensued regarding whether to construct a new café/bistro or simply expand the existing café into the loading dock/receiving area. In addition to compromising outdoor views and natural lighting, a detailed cost analysis of the two options revealed no cost savings with the seemingly more modest approach. This is due, in part, to numerous utility relocations that would have been required to accommodate expansion into the loading dock area.

in the new café/bistro, the simple, straightforward design style reflects Quaker values for high-quality, natural materials.

Features/Services/Amenities: What are the most important features/services/amenities that were incorporated into the project specifically to attract the targeted market?

In addition to providing the new, larger bistro/café area with a range of food options, creating a new identity for the former café was another critical element due to its front door location. Based on resident input, the former café evolved into a coffee shop/ice cream parlor/convenience store. Both the new bistro and the coffee shop are "all day" locations that encourage socialization among residents, staff, and visitors. Providing indoor/outdoor services for coffee, ice cream, and other grab-and-go items is a key feature in making these venues appealing and convenient.

It was important to residents that the formal dining room was maintained, and expanded in space and variation. Residents now have the option of utilizing the serving line and/or soup and salad bar to make their selections or choosing to have full table service, selecting items from the menu to be served to them.

Patio dining was another priority that has been so well received that less than a year after moving into the spaces, Foulkeways has added more seating to the patio and has introduced outdoor grilling to provide another service option. Residents, staff, and family members utilizing the patio tend to linger, watching the putting green and croquet court, as well as enjoying the privacy and view of the community.

Another major challenge was planning and phasing the expansion and renovations to occur in an operating community center that serves 320 residents every day. The project began with the two-story addition housing the main dining room expansion and the new café/bistro. When the time arrived for the addition to be "tied in" to the existing building, dining services were briefly provided in the existing auditorium. Dining services were increased in other campus dining venues, particularly in the personal care residence, which includes a dining room furnished and finished in a manner consistent with a typical Independent Living dining room. In addition, the existing café was maintained until the main dining room and the new lower level bistro/café were completed. When the main dining areas were completed, renovations commenced in the main entrance and gallery, and the existing café was converted into a coffee shop/ice cream parlor.

Innovations: What innovations/unique features were incorporated into the design of the project?

After receiving 246 letters from residents about aspects of the initial design, the team reviewed their input and went back to the drawing board. The resulting new plan for updating the community center cost $2 million less than the original plan and included buy-in from the residents for a comfortable, amenity-rich community center that is unique to Foulkeways. From the punched tin ceiling in the coffee shop/ice cream parlor and the local Mercer tile on the fireplace in the main dining room and pre-dining areas, to the bamboo flooring

Green/Sustainable Features: What are the green/sustainable features that had the greatest impact on the project's design?

Conscientious choice of materials, energy efficiency, and maximizing daylighting.

What are the primary motivations for including green/sustainable design features in the project?

To support the mission and values of the client/provider.

What challenges have you faced when trying to incorporate green/sustainable design features?

There were no challenges to any sustainable design initiatives. The community leaders, residents, and staff wanted as much as possible in the way of sustainable materials.

Aesthetic: Identify which aesthetic your project embraces, why it was chosen and how it was achieved.

While one of the goals for the community center expansion was updating the environment and providing contemporary dining venues, residents were not interested in a hospitality aesthetic. Instead, the reinvented community center features natural materials, abundant natural light, and simple, clean lines.

Common Spaces: What common spaces are included in the project?

Art studio/craft room, bistro/casual dining, coffee shop/grab-and-go, formal dining, large multipurpose room, library/information resource center, and a marketplace/convenience store.

Describe the largest interior common space in the project (excluding dining).

Multipurpose room – 3738 square feet, capacity 268 seats. The multipurpose room renovations and additions expand the room capacity and reorient the main stage to the southeast, providing meadow views from the stage. A secondary, floor level stage is maintained in the previous stage

location. Other additions include a two-sided serving pantry for multiple event refreshments and a green room for pre- and post-show preparations. Updated technology for sound, lighting, electronic window curtains, and video projection was also incorporated.

Describe each dining venue incorporated in the project.

- Formal dining, capacity 200 seats.
- Covered terrace dining, capacity 50 seats – an outdoor grill has been added along with 15 additional seats.
- Bistro/café, capacity 114 seats (including booths).
- Coffee shop/ice cream parlor, capacity 12 indoor and 15 outdoor covered walkway seats.

Design Process: Who did the design team work with to gather information that could be applied to the design of the project?

Current/existing residents, design consultants, and provider administrators.

Which techniques were used with non-design team members to gather information that could be applied to the design of the project?

Focus group/interview, and presentation to a review board.

In addition to the client and designers, who had a key decision-making role?

Current/existing residents, provider administrators, and provider board of directors.

Right: The main dining room was expanded and updated to include an open serving/preparation area.

Photography: Larry Lefever Photography

Marks, Thomas Architects

Gilchrist Center for Hospice Care

Towson, Maryland // Greater Baltimore Medical Center

Facility type: Hospice
Target market: Mixed Income – low income patients are subsidized by foundation and grant gifts to the Hospice.
Site location: Suburban
Project site area (square feet): 11,500
Gross square footage of the renovation(s)/modernization(s) involved in the project: 11,500

Purpose of the renovation/modernization: More in-patient rooms were needed based on demand.
Number of parking spaces added by the project: 0
The site is within 1000 feet of public transportation and everyday shopping and/or medical services.
Provider type: Non sectarian non-profit
Completion date: October 2009

Below: New building entrance – central access to the building
Photography: Quick Fox Photography

Opposite: Living room – this once small ante-room is now an inviting living room centered around the hearth. Located on the ground floor, it was important that the space felt light and airy.
Photography: Tom Terranova

Overall Project Description

In the original Gilchrist Center for Hospice Care at the Greater Baltimore Medical Center, designed in 1989, the lower level home health office area was designed to eventually accommodate the expansion of in-patient rooms. Now that both home health and in-patient needs have grown, the offices needed to expand to allow for new patient rooms and their accompanying program. The 11,500-square foot renovation consisted of 10 private patient rooms, physicians' offices, a lobby, a family lounge and nourishment kitchen, a nurse's station, a medical room, a commercial kitchen, and a charting area. When it became clear that the facility would become an in-patient care hospice, the entry sequence and main location also had to change. The design scope included a new entrance canopy and lobby interior, as well as to redesign the Conference Center for staff training and bereavement counseling. The remainder of the existing building was refreshed with new wall finishes.

Project Goals

What three project goals had the greatest impact on the project?

Creating a homelike environment; creating a caring environment where dying can occur with the most comfort possible for both the patient and their loved ones; and providing visitor support spaces.

- First and foremost, creating a caring environment where dying can occur with the most comfort and dignity possible for both the patient and their loved ones. This includes providing amenities for all patients such as private patient rooms that accommodate visitors overnight; secluded family areas for grief consultation and relaxation; medical facilities and equipment readily available but hidden from view; and a homelike setting in all publicly accessed spaces.

Also important are teaching spaces, areas to "get away," and efficient laundry, dining and pharmaceutical storage, all provided in a non-institutional hospitality setting – more like an inn than a hospice care facility.

- Creating a homelike environment was achieved through the use of elements such as fireplaces, comfortable furniture, patio doors, warm colors, art work, and wood flooring. It was important that institutional elements like metal doors, white bathroom walls, and vinyl flooring be absent.

- Many visitor support spaces are provided. The hospice can accommodate visitors of all ages, with quiet play areas for children and sleeping chairs for adults in rooms that have residential settings, like living rooms and dens. Families feel welcome in the residential environment, with rooms to congregate and spaces for reflection such as the garden and meditation room.

Challenges: What were the greatest design challenges faced by the project?

The greatest challenge was building the renovation while the premises were occupied, which did not allow for wide-sweeping changes to be made. New patient areas have been designed to be similar to the existing areas, but are updated with new and fresh materials.

A second challenge was the revised entry location which is distant from parking and pedestrian access. The solution is a trellised portico with a glass roof that extends to the vehicular drop off, with stone garden walls that separate rooms from the public area.

A third challenge was the location, a steep site. It was difficult to incorporate gardens for the lower rooms. The solution has been to create new bioswales for stormwater management, which provide grade for the garden platform.

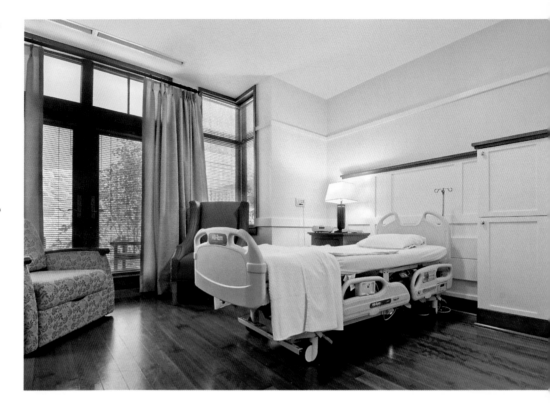

Right: Patient room, headboard and patio – a custom headboard provides storage for the patient while concealing necessary equipment. Each room has access to a landscaped semi-private patio for access to nature and sunlight.

Photography: Tom Terranova

Innovations: What innovations/unique features were incorporated into the design of the project?

Unique features include custom-made patient room doors that feature translucent panes to add detail and create a homelike feel to the extra-wide institutional doors, and custom, built-in headboards that allow hospital beds to look more residential – woodwork conceals vacuum, oxygen and other medical equipment.

Features/Services/Amenities: What are the most important features/services/amenities that were incorporated into the project specifically to attract the targeted market?

- The hospice rooms were designed like "inn" guest rooms, with doors to the gardens, built-ins to conceal medical equipment, and fireplaces in the main lounge spaces to create a warm, homelike feel.

- Bereavement counseling was expanded in the renovation, both for home health customers and in-patient families. Large classroom spaces were added to teach staff how to deal with their feelings, as well as the grief of the patient and their family.

- Doctors working at the hospice had their own special needs. They requested private entries into their offices to avoid frequent interruptions from the families of residents. Their back-of-the-building lower level entry offers them a garden space of their own, plus private access to their office area.

Green/Sustainable Features: What are the green/sustainable features that had the greatest impact on the project's design?

Improved indoor air quality, maximized daylighting, and site design considerations.

What are the primary motivations for including green/sustainable design features in the project?

To stay competitive against other similar/local facilities, to support the mission and values of the client/provider, and to support the mission and values of the design team.

What challenges have you faced when trying to incorporate green/sustainable design features?

Actual and perceived first cost premium.

Aesthetic: Identify which aesthetic your project embraces, why it was chosen and how it was achieved.

Architectural precedents were sought that had a large residential scale but an intimate feel. Craftsman or Arts and Crafts architecture provides both and is broad enough to be creative with details. Also, connections to nature and natural themes were sought by the client, and Arts and Crafts architecture provides these.

Common Spaces: What common spaces are included in the project?

Bistro/casual dining, dedicated classroom/learning space, dedicated conference/meeting space, garden space for each patient room, and religious/spiritual/meditative space.

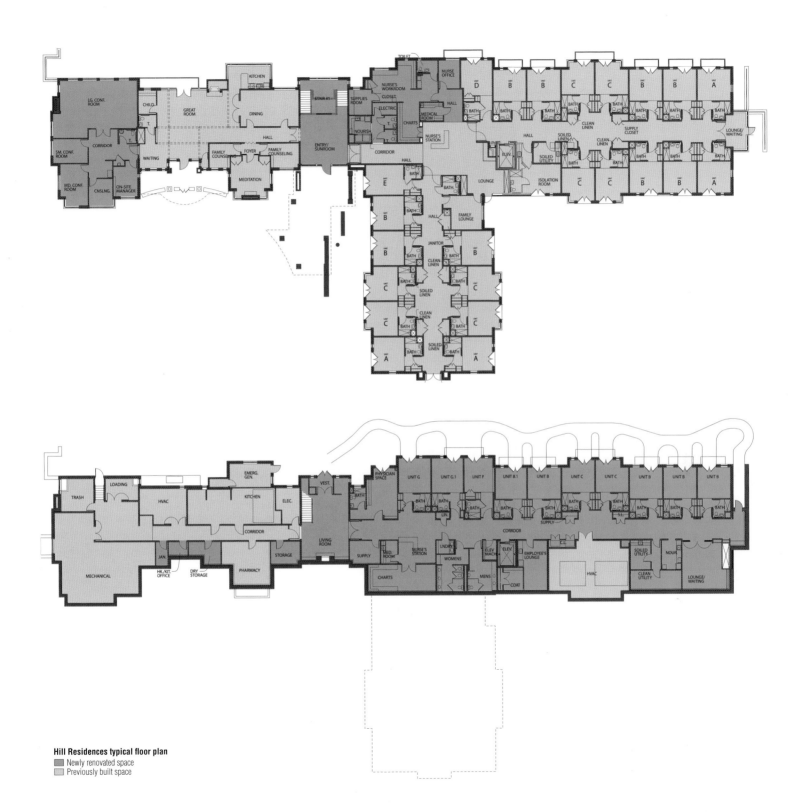

Hill Residences typical floor plan
■ Newly renovated space
■ Previously built space

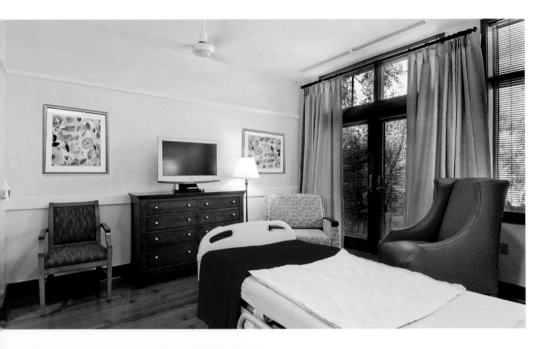

For a typical household wing/facility, describe the common spaces.

The common space for families includes a kitchen, TV area, dining and living room. These spaces allow families to relax and decompress. Counseling rooms are available.

Doctors and nurses offices provide a private conference area for teaching hospice staff, and for in-patient and home health care.

Back-of-house medical care and kitchen facilities conceal the facilities that a hospice needs, but doesn't need to display.

Describe the largest interior common space in the project (excluding dining).

Living room – 400-square foot living area with a seating capacity for two families, which allows each family privacy.

Describe each dining venue incorporated in the project.

An in-room dining service accommodates any requests patients may have.

Design Process: Who did the design team work with to gather information that could be applied to the design of the project?

Care team staff, and provider administrators.

Which techniques were used with non-design team members to gather information that could be applied to the design of the project?

In situ observations.

In addition to the client and designers, who had a key decision-making role?

Provider administrators.

Opposite left: Patients' patios facing east – semi-private patios connected by meandering paths, for patients to have direct access to nature
Photography: Quick Fox Photography

Opposite top right: Bathroom – an earthy paint color warms up this utilitarian space and a seamless floor allows for safe and easy shower access.
Photography: Tom Terranova

Above: Patient room and sitting area – as family is so central to hospice care, each room is appointed with seating for five visitors.
Photography: Tom Terranova

Left: Family lounge – this gathering space gives families an area of refuge during their lengthy visits.
Photography: Tom Terranova

RLPS Architects

Landis Homes: Hybrid Homes

Lititz, Pennsylvania // Landis Homes Retirement Community

Facility type: Independent Living
Target market: Middle/Upper Middle
Site location: Rural; Greenfield site
Project site area (square feet): 4,981,522
Gross square footage of the new construction involved in the project: 72,682

Number of parking spaces added by the project: 45
The project offers transport to nearby shopping, medical, and/or cultural services/amenities.
Provider type: Faith-based non-profit
Completion date: October 2010

Below: Exterior view of pair of hybrid households
Opposite: Exterior view of a hybrid household

Overall Project Description

While providing a new housing option incorporating the features desired by residents, Landis Homes makes use of its land. Density was not to be obtained at the expense of residential character. The resulting hybrid homes now blend the benefits of cottage and apartment living to provide an environmentally and senior-friendly community of up to 13 homes that can be tailored to special interests or economic need.

The hybrid homes provide seniors with a new housing option – multiple exposures, sheltered parking, outdoor living spaces, and an absence of corridors are among the cottage-like benefits. Apartment-like features include indoor access to common areas and opportunities for social connections in a multistory building, which requires less site area. Particularly well-suited to heavily populated suburban areas, hybrid homes offer a higher density model than patio homes but are smaller than a typical apartment building, allowing providers to incrementally expand housing.

The three-story hybrid households are comprised of under-building parking on the first floor with two floors of six hybrid homes each on the floors above.

Designed to achieve LEED Silver Certification, the hybrid homes provide a senior-friendly living environment while achieving responsible stewardship and greater energy efficiency than a traditional building. Under-building parking reduces surface spaces and the associated heat island effects. A geothermal mechanical system, high-performance windows, and increased insulation are projected to help the homes achieve 30 percent higher efficiency than ASHRAE base models. Ultra low-flow fixtures and rainwater harvesting for non-potable uses help to optimize water efficiency. A legacy stormwater management initiative is improving groundwater filtration and recharge.

Project Goals

What three project goals had the greatest impact on the project?

Connecting to nature; offering choice through a diversity of housing options; and providing green/sustainable design.

- Providing choice through a new Independent Housing model that meets the provider's goal of increasing the number of two-bedroom, two-bathroom homes in a higher-density living option. This goal provides a higher-density model that retains features of a patio home, while incorporating the advantages of apartment living. The three-story hybrid households are comprised of under-building parking on the first floor with two floors of six hybrid homes each on the floors above. The hybrid households are paired to share visitor and overflow parking and provide the option for a shared community room and a more moderately priced first floor apartment in one of the households. Each hybrid home includes a private balcony, multiple outdoor exposures, and an open floor plan.

- Maximizing outdoor connections. The homes on each floor are positioned to function as corner units with multiple exposures for improved views and daylight connections. The open floor plan and abundant windows afford multidimensional views of the surrounding countryside. The oversized balcony for each hybrid home is positioned to provide privacy, and plenty of space for outdoor dining, relaxing, and container gardening. The ground floor household patio areas provide opportunities for entertaining and socializing between household members.

- Sustainable design is the third goal. The aim is to reflect a community-wide commitment to sustainable design, and a major focus of

the design solution was achieving LEED Silver Certification. From a geothermal mechanical system to recycled/regional/renewable materials, the hybrid homes are designed to provide a senior-friendly interior environment while achieving stewardship and energy efficiency.

Challenges: What were the greatest design challenges faced by the project?

Meeting the township regulatory process was the greatest design challenge. As part of the project, the flood plain on the property is being restored through a legacy stormwater process, designed to restore an adjacent stream to pre-development conditions rather than employing conventional methods. This involves measures to remove hundreds of years' worth of agricultural sediment that currently limits stormwater capacity and to restore campus stream channels and adjacent floodplains to historical elevations and locations. Based on Landis Homes' commitment to sustainable design, including an anticipated LEED Silver rating for the hybrid homes, the architect and civil engineer worked closely with local officials to educate and solicit endorsement of stewardship initiatives.

Another challenge was designing affordable structured parking. The cost of the parking garage and the associated support space, such as the community room and resident storage, had to be absorbed into the cost of each home.

Meeting floor plan layout design goals for privacy without compromising efficiency or appeal was another challenge. The layout of each home, and particularly the patio/balcony location, was carefully considered to provide privacy and independence to each home, while maintaining an open floor plan that offers interconnectivity of spaces for living, dining, and food preparation.

Innovations: What innovations/unique features were incorporated into the design of the project?

By orienting the households in an "L" formation, each hybrid home benefits from multiple outdoor exposures and enhanced privacy, as well as a first floor household patio/courtyard area defined by the building shape. Pairing hybrid households allows for shared resources, such as overflow/visitor parking and the community room, which in turn allows for an economical first floor apartment in one of the hybrid households.

Features/Services/Amenities: What are the most important features/services/amenities that were incorporated into the project specifically to attract the targeted market?

- Today's elderly consumers expect direct assimilation of floor plans and amenities typical to private residences, such as walk-in closets, laundry centers, eat-in kitchens with daylight exposure, and a home office or den. Hybrid homes are designed to incorporate these amenities more cost-effectively than a single patio home, without losing the sense of community provided in an apartment setting. Six homes on each floor are arranged around a central hearth room, much like the great room in a private residence, reinforcing a residential scale while eliminating the institutional corridors found in a traditional apartment building.

- Covered parking is typically a key consideration for seniors considering a move to a retirement community and one of the benefits of patio homes. Placing parking on the first floor under the homes offers the additional benefits of less surface space being needed.

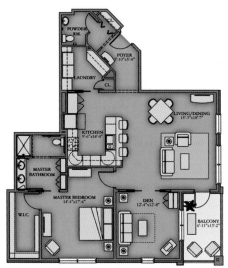

Unit A one-bedroom plus den plan

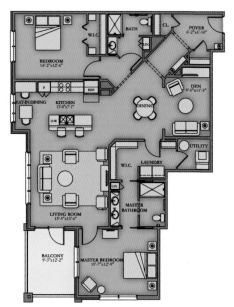

Unit B two-bedroom plan

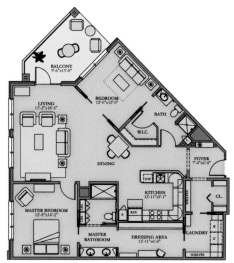

Unit C two-bedroom plan

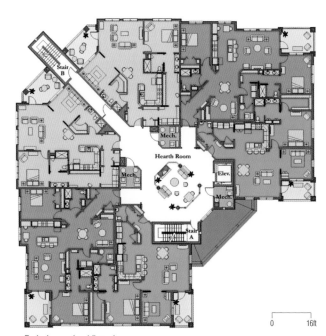

Typical upper-level floor plan

0   16ft

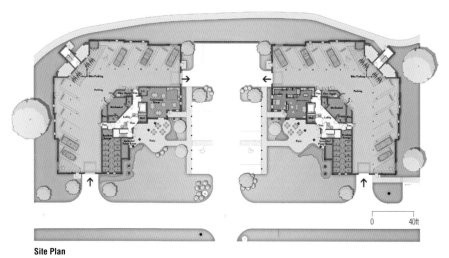

Site Plan

0   40ft

Opposite top left: Hearth rooms on upper floors provide opportunities for social connections.

Opposite top right: The lower level community room provides a larger space for entertaining, meetings and special events.

- Discreetly supportive features and wheelchair-accessible doorways facilitate aging-in-place. Accessibility, from door clearances to space templates, is designed into all homes with consideration for kitchens and bathrooms that can accommodate active residents, those who require assistance from a spouse or care giver, and those who utilize wheelchairs or scooters to maintain their independent mobility. The homes are designed to allow equal access to any user without compromising the residential aesthetic through supportive features such as shower grab rails and elevated vanities. A post-occupancy evaluation revealed a perceived stigma associated with any conspicuous accommodations for aging-in-place, such as roll-in showers and grab bars.

Green/Sustainable Features: What are the green/sustainable features that had the greatest impact on the project's design?

Energy efficiency, improved indoor air quality, and maximizing daylighting.

What are the primary motivations for including green/sustainable design features in the project?

Lower operational costs, to make a contribution to the greater community, and to support the mission and values of the client/provider.

What challenges have you faced when trying to incorporate green/sustainable design features?

Perceived first cost premium, and lack of board or leadership support.

Aesthetic: Identify which aesthetic your project embraces, why it was chosen and how it was achieved.

For the hybrid homes designed to bridge the gap between patio homes and apartments, a homelike/residential appearance was critical for attracting the target market for this rural Lancaster County community. Traditional architectural forms and details were incorporated

Opposite top: Balconies are positioned for privacy and
generously sized
Opposite bottom: Unit B – view from great room to
balcony
Above: Unit A great room with multiple outdoor views

to reflect the local rural vernacular. Similarly, the façade features a mix of local materials that are found on a farmhouse including stone, brick, and cedar trim. Inside, the hybrid homes feature open floor plan layouts and a traditional design aesthetic. The homes on each floor are arranged around a central hearth room, much like the great room in a private residence, reinforcing a residential scale while eliminating the institutional corridors found in an apartment building. The hearth room is highlighted by a stone fireplace and features craftsman-style detailing, which is carried through to the front door for each hybrid home, accessed from the hearth area.

Finally, to maintain a residential idiom as well as affordability, the hybrid homes are built to residential standards, with a wood frame structure and no automatic door openers.

For the residential component, what was critical to the success of the project?

Improving units/private spaces.

Households: Describe the role households had in the project.

A defining feature of this new seniors housing model, hybrid households foster a sense of community between occupants of up to 13 homes per household with social spaces, including a hearth room on each floor and the shared community room, as well as service spaces associated with typical daily routines, such as a mail room or recycling area. These household spaces provide opportunities for spontaneous social interactions, shared hobbies, and lifelong learning.

Common Spaces: What common spaces are included in the project?

Large multipurpose room.

For a typical household wing/facility, describe the common spaces.

- Lobby/sitting area – 333 square feet/capacity 4.
- Covered entry/patio area – 315 square feet/capacity 16.
- Hearth rooms – 430 square feet/2 floors/capacity 10.
- Community room (shared between two households) – 816 square feet/capacity 56.
- Mail room – 57 square feet.
- Resident storage – 648 square feet.

Describe the largest interior common space in the project (excluding dining).

The ground-level community room, typically shared between two households, provides opportunities for shared hobbies, entertaining, life-long learning, and socialization between household members and with other households. The residential kitchen in the community room expands programming options for the space, whether for use in group events or by individual residents to provide refreshments or even meals for a larger group. The patio area outside the community room and front household entrance affords opportunities for outdoor entertaining and socializing.

Design Process: Who did the design team work with to gather information that could be applied to the design of the project?

Contractor/construction team, current/existing residents, market analysts, non-care team staff, potential/future residents, and provider administrators.

Which techniques were used with non-design team members to gather information that could be applied to the design of the project?

Charrette/working session, focus group/interview, and a presentation to a review board.

In addition to the client and designers, who had a key decision-making role?

Provider board of directors.

Off-site Outreach Services: What off-site outreach services are offered to the greater community?

The community rooms may be made available for use by selected community groups to promote intergenerational opportunities and shared resources.

RLPS Architects

Longwood at Oakmont: Hanna Healthcare Center

Verona, Pennsylvania // Presbyterian SeniorCare

Facility type: Long-term Skilled Nursing, Short-term Rehabilitation, Skilled Nursing Dementia/Memory Support
Target market: Middle/Upper Middle
Site location: Suburban
Project site area (square feet): 94,000
Gross square footage of the addition(s) involved in the project: 31,706

Gross square footage of the renovation(s)/ modernization(s) involved in the project: 26,633
Purpose of the renovation/modernization: Upgrade the environment
Number of parking spaces added by the project: 48
The site is within 1000 feet of public transportation and everyday shopping and/or medical services.

The project offers transport to nearby shopping, medical, and/or cultural services/amenities.
Provider type: Faith-based non-profit
Completion date: October 2009

Overall Project Description

To support the transition to a resident-centered care model, the Hanna Healthcare Center represents a multiphased reinvention through a two-story addition and renovations of the existing space to create small, separate households of 12–16 residents. This first phase of new construction provides 32 private rooms with European showers, walk-in closets, and walk-out bay windows to expand views and orientation to the Oakmont Country Club and golf course.

The two new 16-bed neighborhoods are organized around an open and spacious family room, dining room, and activity center. Nursing support is presented in a hospitality design solution that is fully integrated into the resident program areas. A fireplace parlor provides each neighborhood with a focal point for organizing activities and serving as an area to assemble prior to meals.

Each reconfigured household has its own communal living areas, dining room, and spa bathing room providing a comfortable, residential environment with more privacy, as well as social spaces for family visits and interaction among residents. The reinvented residential-style kitchens with open cooking areas serve as a focal point of activity. In each household a separate activity kitchen is provided directly between the living and dining room, so activities can take place even when the country kitchen is being used by staff for meal preparation. The nurses station, medications, and other service areas are tucked away to allow the resident areas to be the new centerpiece of the household.

Project Goals

What three project goals had the greatest impact on the project?

Creating a homelike environment; offering choice through a diversity of housing options; and incorporating the adoption of the household/neighborhood concept by decentralization into neighborhoods, and promoting a sense of community among residents, staff, visiting families/friends, and/or neighbors from the greater community.

- Creating a homelike environment was the most influential driver of the project, together with the owner's vision and conviction in creating both a resident-centered care operation and a supportive physical environment. Architectural decisions to reinvent the environment were based on establishing a functional program of creating a home. Design decisions were based primarily on the ability to reinforce this functional objective and were applied selectively to have the most impact. The resulting households are warm and inviting, eliminating overhead paging, medical carts, and other instruments of care, thereby enabling the communal living areas and country kitchens to take center stage. The interior also assumes a "country club" aesthetic, taking its cues from the Oakmont Country Club across the street.

- Following from the adoption of the all-private-room and household concept to support the operational shift to resident-centered care, the environment needed to facilitate this change by reorganizing the existing institutional nursing units into smaller, residential-style households, reinforced by separate household living and dining areas.

- Promoting a sense of community and resident/staff relationships, the new households, and particularly the dining rooms/country kitchens/activity kitchens, enable the provider to be both more resident and team member focused. Eliminating the traditional nursing station breaks down a significant physical and psychological barrier between staff and residents.

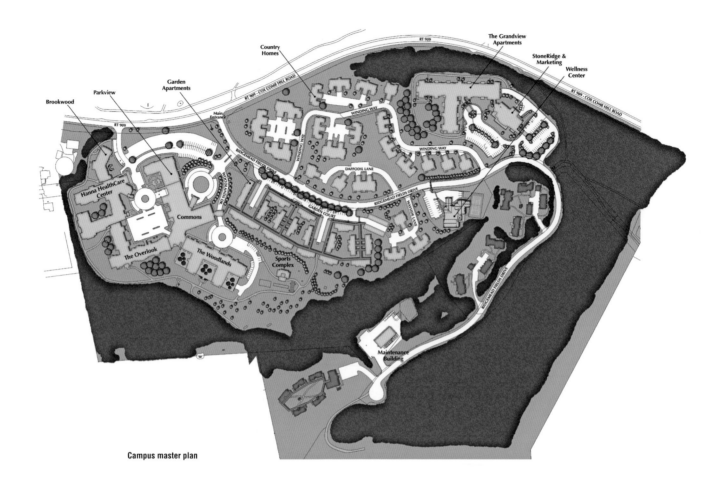

Campus master plan

Labels on map: Brookwood, Parkview, Garden Apartments, Country Homes, The Grandview Apartments, StoneRidge & Marketing, Wellness Center, Hanna HealthCare Center, Main Entrance, Commons, The Overlook, The Woodlands, Sports Complex, Garden Court, Daffodil Lane, Winding Way, Ridgemead Fields Drive, Maintenance Building, RT 909 - COX COMB HILL ROAD

Challenges: What were the greatest design challenges faced by the project?

The greatest challenge was overcoming the logistics of building a new, two-story social household model Skilled Nursing center immediately adjacent to an existing Independent Living apartment building, and mitigating concerns relating to the future marketability of those Independent Living Units. The site adjacent to the apartments was the only remaining buildable area. Bay windows, covered porches, bright colors, extensive glass at social spaces, and other residential detailing provide a seamless transition between the two areas.

A second challenge was found in the overriding goal for the project: to convert a medical model Health Center, comprising primarily semi-private rooms, into a social household model with all private rooms. This goal suggested that the first phase, two-story healthcare addition be large enough to allow all of the Skilled Nursing residents to be relocated there upon completion, allowing the phase two renovations to take place in the existing vacated building. Any hurdles during the various phases were addressed so that both the Skilled Nursing and neighboring Independent Living residents' lifestyles were not compromised.

This goal was only achievable through a strong team effort, including the owner, contractor, and architect/engineers.

A third challenge was balancing the goals of the project with the constraints of the budget, site, and existing building. Careful prioritization and analysis of the tradeoffs between various options helped lead the design team in complex choices for both the new addition and renovated areas. The design decisions were based on where they would have the most impact.

Innovations: What innovations/unique features were incorporated into the design of the project?

Every resident is provided with an experience that reinforces a sense of "home." This is achieved through the additions and renovations in all private and shared-bathroom private rooms, ensuring privacy is not compromised. Each private bedroom space also includes a walk-in closet for the resident's personal belongings. Bed linens, towels, and other supplies for that resident are also stored in the walk-in closet, eliminating the need for service carts. Each room also has a fully accessible bathroom including a shower.

In addition to the residential country kitchen, a second activity kitchen is provided directly between the living and dining rooms. This allows kitchen/cooking activities to take place in an area removed from the serving/staff component of mealtimes. This area serves as a hub of activity and also provides staff members with another activity area option.

Features/Services/Amenities: What are the most important features/services/amenities that were incorporated into the project specifically to attract the targeted market?

The first priority for this reinvention project was creating neighborhoods, each with its own communal living spaces. A close second was improving resident rooms to facilitate greater privacy, dignity, and comfort. The first phase of new construction provides 28 private rooms with private European showers, and four rooms with separate bedroom areas and a shared bathroom with European shower. All of the rooms include walk-in closets and walk-out bay windows. Indirect lighting complements wall sconces and table lamps to create a glare-free residential atmosphere. Similarly, the introduction of European showers in the rehabilitation neighborhood reinforces dignity and privacy for those residents. Finally, the elimination of the traditional nurses' stations makes staff members accessible to residents. Carts, medications, and other implements of care are tucked away to allow the resident areas to become the new centerpiece of the households. Corridors are animated by curio cabinets displaying personal items rather than carts or medical equipment.

Green/Sustainable Features: What are the green/sustainable features that had the greatest impact on the project's design?

Energy efficiency, improved indoor air quality, and maximizing daylighting.

What are the primary motivations for including green/sustainable design features in the project?

Lower operational costs, to support the mission and values of the client/provider, and to support the mission and values of the design team.

What challenges have you faced when trying to incorporate green/sustainable design features?

Actual first cost premium.

Above left: Staff desk; other functions are tucked behind the scenes.
Above right: Activity kitchen, adjacent to dining area, serves as an activity hub.

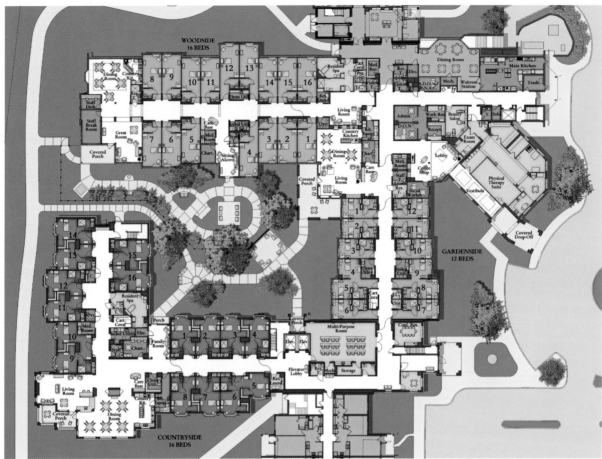

Floor plan of new neighborhood addition and renovated Rehabilitation and Memory Care neighborhoods

Private room unit plan

Semi-private unit plan

Aesthetic: Identify which aesthetic your project embraces, why it was chosen and how it was achieved.

The aesthetic for the Hanna Healthcare Center is homelike/residential. A guiding principle for the design team was to minimize or eliminate features not typically found in a traditional home. The design team looked to the neighboring Oakmont Country Club for inspiration, resulting in rich wood tones, soft arches, and elegant lighting. The gracious and inviting corridors feature floor-to-ceiling curio cabinets, artwork, direct and indirect lighting, crown molding, and stained wood paneling.

For the residential component, what was critical to the success of the project?

Improving units/private spaces.

Households: Describe the role households had in the project.

Introducing households was a major priority of this healthcare center reinvention project.

This was accomplished with a two-story addition, comprising a 16-bed household on each floor. The addition, in turn, allowed for the renovation of the existing health center into a 12-bed Rehabilitation household and a 16-bed Memory Care household, each with its own dining and living areas.

Common Spaces: What common spaces are included in the project?

Coffee shop/grab-and-go, dedicated conference/meeting space, large multipurpose room, and salon.

For a typical household wing/facility, describe the common spaces.

- Family rooms – 124 square feet, capacity 4.
- Living rooms/lounges – 518 square feet, capacity 17.
- Sitting areas – 240 square feet, capacity 8.
- Dining room – 639 square feet, capacity 20.
- Bathing spa – 237 square feet.

Describe the largest interior common space in the project (excluding dining).

962-square foot multipurpose room, with a capacity of 32 seats. The multipurpose room is used for a variety of staff and resident functions including meetings, educational seminars, training, performing arts, and special events.

Describe each dining venue incorporated in the project.

Each neighborhood now includes a dining room with country kitchen (20 resident capacity), which replaces the former nursing station as the hub of activity. Today, 90 percent or more of Hanna's residents eat in the country kitchens, compared to 40 percent in the previous dining room. A separate activity kitchen is provided between the living and dining rooms so that it can be used while staff are preparing meals in the country kitchen.

Design Process: Who did the design team work with to gather information that could be applied to the design of the project?

Care team staff, contractor/construction team, current/existing residents, potential/future residents, and provider administrators.

Which techniques were used with non-design team members to gather information that could be applied to the design of the project?

Charrette/working session, focus group/interview, presentation to a review board, and a survey.

In addition to the client and designers, who had a key decision-making role?

Care team staff, contractor/construction team, and provider administrators.

Opposite: Resident rooms include bay windows, walk-in closets and private bathrooms with European showers.

Photography: Larry Lefever Photography

EGA PC

Mary's Meadow at Providence Place

Holyoke, Massachusetts // Sisters of Providence

Facility type: Long-term Skilled Nursing, Short-term Rehabilitation
Target market: Mixed Income – built by the Sisters of Providence to replace their existing long-term care facility, the project houses the elderly members of their order, most of whom are low income and live on various subsidies, and individuals from the larger community.

Site location: Suburban; Greenfield site
Project site area (square feet): 535,788
Gross square footage of the new construction involved in the project: 30,135
Number of parking spaces added by the project: 42
The site is within 1000 feet of public transportation.
Provider type: Faith-based non-profit
Completion date: August 2009

Opposite: Houses – massing broken into recognizable residential elements
Left: Garden – one of four unique gardens

Photography: Jarred Sadowski

The kitchen, living, and dining spaces all look like the spaces found in a typical home. Each house has access to its own garden, designed to respond to the orientation/climate of the particular location.

To the extent possible, service spaces are removed from residential spaces, while still being a short distance away for staff convenience.

- Responding to site constraints. The site available was both small and had a significant slope. The Sisters' wish to have the houses joined together at a central chapel and the need to minimize level changes for the frail elderly left little room for movement in the overall design. Factoring in parking and stormwater management nearly filled the site.

The challenge was to provide as much natural light as possible to the common spaces of the building (each private room has a large bay window with a window seat). To accomplish this, the buildings are articulated in such a way as to carve out a separate entrance and garden for each house, and a large wall of windows face into the gardens from each dining room. Additionally, large and small skylights are used to bring more natural light into the interior spaces that otherwise would have no direct connection to the outside.

- Promoting a sense of community was part of the larger goal of the residential model of long-term care. The goal was to create an environment that promotes improved health and wellbeing for the residents as they live out their lives.

Overall Project Description

The project was built to replace an existing long-term care facility previously located on a secure floor within a hospital that otherwise serves those with mental illness. The Sisters of Providence wanted to return their elderly sisters to a new facility closer to their Motherhouse, on a portion of their campus adjacent to the Motherhouse that had yet to be developed. The project consists of 40 new long-term care beds in four 10-bed houses connected by a central chapel. At least one of the 10-bed houses can be used for short-term rehabilitation, depending on the need in the larger community. The adjacent Motherhouse provides some support to the long-term care facility in the form of administrative services and maintenance, but otherwise the project is self-sufficient.

Project Goals

What three project goals had the greatest impact on the project?

Creating a homelike environment; promoting sense of community and responding to local conditions.

- Creating a homelike environment in the "small house" residential model of long-term care, which seeks to provide all of the typical services found in a traditional nursing home. By separating a typical nursing unit into four 10-bed houses, it is possible to break down the scale of all of the required elements while simultaneously reducing travel distances, which may make it easier for the less mobile residents to participate in the active life of the household.

Each resident has their own private room, all of which are nearly equally close – by nursing standards – to the common spaces.

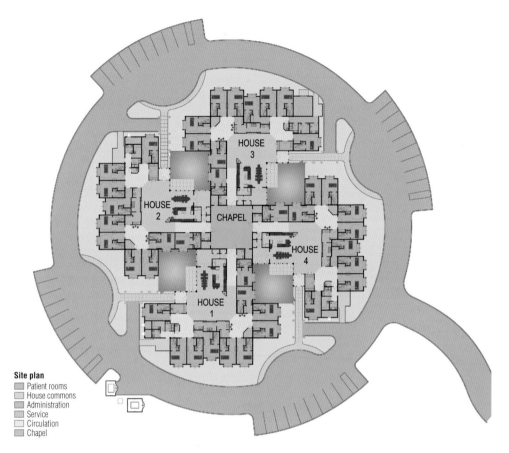

Site plan
- Patient rooms
- House commons
- Administration
- Service
- Circulation
- Chapel

HOUSE 3

HOUSE 2

CHAPEL

HOUSE 4

HOUSE 1

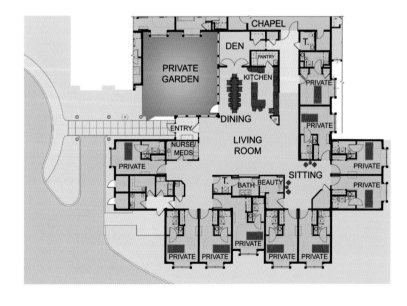

Typical house floor plan
- Patient rooms
- House commons
- Administration
- Service
- Circulation
- Chapel

CHAPEL

DEN

PANTRY

PRIVATE GARDEN

KITCHEN

PRIVATE

T.

DINING

ENTRY

PRIVATE

NURSE/ MEDS

LIVING ROOM

PRIVATE

PRIVATE

SITTING

PRIVATE

T. BATH BEAUTY

PRIVATE

PRIVATE PRIVATE PRIVATE PRIVATE

The scale of the houses, the residential feel of the commons spaces, and the reduction in focus on the service areas are the architectural elements that help to foster this sense of community. Equally important are the staff and resident interactions within these spaces, and the relationships they develop over time.

Challenges: What were the greatest design challenges faced by the project?

The site presented the greatest challenge. It was both small and had significant grade change across its width. Linking the four houses together at a common chapel meant that the houses needed to be at essentially the same grade, so the site needed to be flattened more than may otherwise be desirable. Linking the houses reduced the amount of available exterior wall for windows into common spaces.

Limited space for dealing with stormwater was addressed by putting some of it below the drive and parking areas, and the rest in an area of the site not used for buildings. The shape of the detention basins respond to the shape of the available land.

The buildings for each of the houses pinwheel off from the chapel, and each of the houses is shaped so as to allow each a separate entrance and a private garden.

A second challenge was that the project was the first of its kind licensed in Massachusetts. As such, the regulatory review process was involved and required a significant amount of discussion/revision with the Department of Public Health. In the end, 30 physical plant waivers were required to achieve the desired outcome, many of which reflect the smaller scale found in this model.

Innovations: What innovations/unique features were incorporated into the design of the project?

As a residential model long-term care facility in Massachusetts, the whole concept ranks as unique. The scale and outfitting of the kitchen, the short

travel distances from resident rooms to commons, the minimization of staff spaces including administration and service, the easily accessible private gardens, and the shared chapel spaces are innovative in the realm of long-term care.

Each resident room has a ceiling-mounted lift to minimize staffing requirements and injuries. Each garden responds to the exposure/orientation of its particular location.

Features/Services/Amenities: What are the most important features/services/amenities that were incorporated into the project specifically to attract the targeted market?

• 10-bed nursing units in a residential model

• Private rooms with private baths

• Short-stay rehabilitation facilities in a residential model.

Green/Sustainable Features: What are the green/sustainable features that had the greatest impact on the project's design?

Conscientious choice of materials, maximizing daylighting, and water efficiency.

What are the primary motivations for including green/sustainable design features in the project?

To support the mission and values of the client/ provider.

What challenges have you faced when trying to incorporate green/sustainable design features?

Actual first cost premium, and lack of knowledge about green/sustainability.

Aesthetic: Identify which aesthetic your project embraces, why it was chosen and how it was achieved.

The project strives for a residential appearance, but that effort is constrained by a host of competing

issues, including usability by the elderly (height of seat/arm), flammability of furnishings, cleanability/ durability of carpets and wall coverings, hospital beds, and other issues that tend to push towards a more hospitality-based aesthetic.

The goal of the small house model of long-term care is to create an environment that is as homelike as possible, so the project strives to feel like a home, albeit one with 10 residents and most of the state-enforced requirements of long-term care (such as corridor widths and door widths.)

Top left: Site plan – location plan showing relationship to Motherhouse

Photography/Illustration: EGA PC / Google Earth

Top right: Chapel – shared central chapel linking four houses

Photography: Ned Gray

The architecture pushes the residential feel by the small scale of the spaces, the trims, the finishes and equipment in the kitchen, the arrangement of the spaces in a grouping rather than along a corridor, diminishing the impact of the service spaces, and other similar means. The furnishings and finishes also attempt to foster a residential feel while addressing usability and durability issues.

Households: Describe the role households had in the project.

The project is the first small house residential model long-term care facility in Massachusetts, and as such, is entirely based upon a household model.

Common Spaces: What common spaces are included in the project?

Formal dining, religious/spiritual/meditative space, dedicated rehabilitation/therapy gym, resident-maintained gardening space, and salon.

For a typical household wing/facility, describe the common spaces.

- Kitchen (220 square feet) – preparation of all resident meals and activity space.
- Dining (250 square feet) – long table with 12 seats for sharing meals and doing activities.
- Living room (415 square feet) – casual seating for eight plus activity table for four with a fireplace.
- Den (180 square feet) – used as the television room and a quieter area for small gatherings.
- Chapel (1150 square feet) – shared among the four households for worship services and quiet contemplation.

Describe the largest interior common space in the project (excluding dining).

The chapel is the largest common space at 1150 square feet. It includes seating for up to 30. It is used for daily worship services and for quiet personal contemplation.

Describe each dining venue incorporated in the project.

Each household has a residential dining room with a large table seating 12. At least one meal per day is shared among all residents, with flexibility, based on resident wishes, for other meal options.

Design Process: Who did the design team work with to gather information that could be applied to the design of the project?

Care team staff, city planners/code officials, contractor/construction team, design consultants, non-care team staff, potential/future residents, and provider administrators.

Which techniques were used with non-design team members to gather information that could be applied to the design of the project?

Charrette/working session, full-scale mock-up, and presentation to a review board.

In addition to the client and designers, who had a key decision-making role?

Care team staff, contractor/construction team, and provider administrators.

Opposite: Kitchen – typical house kitchen
Top left: Bedroom – typical resident room with bay
Top right: Dining – typical house dining room with view to garden

Photography: Jarred Sadowski

Cummings & McCrady Inc

Read Cloister Nursing Community Transformations

Charleston, South Carolina // Bishop Gadsden Retirement Community

Facility type: Long-term Skilled Nursing
Target market: Upper
Site location: Suburban
Project site area (square feet): 3072
Gross square footage of the renovation(s)/ modernization(s) involved in the project: 3072

Purpose of the renovation/modernization: Upgrade the environment
Number of parking spaces added by the project: 0
The project offers transport to nearby shopping, medical, and/or cultural services/amenities.
Provider type: Faith-based non-profit
Completion date: 2011

Below: Main dining area for the residents
Opposite: Skylight bathes the room in natural light.

To resolve this, a 10-by-10-foot skylight was installed, becoming a dramatic feature in the room and allowing for ample natural light where it was most needed.

Project Goals

What three project goals had the greatest impact on the project?

Offering daily choice through extensive amenities; promoting a sense of community and providing a hospitality/resort feel.

- Offering daily choice through extensive amenities. This project supports culture change initiatives and improves resident quality of life by increasing choices, options, and flexibility in the dining experience for Skilled Nursing residents. A full-production servery area gives residents access to a wide variety of fresh, made-to-order meals to satisfy their preferences at any given moment. From the hot-grill and griddle – where everything from stir-frys to burgers to grilled fish is available daily – to the sandwich and salad deli bar, to the comforting soups and hot entrees, and the ice cream topping bar with homemade desserts, the variety and flexibility is extensive. The fully accessible servery allows residents to see and smell the food as it is being prepared, as well as interact with the chef and dining staff. Residents may serve themselves, have staff assist them in the serving line, or they may be seated and wait staff will take their order from a menu.

- Promoting a sense of community. The Skilled Nursing dining room historically was too small and uninviting for residents to host guests. This renovation doubled the square footage, allowing ample seating for residents to regularly host friends and family. An example of this success is seen at holiday meals when unprecedented numbers of guests are

Overall Project Description

In 2007, as part of a master planning process, the owner began the replacement of its Skilled Nursing and Memory Care areas. Gathering input from residents, staff, resident families, and board members, a plan was created for a state-of-the-art building to include a flexible and resident-centered café for meal service. In the wake of the economic downturn, these plans were shelved. However, an office and a dry food storage area were moved to other locations down the exterior corridor adjacent the dining room. The dining room itself has been updated, with the following goals foremost in the upgrade.

- Create a new focal point/centerpiece for the room. The servery functions as the action centerpiece for the room. Its luxury finishes, glass tiles, lively lighting, and metallic accents all create a clean, sleek focal point that draws attention to the fresh, made-to-order selections awaiting residents.

- Keep a separate but open area for residents needing total assistance. The layout of the dining room was planned so that there is a natural separation between residents who need total assistance with dining and those who do not, to preserve the dignity of those needing assistance and maximize the dining satisfaction for both groups. The room was prepped with electricity for optional lighted, translucent, moveable room dividers to allow the highest flexibility and success in dividing the room.

- Maximizing natural light. This was a particularly important goal since the room initially only had one large triple-window, leaving much of the room without direct access to natural light. Relocating one of the offices on the exterior adjacent hall produced a second large triple-window looking out to a courtyard. Still, half of the room was perceived as dark and without natural light.

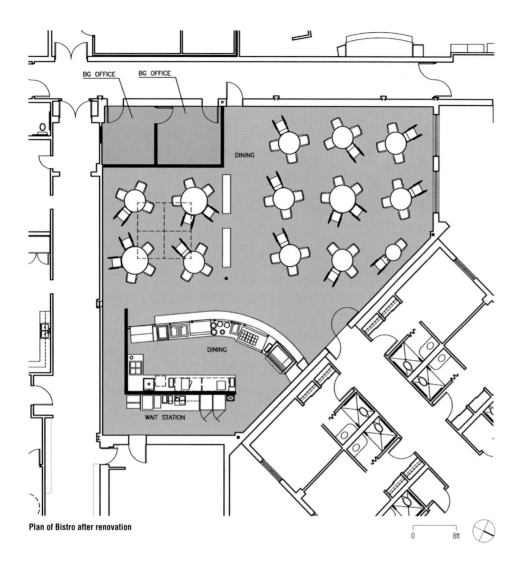

Plan of Bistro after renovation

0   8ft

served in the bistro. The additional space and welcoming atmosphere also gives residents the opportunity to have friends from other areas of the community (such as Independent Living or Assisted Living) join them for a meal. The bistro strengthened the sense of community on campus, eased transition resistance, and helped residents become familiar and comfortable with the Skilled Nursing environment.

- Providing a hospitality/resort feel. A goal of the renovation was to bring the quality of the Skilled Nursing environment up to the level seen throughout the rest of the campus. The provider was committed to the intention that while resident need and care levels may be revealing, one would not recognize the environment in the dining room as Skilled Nursing by the surroundings. The high-quality finishes and contemporary design promote a resort-type environment and eliminate any institutional characteristics. From the transitional glass tile to modern spot and drop lights, the environment feels more like a restaurant than a Skilled Nursing facility.

Challenges: What were the greatest design challenges faced by the project?

There were no readily available prototypes or models for this type of food service program in Skilled Nursing. The owner's experienced Food Service Director had a varied background including institutional and restaurant start-up experience and was able to select the equipment and work with the architect to provide a general layout of the production space. Key to the project's success was ensuring the servery concept would be functional and that food quality would be as much a hallmark of this dining venue as the aesthetic/design quality. Because this design was innovative, it required extensive consultation and planning with state code and health regulatory

Left: Residents have an abundance of choices.

cooking staff to easily accommodate requests and customize orders. The open hours and welcoming environment provide residents and families with a destination, not only at traditional meal times, but also for refreshments or meals at any time of day. Dining staff may be found frying eggs just before lunch for a late riser, serving coffee and pie for an afternoon snack, or preparing a wrap for a light supper. The servery design supports the innovative change from institutional culture to a resident-centered dining experience.

officials. Following discussions of the culture change and resident-centered care goals for the project, state health facilities' construction staff endorsed the project and assisted in the effort to produce a compliant and effective project.

Because the dining space is an interior room, capturing the necessary square footage to incorporate a functional servery/production area, as well as gain additional seating for guests, was another challenge. The design team was able to creatively move offices, bathrooms and a dry food storage area in order to incorporate that space, which was key to the design's success.

Providing maximum exposure to natural light was an important goal of the upgrade. As an interior room, more than half of the dining room did not have access to windows or an exterior wall. A design incorporating a large skylight answered this concern. The generous scale of the skylight admits ample natural light and serves as a dramatic feature.

Innovations: What innovations/unique features were incorporated into the design of the project?

The fully functional and accessible production servery is unique to the Skilled Nursing environment. The ability of Skilled Nursing residents to see, smell, and choose from a variety of options made-to-order is unique. Prior to designing and developing this concept, the Skilled Nursing dining system was a cycle menu. Residents (and often their care givers or family members) would make food selections days in advance from a printed paper menu with limited choices. There was a distinct disconnect between the residents' personal preference at the moment the meal was served and the choices they may have made at a previous point in time without the benefit of seeing and smelling the food. Now, residents decide what they want based on what looks and smells appealing to them at each meal. They are able to interact with the chefs to make their preferences known, and the functionality of the production space allows

Features/Services/Amenities: What are the most important features/services/amenities that were incorporated into the project specifically to attract the targeted market?

Residents in Skilled Nursing who transition through the continuum on-campus are accustomed to a hospitality/resort-type environment and the choices offered in other dining areas. The options and flexibility offered in the bistro are important features to residents and their families. This represents a change in culture from institutional dining service, eliminating the limited menu and defined meal times. The high-end finishes and contemporary, upbeat look of the room are consistent with the quality of the environment seen elsewhere on the campus and enhance the feeling of "going somewhere" for a meal.

Green/Sustainable Features: What are the green/sustainable features that had the greatest impact on the project's design?

Energy efficiency, improved indoor air quality, and maximizing daylighting.

What are the primary motivations for including green/sustainable design features in the project?

Lower operational costs, to make a contribution to the greater community, and to support the mission and values of the design team.

Aesthetic: Identify which aesthetic your project embraces, why it was chosen and how it was achieved.

The Skilled Nursing facility is undergoing a transformation to match the environment found throughout the rest of the campus. The community as a whole is best described as having a Southern hospitality/resort-type appearance. Management of the community is continually engaging in an effort to update and modernize in order to meet the expectations of the market. For the Skilled Nursing dining room renovation project, a distinctly contemporary, casually elegant approach to the interiors was chosen, and this style is being carried through in the ongoing renovation of the Skilled Nursing area. Contemporary lighting fixtures, tile work, and a coffered ceiling highlight the style, providing both a comfortable setting for current residents, and a fresh, up-to-date look for the market and future residents.

For the residential component, what was critical to the success of the project?

Improving common spaces/amenities.

Common Spaces: What common spaces are included in the project?

Bistro/casual dining and coffee shop/grab-and-go.

Describe each dining venue incorporated in the project.

This project was the renovation of Skilled Nursing dining from a traditional-style service to a casually elegant, flexible café/bistro facility. Open from 7:00am to 7:00pm, the Schlemmer

Servery plan
1   Custom front counter
2   Exhaust hood system
3   48" with 36" griddle and 12" char-broiler
4   Refrigerated equipment stand
5   Refrigerated sandwich unit
6   Drop-in cold pan unit
7   Drop-in soup well
8   Drop-in heated bowl dispenser
9   Drop-in heated plate dispenser
10 Undercounter refrigerator
11 48" heated shelf
12 Drop-in hot food well
13 Drop-in cold pan unit
14 Drop-in refrigerated frost top unit
15 Refrigerated display case
16 Custom counter
17 Drop-in ice cream dipping cabinet
18 Drop-in dipperwell
19 Drop-in sink
20 Half-height heated cabinet
21 Trash container (3)
22 Undercounter rerfrigerator
23 Not used
24 Undercounter freezer
25 Not used
26 Hand sink
27 Glass door refrigerator (by owner)
28 Reach-in freezer
29 Wall-mounted cabinet
30 Custom beverage counter
31 Drop-in ice and water station (by owner)
32 Coffee brewer (by owner)
33 Tea brewer (by owner)
34 Juice dispenser (by owner)
35 Ice and soda dispenser (by vender)
36 Ice maker w/bin (by owner)
37 Custom sneeze guard
38 Storage cabinet
39 Wall-mounted shelf
40 Post station (by owner)

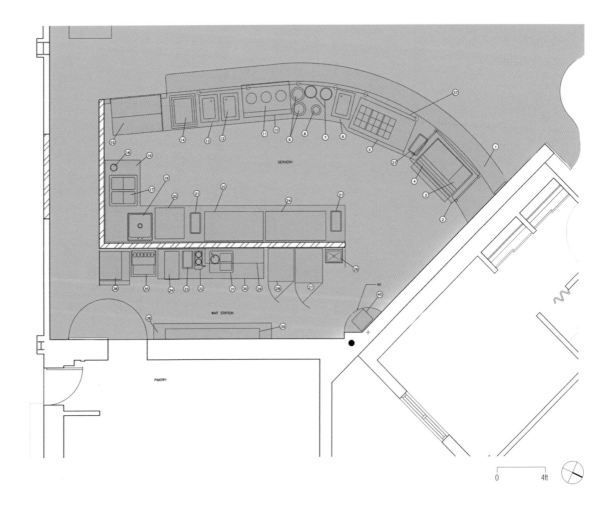

0   4ft

Bistro operates from a fully functional production servery featuring made-to-order grill items, sandwiches, entrees, soups, salads, and homemade desserts. The bistro seats 54 at any one time to easily accommodate residents and guests in this 48-resident area.

Design Process: Who did the design team work with to gather information that could be applied to the design of the project?

Care team staff, city planners/code officials, current/existing residents, design consultants, family or friends of residents, non-care team staff, and provider administrators.

Which techniques were used with non-design team members to gather information that could be applied to the design of the project?

Charrette/working session, focus group/interview, in situ observations, and a presentation to a review board.

In addition to the client and designers, who had a key decision-making role?

Care team staff, city planners/code officials, non-care team staff, provider administrators, and provider board of directors.

Below: View of the servery from the dining area
Photography: W. Baker and GMK

Kava Massih Architects

AgeSong at Bayside Park

Emeryville, California // AgeSong, Inc. & Long Wharf Real Estate Partners, LP

Facility type: Assisted Living, Assisted Living Dementia/ Memory Support, Hospice – AgeSong is licensed to provide residents with hospice care in their resident units
Target market: Middle/Upper Middle
Site location: Urban; Brownfield site
Project site area (square feet): 30,000
Gross square footage of the new construction involved in the project: 116,366

Number of parking spaces added by the project: 37
The site is within 1000 feet of public transportation and everyday shopping and/or medical services. The project offers transport to nearby shopping, medical, and/or cultural services/amenities.
Provider type: For profit
Completion date: February 2010

Below left: Main street entrance with glass canopy above and street-level steel sculptures beyond
Below: Southeast corner of building – ground-floor shared resident spaces open to street.
Opposite: The generous main lobby serves as the heart of the community providing access to various shared services.

Overall Project Description

The five-story project located in an urban area was designed to accommodate upwards of 160 residents. The first floor includes common resident spaces, administrative offices and indoor parking, the second and fourth floors provide Assisted Living units and support spaces, the third floor provides Forgetfulness Care and the fifth floor provides Independent Living units. This project was undertaken to enable the client to bring their philosophy of providing senior care to a new community. The client believes that aging is a resource, not a liability, and their goal is to re-establish the role of eldership in the community. Many highly visible common spaces are included that actively – through their many programs – promote a sense of community and friendship among the residents and develop a synergy with the surrounding community. On any given day there will be craft activities, an art sale, a jazz concert or a lecture at AgeSong. School children come to converse with residents and university students offer counseling and companionship.

The "Kneipp" philosophy is a holistic approach to health and healing that is integrated into the building and therefore the residents' lives. It is structured around five focuses: water, plants, exercise, nutrition, and balance. These are incorporated into the building in the form of hydrotherapy facilities, planted courtyards, exercise rooms, menus offering local organic food, and meditation services.

Project Goals

What three project goals had the greatest impact on the project?

Integrating with the surrounding neighborhood/ greater community; promoting holistic wellness, a sense of community among residents, staff, visiting families/friends, and/or neighbors from the greater community; and to design a building that reflects the client's care philosophy.

The key to accomplishing these goals relies on three important planning directions:

- The common spaces look onto the adjacent commercial street. Large windows make the residents a part of the street action.

- A variety of outdoor spaces are provided, including a central courtyard, a roof garden, green roofs, and several decks.

- The clustering of the common spaces maximizes the energy and sense of vitality about all the spaces.

Another key goal was to construct the project within budget. Although the project was designed to budget, subsequent to the start of construction some previously unknown issues required a large increase in site development expenses. As a result, a number of value engineering decisions were initiated: the finished roof material, originally scheduled to be pavers, was changed to a concrete topping slab; the overall accessible roof area was reduced in size; the lobby floor, originally intended to be stone, was changed to porcelain tile; and the installation of solar panels was delayed. These value engineering decisions were made so that no resident amenities were eliminated.

It was also a key project goal to respect the surrounding architecture. Historically the area has been a hub of small, light industrial buildings. Many of these buildings are still standing today. They tend to be brick and have a simple, regular rhythm of punched window openings. They also tend to have a tripartite façade design. The project relates to the existing architecture in several ways: there is a clear bottom, middle, and top to the façade design; the center portion of each façade is a regular array of windows with a projecting steel frame to provide shading and definition; and overall, the façade is broken up with glass corners, so that the perceived scale of the building melds with the scale of the older structures.

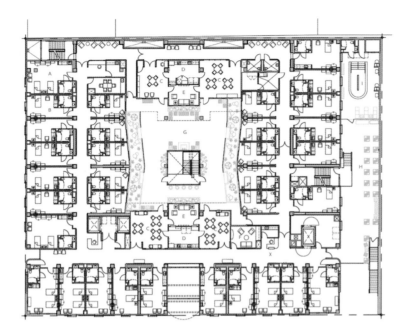

Second floor plan
A Typical single unit
B Typical double unit
C Dining
D Warming kitchen
E TV lounge
F Quiet living room
G Central courtyard
H East courtyard/
   vegetable garden
I Kneipp pool

First floor plan
A Cafe
B Beauty salon
C Meditation space
D Fitness center
E Lobby
F Expressive arts
G Dining
H Kitchen
I Library
J Staff lounge
K Administrative offices
L Parking garage

HORTON STREET

40TH STREET

0   32ft

Challenges: What were the greatest design challenges faced by the project?

The greatest challenge was to maximize the program without having the site appear to be overbuilt. This was accomplished in several ways:

- The building used a post-tension construction system that avoided deep beams. This in turn allowed for a lower floor to floor dimension while maximizing the clear ceiling height. The typical ceiling height in resident units is nine feet and three inches, and the typical ceiling height of the first floor common spaces is 13 feet.

- Both the first and the fifth floors are set back from the rest of the façade.

- Large expanses of glass at the corners of the building minimize the perceived overall building mass.

A linked design challenge was building five floors within the 55-foot height limit. This was accomplished by utilizing the post-tension slab system described above.

A third challenge was maintaining a strong design connection to the exterior. Strong, clear connections between the interior and the exterior were accomplished in several ways:

- A central courtyard allows light to enter the interior spaces of the building.

- On each floor, large windows are located at the ends of every main east–west corridor.

- The main resident corridor is broken up with a lounge area that features a full wall of glass looking onto the commercial street.

- Areas such as the dining and café include exterior spaces.

Innovations: What innovations/unique features were incorporated into the design of the project?

The Kneipp philosophy of care inspired some of the innovative features of this project. Foremost of these is the inclusion of a wellness walking pool on the second floor deck. Adjacent to the pool are hot/cold foot and arm therapy tubs designed for use as part of the Kneipp wellness program. Other innovations include a public café, which residents can access directly from within the building, a meditation room, and an art consignment center located in the lobby. This center is a changing art gallery and also offers resident-produced art for sale.

Architecturally, the roof is equipped with a large resident deck offering views of the surrounding area. Planted with drought-resistant native plants, the green roof filters particulate rainwater runoff to reduce pollution in the bay area. The roof has

heat-pumps that make up part of the efficient split heat-pump mechanical system. Provisions have also been made for future passive solar collectors on the roof.

Features/Services/Amenities: What are the most important features/services/amenities that were incorporated into the project specifically to attract the targeted market?

- Market-sized, high-quality residential units brought in a wide age-range of residents. This adheres to the care giving goal of having seniors as a part of the larger community.

- The abundance of outdoor green spaces is unique to this area.

- Another targeted audience is the greater community. The project sought to bring the community into regular contact with the residents and vice versa. Both the large

common space that is the main lobby and the street-side café blur the edge between the seniors' zone and the community, ultimately bringing the two together.

Green/Sustainable Features: What are the green/sustainable features that had the greatest impact on the project's design?

Maximizing daylighting, site selection, reducing solar gain/heat island effect, and planting including rainwater filtration planters and green-roofs.

What are the primary motivations for including green/sustainable design features in the project?

To make a contribution to the greater community, to adhere to the Kneipp philosophy of "wellness and healing," and to support the mission and values of the client/provider.

What challenges have you faced when trying to incorporate green/sustainable design features?

Actual and perceived first cost premium.

Aesthetic: Identify which aesthetic your project embraces, why it was chosen and how it was achieved.

This project is a physical manifestation of the client's philosophy. Thus the project is prominently located on a busy intersection in an up-and-coming multigenerational area.

The design aesthetic was a reflection of the owner's goal to change the stereotype of elders. The building represents "today" and the power and vitality of "now." The architecture is outward-looking, a contemporary interpretation of the light industrial buildings that remain in the area.

It is designed heavily with glass, connecting it to the wider world. The interiors follow the same philosophy. They are clean and modern with strong color accents, reflecting the energy that is the community.

Art is an integral part of the design and enhances the message that the community is vital and that the elders are a part of that community. Custom pieces are designed and fabricated by local artists. They include planters and sculpture on the entry side of the building, patterned glass over the entry, a sculptural stair leading to the second floor, and a curated collection of prints and drawings.

For the residential component, what was critical to the success of the project?

Improving common spaces/amenities.

Households: Describe the role households had in the project.

Creating households was an important factor in the planning of the Assisted Living and Forgetfulness Care floors. Generally each household consists of 16 rooms, and each household has its own dining room, lounge area, and staff support space. The formation of households was not an important factor in planning the Independent Living floor.

Common Spaces: What common spaces are included in the project?

Art studio/craft room, bistro/casual dining, coffee shop/grab-and-go, dedicated conference/meeting space, dedicated exercise classroom, dedicated fitness equipment room, formal dining, library/information resource center, massage/aromatherapy room, religious/spiritual/meditative space, resident-maintained gardening space, salon, and pool/aquatics facility.

Above: The backlit "Holy Wall" in the meditation room contains multidenominational niches.
Right: The main dining room with full height windows onto outdoor dining and the public street beyond
Opposite left: Light-filled corner units afford views of downtown Oakland and the San Francisco Bay.
Opposite right: Typical 1- bedroom Independent Living unit

Photography: Bruce Damonte Photography

For a typical household wing/facility, describe the common spaces?

Each household has (two) small dining rooms each accommodating 14-16 residents with a shared kitchen between. Additional common spaces include a TV lounge, a quiet reading lounge, art studios and various corridor conversation alcoves.

Describe the largest interior common space in the project (excluding dining).

The largest interior common area is the entry space – it acts as a town square. People entering the building from both the main entrance and the entrance from the parking garage go through this space. It is the nexus of all activities. It opens onto the primary common areas (dining, crafts, and exercise), putting these spaces front and center and encouraging residents to partake in the ongoing activities. The space can accommodate up to 150 people.

Describe each dining venue incorporated in the project.

The main dining room accommodates 54. The street-side outdoor terrace outdoor terrace, adjacent to the main dining room, accommodates eight. A public café seats 28 inside and has an additional eight seats outside. Each Forgetfulness Care household has two dining rooms, each accommodating 14-16. Assisted Living residents generally dine in the main dining room on the ground floor, but also have access to a private dining room on their own floor.

Design Process: Who did the design team work with to gather information that could be applied to the design of the project?

Care team staff, city planners/code officials, design consultants, market analysts, neighbors/members of the greater community, non-care team staff, an orthopedic surgeon, and "Healing Environments Org."

Which techniques were used with non-design team members to gather information that could be applied to the design of the project?

Charrette/working session, full-scale mock-up, and presentation to a review board.

In addition to the client and designers, who had a key decision-making role?

Care team staff, city planners/code officials, non-care team staff, and provider administrators.

Blanche Robertson Garden Cottage at Penick Village

Southern Pines, North Carolina // Penick Village

Facility type: Assisted Living
Target market: Middle/Upper Middle
Site location: Suburban
Project site area (square feet): 47,916
Gross square footage of the new construction involved in the project: 6997

Number of parking spaces added by the project: 8
The site is within 1000 feet of public transportation and everyday shopping and/or medical services. The project offers transport to nearby shopping, medical, and/or cultural services/amenities.

Provider type: Faith-based non-profit
Completion date: March 2010

Opposite: The Garden Cottage blends with neighboring Craftsman bungalows in historic Southern Pines, North Carolina.
Left: A view towards the southwest shows the scale of the Garden Cottage.

Overall Project Description

After much research, the Board of Directors of Penick Village decided that small, single-family home living provides life-affirming, life-enhancing care to elderly residents in both Assisted Living and Skilled Nursing settings. Committed to holistic, resident-centered care, the Board studied similar facilities in operation in other states, and decided that none suited the delivery of care philosophy that Penick Village imagined for its residents. The Board and executive team felt compelled to develop their own care delivery systems, and design and build the facilities to support the systems. This project is Garden Cottage, the first of a total of six planned cottages. The result of a year of cooperative efforts by the Division of Health Service Regulation (DHSR) and Penick Village partnership, the Garden Cottage is the first licensed, free-standing single-family Assisted Living home of its kind in North Carolina. In keeping with Penick Village's holistic philosophy, it is also the first Assisted Living facility in North Carolina to be Certified under the LEED for Homes program (LEED Silver).

Project Goals

What three project goals had the greatest impact on the project?

Creating a homelike environment; promoting a sense of community; and providing green/sustainable design.

- Creating a homelike environment. The goal was to create a home for 10 Assisted Living residents. Every aspect of the design was measured by the simple question, "Would you have this in your home?" The house is designed with single bedrooms and single baths, ample in size to accommodate the residents' choice of furnishings, books, and artwork, and to be a place where each resident can enjoy privacy. The kitchen, dining room, and living room are all open to each other and to the hallways and are visible from most resident room entry doors. This arrangement allows residents to group together easily with short travel distances or to remain on the periphery of activity as they choose.

- Promoting a sense of community. The philosophy behind the Garden Cottage is to house 10 Assisted Living residents in a single-family setting attended by caregivers. Residents and staff choose their meal menus together, prepare the food together, eat together at one big dining table, and clean up together. The kitchen is always open to the residents and food is available anytime a resident wants it. Residents decide what to do, and routine chores are performed by caregivers, with as much involvement of residents as the residents would like. The small, intimate size of the home reduces travel distances to the minimum. The view of the great room from almost every resident room door affords residents an awareness of group activities.

- Providing green/sustainable design. The design team discovered ways to achieve LEED Silver Certification without a significant increase in construction cost. Landscaping is drought tolerant and consists of native plant varieties. All stormwater is managed on site and the Garden Cottage is within half a mile of 14 public amenities. The large French doors and high clerestory windows in the common room allows daylight to reach deep into the house. Low-VOC paints and finishes are used throughout the Cottage. Other sustainable design features include the use of recycled materials (for example, carpet), regional materials (brick and tile), Energy Star appliances, and enhanced outdoor air ventilation.

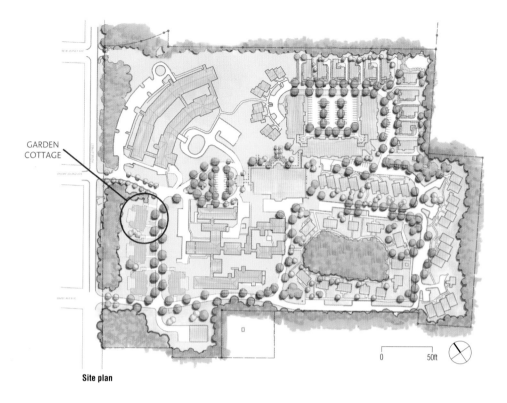

GARDEN COTTAGE

Site plan

0   50ft

Challenges: What were the greatest design challenges faced by the project?

Until now, North Carolina's Division of Health Service Regulation (DHSR) has not permitted licensing as Assisted Living for a small, free-standing, 10-resident, single-family home. The project owners and architects asked the Chief of DHSR to join the design team early on to explore how to interpret the governing regulation by use of equivalency measures to remove barriers to single-family living in a licensed environment. This collaborative effort succeeded, and the Garden Cottage is the first of its kind in North Carolina – a purpose-built, free-standing, single-family house licensed for Assisted Living.

Another challenge was that the Garden Cottage was the first Assisted Living facility in North Carolina to be certified under the LEED for Homes program. LEED for Homes was a new program at the time, and the architect worked closely with the U.S. Green Building Council (USGBC) during this pilot phase to help determine specifics of implementation and certification requirements.

Innovations: What innovations/unique features were incorporated into the design of the project?

The ceiling of the common room was increased from nine feet (the ceiling height throughout the rest of the house) to 13 feet 8 inches, creating a clerestory on the exterior wall, allowing for high windows in addition to the French doors across the room's exterior wall. This allows daylight to reach deep into the house, adding to the views of the garden. The open views of the common room from almost every resident room afford residents awareness of group activity. The short travel distance to the common room encourages less mobile residents to venture out and join in. Universal design elements are employed throughout the Garden Cottage. Features such as lower kitchen counters encourage residents to participate in food preparation from a

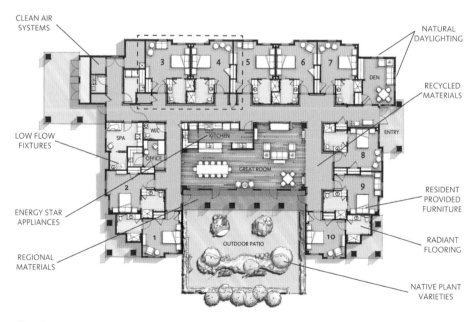

CLEAN AIR SYSTEMS

NATURAL DAYLIGHTING

RECYCLED MATERIALS

LOW FLOW FIXTURES

RESIDENT PROVIDED FURNITURE

ENERGY STAR APPLIANCES

RADIANT FLOORING

REGIONAL MATERIALS

NATIVE PLANT VARIETIES

DEN

ENTRY

SPA

WIC

OFFICE

KITCHEN

GREAT ROOM

OUTDOOR PATIO

Floor plan

Above: The great room is the gathering space for staff
and residents.

Above: Universal height counter makes it easy for residents to help with meal preparation.
Top right: Bathing spa and salon
Right: The kitchen is like one would find in any home.
Opposite: Residents enjoy the courtyard with its native landscaping.

comfortable sitting position, while features such as a ceramic tile no-threshold shower in every resident bathroom, ample space for accessible travel indoors and out, and no trip hazards, encourage mobility and participation.

Features/Services/Amenities: What are the most important features/services/amenities that were incorporated into the project specifically to attract the targeted market?

- All resident rooms are single-occupancy and have a full bathroom. The rooms are ample in size to accommodate the residents' choice of furnishings, books, and artwork, with an abundance of storage and display space. Each bath has a large ceramic tile, no-threshold shower. Windows in the resident rooms are sized and placed to provide daylight and views to the outside.

- Each resident room has its own 25-SEER, mini split-system heat pump with individual remote control and enhanced fresh air ventilation, so every resident can control the temperature in his or her room.

- Wireless communication components, including internet access, are provided throughout the house and are available in every resident's room.

Green/Sustainable Features: What are the green/sustainable features that had the greatest impact on the project's design?

Conscientious choice of materials, maximizing daylighting, and site design considerations.

What are the primary motivations for including green/sustainable design features in the project?

To make a contribution to the greater community, to support the mission and values of the client/provider, and to support the mission and values of the design team.

Above: A typical resident bedroom
Opposite top left: Each resident room has a
  private bath with lots of storage.

Photography: ©JamesWest/JWest Productions

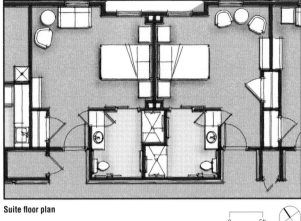

Suite floor plan

0   5ft

What challenges have you faced when trying to incorporate green/sustainable design features?

Actual and perceived first cost premium; lack of Board or leadership support; and lack of resident support.

Aesthetic: Identify which aesthetic your project embraces, why it was chosen and how it was achieved.

The appearance of the Garden Cottage is homelike and residential both inside and out, consistent with the sponsor's commitment to deinstitutionalization of the aging experience. On the interior, this goal is achieved by using residential materials, trim, and furnishings. The exterior is designed to reflect the predominant style of homes in the neighborhood.

For the residential component, what was critical to the success of the project?

Improving common spaces/amenities.

Households: Describe the role households had in the project.

The Garden Cottage is a household.

Common Spaces: For a typical household wing/facility, describe the common spaces.

The Cottage is a free-standing house, with rooms and spaces typical of a house. The Cottage includes: resident bedrooms with attached single bath (average 307 square feet each); a kitchen (221 square feet); a dining area (359 square feet); and a great room (404 square feet). The kitchen, dining, and great room areas are all open to one another. The Cottage also includes a den (195 square feet) and a spa (170 square feet).

Describe the largest interior common space in the project (excluding dining).

The great room (404 square meters) provides seating for up to eight people, plus space for wheelchairs. It is used for socializing, television watching, household meetings, games, puzzles, cards, and reading. It includes a small seating area focused on the television and a game table. The room is open to the dining area and there is room to pull over dining chairs for additional seating if needed.

Describe each dining venue incorporated in the project.

One casual dining area seating 12.

Design Process: Who did the design team work with to gather information that could be applied to the design of the project?

Care team staff, city planners/code officials, current/existing residents, and provider administrators.

Which techniques were used with non-design team members to gather information that could be applied to the design of the project?

Charrette/working session, and a focus group/interview.

In addition to the client and designers, who had a key decision-making role?

City planners/code officials.

JSA Inc

The Boulders and The Ridge at RiverWoods

Exeter, New Hampshire // RiverWoods at Exeter

Facility type: Assisted Living, Independent Living, Long-term Skilled Nursing, Skilled Nursing Dementia/Memory Support, Wellness/Fitness Center
Target market: Middle/Upper Middle
Site location: Rural; Greenfield site
Project site area (square feet): 5,009,400
Gross square footage of the new construction involved in the project: 558,000

Number of parking spaces added by the project: 471
The project offers transport to nearby shopping, medical, and/or cultural services/amenities.
Provider type: Non sectarian non-profit
Completion date: 2009

Below: The third community, The Boulders, opened in 2010.

Photography: Rob Karosis

Opposite: The shingle style of The Ridge is designed to depart from the original design to complement The Woods' community.

Photography: Warren Jagger

functional planning, asymmetrical massing, and picturesque composition as the keys to developing a design solution. The building envelopes employ the illusion of varied rooflines and heights as they embody a casual, residential character with large bay windows and two-story asymmetrical end gables.

Project Goals

What three project goals had the greatest impact on the project?

Offering choice through a diversity of housing options and alternatives in skilled care; offering daily choice through extensive amenities; and repositioning to appeal to the market.

The primary goal was offering choice through a diversity of housing options. The driving force behind expansion was to provide the RiverWoods way of life to more people, and also to provide added financial security to the organization. A potential for greater operational efficiency and an increase in programs and services was also a factor. To achieve this and optimize the development of their 115-acre expansion parcel, RiverWoods eventually developed a 558,000-gross-square foot, $79 million expansion, accommodating a total of over 600 residents in all three neighborhoods.

This presented design challenges to the rural context of the greater Exeter community, which stands in contrast to the development pro forma. To address this, the design visually reduces the scale of the project by:

- Breaking the expansion into two distinct neighborhoods, each with differing architectural character.

- Using architectural tools to help reduce the scale and overall impact of the design, such as eaves that reach down to the lowest levels in critical locations, and using residential forms.

- Adding single family and duplex cottages to each neighborhood development.

Overall Project Description

RiverWoods of Exeter is a Continuing Care Retirement Community (CCRC) comprising three distinct neighborhoods: The Woods, The Ridge, and The Boulders. While the overall community shares services and resources, what makes RiverWoods unique is that each neighborhood has its own distinct character, culture, architecture, interior design, and amenities, offering a variety of lifestyle options.

The original Woods campus was opened in 1994 and was the dream of a small group of Seacoast area residents. By the late 1990s RiverWoods was a CCRC consisting only of The Woods, and began to explore the potential for expansion due to a long waiting list, and an increase in demand. A market study was done that indicated that the demographics were growing, and there was capacity for another campus. In addition, there was an interest in creating more diversity in apartment style. The resulting master plan identified the

location for The Ridge but limited its footprint in anticipation of potential future development – the remaining site later became The Boulders.

Design: The Ridge was designed to depart from, while complementing the design of, The Woods. Similarly, when it came time to expand again, the same logic was used to design The Boulders to provide further diversity and choice represented by another variation on programs and architectural forms.

Another significant result of separating the community into smaller, uniquely designed buildings, is its intimacy and reduction in scale. The three smaller communities are consistent with traditional New England inns, resorts, and campus communities.

Zoning restrictions limit the facility to three stories and/or 35 feet to the roof peak. The wooded location and its New England setting created a relaxed, shingle-style vocabulary, characterizing

- Developing separate vehicular circulation patterns that reduce traffic through each of the sites.

In addition to increasing the overall size of the community, the new neighborhoods afforded the opportunity to provide residents with larger units, open kitchens and solariums and porches.

The second key goal was offering daily choice through extensive amenities. Recognizing the need to provide a broad array of services and amenities for its residents, programming spaces and places that offer daily variety within each neighborhood, as well as to the entire campus, became a key component of the design. Some of the amenities were:

Food venues:

- Formal dining
- Bistro
- Take out
- Dessert/pastry demonstration
- Self-serve
- Wait service
- Sports bar
- Pizza oven.

Wellness/Fitness:

- New and larger pool
- Dedicated cardio equipment
- Dedicated aerobics/dance room
- Wellness suite
- Wii Sports
- Both The Ridge and The Boulders have their own enclosed swimming pools and fitness/cardio rooms to promote therapeutic exercise. Each building also has dedicated physical therapy facilities and staff to aid residents with any necessary treatment. The Boulders is designed with a visiting physician's suite, equipped with several exam rooms, to provide a venue for physicians or home health care workers to visit residents from any part of the facility.

Multipurpose:

- Theater, performing arts space
- Meeting rooms
- Event space, RiverWoods fundraiser
- Religious services
- Spaces of different sizes and characteristics for large to medium sized events.

Other:

- Library
- General look and interior design; more contemporary detailing
- Hotel-style guest rooms for visiting family members.

Our third goal was repositioning to appeal to the market. As RiverWoods expanded, the design goals to address the younger age of those considering retirement communities resulted in a focus shift. Fitness and pool areas became more prominently positioned and accessible, the dining design became more open and interactive, and new concepts were introduced, like the Boulders Bistro, which is complete with pizza oven and cappuccino machine. The timing afforded by the phased development of the community and each subsequent neighborhood provided the opportunity to capitalize on generational differences.

Above: The Ridge and The Boulders are the two newest communities at RiverWoods at Exeter.
Illustration: JSA Inc

Challenges: What were the greatest design challenges faced by the project?

The site, while located in proximity to The Woods, was also surrounded by opposing abutters. The site design accommodated this challenge by negotiating with the town to accept a narrow, winding connection to the existing neighborhood. This narrowed connection gives the appearance of a residential driveway rather than a connecting road. This passive form of traffic calming was acceptable to all parties and reinforces the rural, residential character of the neighborhood. Also, as a buffer, cottages were arranged as a partial subdivision to act as a transition to the neighbors.

A second challenge was that the existing topography on the 115-acre parcel contained over 28 acres of wetlands. The site and building design for both projects respect the wetland setback line, only traversing the wetlands with access roads. The meandering nature of the building design is consistent with the nature of the land.

A third challenge was RiverWoods' resident involvement. The Ridge residents were invited to take part in the planning and programming of the subsequent phase, The Boulders. This involvement presented a number of challenges regarding access, identity, and amenities. The resulting design of The Boulders responds in a way that complements the design of The Ridge.

Innovations: What innovations/unique features were incorporated into the design of the project?

The wooded site has many protected wetlands. These wetlands played a pivotal role in shaping the organization of the project, but also provide a natural amenity that benefits the residents. Walking trails take residents from a paved perimeter to woodland trails and back.

The Ridge, located on the highest ground of the new site, inspired its name. Intentionally designed to depart from, while complementing

the design of the Woods, it employs a shingle-style vocabulary. The second site has with boulders of all shapes and sizes, some as large as a single story house. The residents themselves were instrumental in selecting the name "The Boulders," which is represented by the amount of stone incorporated into the overall design.

Resident committees participating in the design process urged the developer to adopt environmentally sustainable building practices. Adopting both active and passive initiatives, the design includes an enhanced building envelope, an array of photovoltaic collectors, water/energy reducing fixtures, and features to mitigate stormwater run off and wetland contamination.

Features/Services/Amenities: What are the most important features/services/amenities that were incorporated into the project specifically to attract the targeted market?

- Opportunity for choice, where to live, and how to live. The addition of duplex cottages and single family homes to The Ridge and The Boulders programs embodies the direction taken to attract residents looking for alternatives to the lifestyle options offered at The Woods. Floor plans are open, and contain great rooms with kitchens, interconnected dining, and living/family spaces. Each home features a two-car garage, and optional second floor home office and guest rooms.

- A progressively contemporary community incorporating contemporary lifestyles, examples of which are the informal bistros and fitness/wellness facilities. The Boulders pizza, sports, and cappuccino bistro is an example.

- For many RiverWoods residents, retirement affords them the opportunity to refocus their lives on giving back. RiverWoods has, since the beginning, reached out to the greater Exeter

community to engage in educational, social, and philanthropic programs. The Boulders includes a multipurpose room designed to accommodate a wide variety of functions.

Green/Sustainable Features: What are the green/sustainable features that had the greatest impact on the project's design?

Conscientious choice of materials, and energy efficiency.

What are the primary motivations for including green/sustainable design features in the project?

To promote good public relations, to make a contribution to the greater community, and to support the mission and values of the client/provider.

What challenges have you faced when trying to incorporate green/sustainable design features?

Actual and perceived first cost premium; and lack of support from development consultant.

Aesthetic: Identify which aesthetic your project embraces, why it was chosen and how it was achieved.

The three RiverWoods' neighborhoods represent a transition from traditional residential design to a more contemporary hospitality vocabulary as they progress from the original Woods to the Ridge and the most recent Boulders.

The transition, while purposely subtle, is apparent on the interior. Colors are deep and rich, details are crisp and simple, and furniture is light and clean yet comfortable. The overall design intent for RiverWoods is to maintain a cohesive community.

For the residential component, what was critical to the success of the project?

Improving common spaces/amenities.

Households: Describe the role households had in the project.

Assisted Living, Skilled Nursing and Skilled Nursing Dementia at The Ridge and The Boulders are organized around households.

Common Spaces: What common spaces are included in the project?

Art studio/craft room, bistro/casual dining, coffee shop/grab-and-go, dedicated conference/meeting space, dedicated exercise classroom, dedicated fitness equipment room, dedicated rehabilitation/therapy gym, formal dining, large multipurpose room, library/information resource center, marketplace/convenience store, resident-maintained gardening space, salon, and swimming pool/aquatics facility.

For a typical household wing/facility, describe the common spaces.

Typically common spaces consist of central living, dining, kitchen, and activity spaces. However, some common areas also include porches, crafts, therapy, library, and outdoor terraces. Accommodations vary per household depending on function and overall size, but on average comprise 2450 net square feet each, or 162 net square feet per resident.

Describe the largest interior common space in the project (excluding dining).

The Boulders includes a 2500-square foot multipurpose room designed to accommodate a wide variety of functions, such as music, theater, lectures, dinners, and dances, as well as an annual philanthropic event supported by the community. The space includes a raised stage and 15-foot clear ceilings, affording sightlines for all venues. Capacity is between 150 and 175.

The Boulders floor plan
- Independent living—residential
- Independent living—common
- Assisted living
- Skilled nursing

0   80ft

Opposite: The Boulders includes a 2500 square foot multipurpose room designed to accommodate music, theater, lectures, dinners, and dances.
Left: The dining experience is designed around a marketplace concept, providing for more personal choices.
Below: Formal dining room at The Boulders

Photography: Rob Karosis

Above left: In The Ridge formal dining room, lunch is self-service with full table service offered for the evening meal.
Above right: Outdoor dining terrace at The Ridge

Photography: Warren Jagger

Describe each dining venue incorporated in the project.

The Ridge – the formal dining room accommodates two service options: lunch is self-service (assistance is available if needed) and full table service is offered for the evening meal. The dining room is designed to serve all (approximately 100) Independent Living residents at one seating, although typically meals are served over an extended period of time. Tucked away in a corner of the formal dining room is a bakery. A demonstration window is provided for viewing preparation and baking.

Private dining can accommodate 16, and outdoor dining is also available.

The bistro is an informal dining venue serving breakfasts, sandwiches, and fast foods. The bistro also offers a take-away service and boxed meals, along with a grab-and-go option for prepared foods and drinks. Seating in the bistro is limited to 16 to 20.

The Boulders – the formal dining room is designed for a single seating in excess of 100, accommodating all Independent Living residents in one seating.

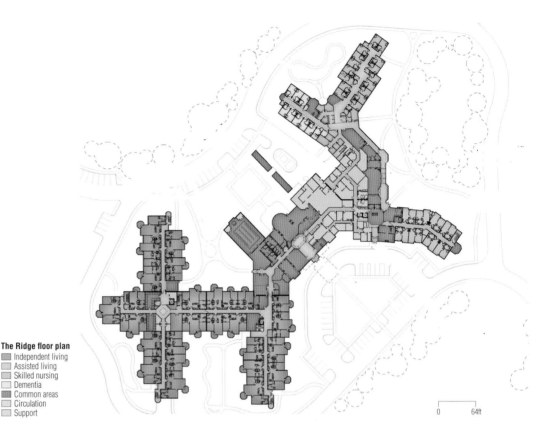

The Ridge floor plan
- Independent living
- Assisted living
- Skilled nursing
- Dementia
- Common areas
- Circulation
- Support

0   64ft

Like the Ridge, meal times are extended to allow for flexibility. However, the dining experience is designed around a marketplace concept.

Private dining can accommodate 16, and outdoor dining is also available.

The bistro is designed to suggest a sports bar. It features televisions, a pizza oven, and a cappuccino machine. Informal dining includes hot and cold foods, take-away, and grab-and-go options. Seating is split between bar stools and tables, and can serve 20 to 24. It is a social space as much as it is a dining venue.

Design Process: Who did the design team work with to gather information that could be applied to the design of the project?

Care team staff, city planners/code officials, contractor/construction team, current/existing residents, design consultants, family or friends of residents, market analysts, neighbors/members of the greater community, non-care team staff, potential/future residents, and provider administrators.

Which techniques were used with non-design team members to gather information that could be applied to the design of the project?

Charrette/working session, focus group/interview, in situ observations, 3D renderings, hand-drawn sketches, photographic computer-generated renderings, presentation to a review board, reduced-scale mock-up, and a survey.

In addition to the client and designers, who had a key decision-making role?

City planners/code officials, contractor/construction team, provider administrators, and provider board of directors.

Perkins Eastman

Franciscan Sisters of St. Joseph
Hamburg, New York // Franciscan Sisters of St. Joseph

Facility type: Independent Living, Long-term Skilled Nursing, Wellness/Fitness Center
Target market: Low Income/Subsidized
Site location: Suburban; Brownfield site
Project site area (square feet): 420,354
Gross square footage of the new construction involved in the project: 114,000

Number of parking spaces added by the project: 46
The site is within 1000 feet of public transportation. The project offers transport to nearby shopping, medical, and/or cultural services/amenities.
Provider type: Faith-based non-profit
Completion date: December 2010

Below: The Motherhouse offers a modern, energy efficient home appropriate for aging in place and transition to other laity use.
Opposite: A new Chapel sits in the midst of a large exterior courtyard.

Photography: Perkins Eastman

Overall Project Description

This project is seen by the Franciscan Sisters of St. Joseph as a step to provide an age-in-place replacement convent for their membership, to serve the needs of their aging Sisters. The new building will ultimately, once the Sisters have passed on, be used as affordable senior housing for the community at large.

The current Motherhouse (convent) dates back to the 1930s, and is large, has long corridors and stairways, and is expensive to continue to operate. It is also underutilized, having been designed for a population of 250–300 Sisters. Based on current and projected demographics, the main mission will be to provide aging-in-place residences and Skilled Care for the Sisters over the next 25 years. The new Motherhouse will provide 40 beds of Skilled Care in two neighborhoods, and four Independent Living households of eight Sisters each.

The community will be sustainable, with the admonition that it be "low, wide, and green." The new Motherhouse has been designed to the U.S. Green Building Council's (USGBC) LEED for Homes standards, and has achieved a Platinum Rating.

The new Motherhouse is built on a 9.65-acre site directly across the street from the existing Motherhouse. The new building, in addition to the residential/care households, includes a pool and exercise room, library, heritage room, two guest studios, a new 60-seat Chapel, a full commercial kitchen, dining rooms for Independent Living and Skilled Care residents, a multipurpose room, two outdoor gardens, administrative offices and a Board Room, as well as mechanical/service and staff spaces. There is also a detached garage structure on the site to house a van and other Order vehicles.

Project Goals

What three project goals had the greatest impact on the project?

Aging-in-place; promoting a sense of community; and providing green/sustainable design.

- The primary goal of this project was to provide an aging-in-place Motherhouse for the Franciscan Sisters of St. Joseph that will support the mission and charism of the Order as the Sisters age, and also provide an environment that will accommodate and help provide for both Independent Living and Long-term Nursing Care for the members of the Order. Additionally, this new building would eliminate the long walking distances and multiple stairways, as well as the remoteness of outdoor devotional space, that existed in the old Motherhouse. The solution created a predominately single-story structure in which Skilled Care and Independent Living areas are equal distances from the Chapel, which is the center of the spiritual and daily life of the community. Formal dining areas for both populations are also located close to their respective households. Additionally, outdoor garden and devotional areas are located between the Skilled Care neighborhoods, as well as adjacent to the Chapel. The outdoor spaces are accessible, walkable, and provide ample seating opportunities.

- The second major goal of the project was to be "low, wide, and green." The Sisters insisted that the new building be respectful of the environment and use systems that will be energy efficient. The design accomplishes this goal by designing to the USGBC LEED for Homes standards, and obtaining Platinum Certification. The Sisters have created a demonstration area and give educational tours to explain the systems and materials that are incorporated into the building. Some of these include high-efficiency boilers; radiant floor heating; wall and roof insulation with a combination of fiberglass batts and icynene; double-glazed, thermally broken, low-E glass on windows; heat recovery from all ducted returns; and hybrid heating and cooling systems in Independent Living households that use ceiling fans, not air conditioning, with reheat coils as part of the air distribution system for winter heating. Also included are the use of indigenous plantings and virtually no irrigation for landscaping; a high-efficiency lighting system with motion detectors in public areas; premium efficiency motors in MEP equipment; and the building has been wired so that photovoltaic panels can be added in the future. Additionally, the site is one third wetlands, and the decision was made not to encroach on any part of the wetlands as the basis for site design and building and road locations.

- The Sisters' third major goal was to leave behind a legacy that will help the community once they no longer occupy this new Motherhouse. This was incorporated into the overall planning of the building, and the design has been developed to anticipate a lay community of affordable senior housing that could provide both Independent Living and Long-term Care. To meet these criteria, the 300-square foot Independent Living studios meet market needs and the Skilled Care rooms are of equal size. A fitness and pool area has been provided. A full commercial kitchen, multipurpose and meeting space, two guest suites (similar to Independent Living studios), a library, and various meeting rooms are designed to meet and anticipate future market needs.

Challenges: What were the greatest design challenges faced by the project?

The greatest design challenge was deciding to have a new Motherhouse at all. The original charge was to see how the existing Motherhouse and attached Skilled Care building might be

First floor plan

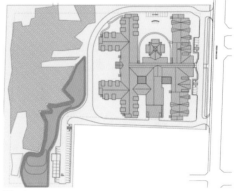

Site plan

renovated. When that study indicated the large cost and less-than-optimal improvement in living conditions, a new building was indicated. The Sisters debated on the need for individual private studios with dedicated bathrooms. Also, there were debates on the need for outdoor landscaping, fitness and pool areas, as well as multipurpose and meeting rooms. This challenge was resolved. These building and program elements make the building acceptable to a future sponsor and/or potential residents.

Another challenge faced by the design team was the goal of making the project "low, wide, and green." The initial concept had the entire building as a single-story structure, with all four Independent Living households on the first floor. This pushed the footprint further back on the site, with encroachment on the wetlands. The Sisters were willing to create a small second floor to house two of the Independent Living households. This compromise enabled them to avoid building

on the wetlands, which also saved delays in construction by avoiding significant submissions and reviews by the Army Corps of Engineers.

Innovations: What innovations/unique features were incorporated into the design of the project?

The LEED for Homes program encouraged innovation. See the previous description of energy efficient elements of the building.

Features/Services/Amenities: What are the most important features/services/amenities that were incorporated into the project specifically to attract the targeted market?

All Independent Living studios and Skilled Care rooms are fully accessible. A compact floor plan with accessible corridors, outdoor spaces, and reduced walking distances creates a community that is supportive of all levels of physical ability and aging-in-place.

A major design priority was to allow for natural light and connection and views to nature from

major activity areas throughout the building. This aids in individual wellbeing, as well as way-finding and orientation throughout the day. The natural lighting is bright enough so that even on cloudy days lighting can be turned off in major public areas, creating a softer, more "homelike" environment and saving energy.

Green/Sustainable Features: What are the green/sustainable features that had the greatest impact on the project's design?

Energy efficiency, improved indoor air quality, and site design considerations.

What are the primary motivations for including green/sustainable design features in the project?

Lower operational costs, to make a contribution to the greater community, and to support the mission and values of the client/provider.

What challenges have you faced when trying to incorporate green/sustainable design features?

Perceived first cost premium.

Aesthetic: Identify which aesthetic your project embraces, why it was chosen and how it was achieved.

Because the building is both a convent and a senior living residence, there are two aspects to the feel of the building. The design team drew on two architectural sources for the overall appearance of the building: the basilica image of a church with a strong center and two lower side portions, and also low-rise Carpenter Gothic wood farm buildings. Interior finishes in the neighborhoods are low-key and residential. There are natural woods throughout, as well as biophilic carpet and wall-covering patterns. Lighting is kept at adequate levels, but is also soft and residential-feeling.

For the residential component, what was critical to the success of the project?

Improving units/private spaces.

Households: Describe the role households had in the project.

The project is based entirely on household concepts, both for Skilled Care and for Independent Living. Because this is a convent, however, there are also common dining areas that allow the community to come together for meals. Independent Living households have the option to cook for themselves or join the whole group for meals.

Common Spaces: What common spaces are included in the project?

Dedicated fitness equipment room, dedicated rehabilitation/therapy gym, formal dining, large multipurpose room, library/information resource center, grotto, heritage room, two parlors, religious/spiritual/meditative space, salon, and swimming pool/aquatics facility.

For a typical household wing/facility, describe the common spaces.

Skilled Care – nursing support areas, a bathing room (260 square feet), a laundry room (143 square feet), a sun room (240 square feet), and dining/activity/common living area (900 square feet).

Independent Living – private parlor, laundry/sewing (160 square feet), bathing room (120 square feet), kitchen (165 square feet), dining area (285 square feet), living room/activity room (484 square feet), sun room (312 square feet).

Describe the largest interior common space in the project (excluding dining).

The largest interior common space is an activity room between the two Skilled Care households (2000 square feet). Seating capacity is 40 seats at five activity tables, or 120 individual seats in an auditorium arrangement. Along one side is a continuous counter with residential kitchen appliances and cabinetry for use in activities involving cooking, or for providing food related to activities. It serves as a common meeting space for Sisters in the whole community and is used for quarterly assemblies and other whole-Order functions. The opposite side of the room offers closets for chair/table/activity storage. One of its long walls has French doors that open directly to a terrace and garden; the other long wall opens to a large foyer/pre-function space that also connects to the two Long-term Care neighborhoods. This pre-function space is also for informal receptions and holiday buffets.

Describe each dining venue incorporated in the project.

Skilled Care dining (48 seats) – this is a dedicated, formal dining area, and the meals are brought to the table.

Independent Living dining (40 seats) – this has self-serve cold and hot beverages with a buffet for self-serve main course, salads, and desserts.

Design Process: Who did the design team work with to gather information that could be applied to the design of the project?

Care team staff, contractor/construction team, current/existing residents, non-care team staff, potential/future residents, and provider administrators.

Which techniques were used with non-design team members to gather information that could be applied to the design of the project?

Charrette/working session, focus group/interview, in situ observations, and a presentation to a review board.

In addition to the client and designers, who had a key decision-making role?

Current/existing residents, potential/future residents, provider administrators, and provider board of directors.

Opposite left: Resident rooms are within walking distance of dining areas, Chapel and gardens, and organized around a central activity or Living Room that opens onto an outdoor courtyard or balcony.
Opposite right: Resident rooms have large operable windows for independent environmental control and a unique system of ceiling fans and natural ventilation that takes advantage of the Buffalo summer climate.
Below: The devotional grotto is within a short walk of the household neighborhoods and Chapel.

Photography: Sarah Mechling/Perkins Eastman

RLPS Architects

The Houses On Bayberry: Arbor Acres United Methodist Retirement Community

Winston-Salem, North Carolina // Arbor Acres United Methodist Retirement Community

Facility type: Independent Living
Target market: Mixed Income – Arbor Acres serves all economic levels
Site location: Suburban
Project site area (square feet): 60,674
Gross square footage of the new construction involved in the project: 12,296

Number of parking spaces added by the project: 11
The project offers transport to nearby shopping, medical, and/or cultural services/amenities.
Provider type: Faith-based non-profit
Completion date: January 2010

Below: Exterior view of Houses on Bayberry
Opposite: Exterior view of second cluster of Houses on Bayberry at dusk

house clusters are arranged to create small-scale public spaces or garden commons, fostering a sense of community and outdoor connections.

Project Goals

What three project goals had the greatest impact on the project?

Addressing affordability/budgetary concerns; repositioning to appeal to the market; and responding to local conditions.

- Addressing affordability/budgetary concerns – this was achieved with the design of an attractive, affordable home that will not visually compromise the adjacent market-rate housing. The Houses on Bayberry feature careful detailing and compact one- and two-bedroom floor plans. The positioning of the clusters is such that two one-bedroom homes join as a duplex and flank two two-bedroom homes to create a common garden courtyard. A cathedral ceiling and dormers create volume within a small living space to allow for the infusion of natural light, create an overall feeling of openness, and ultimately achieve a sense of spaciousness within limited square footage.

- Responding to local conditions – the Houses on Bayberry are now carefully phased into this location at the center of the campus. The project's phasing strategy permits the owner to build new replacement homes over a five-year period. The multiphased plan introduces the first phase of new housing without requiring the demolition of any existing homes. Later phases will incrementally replace the existing stock with the new cluster homes.

- Repositioning to appeal to the market – this replacement of independent housing maintains the appealing aspects of the existing affordable housing – interconnected porches and gardens – but provides a senior-friendly, marketable option that reflects the overall campus aesthetic.

Overall Project Description

Arbor Acres needed to replace 25-year-old affordable housing. Seniors in Winston-Salem needed affordable access to continuing care. However, the existing houses were deemed affordable more by default than design. The dilapidated appearance of the houses, lack of market-rate amenities, and absence of any accessibility features drove the accepted entry fees to evolve into the "affordable houses on campus." Two redeeming physical features of the homes were the connected porches and the gardens they defined. The challenge was to design a replacement affordable product that would retain the charm and character of the porches and gardens without sacrificing any design integrity.

This new neighborhood of up to five small house clusters responds to the need for affordable, moderately sized, higher-density homes near the center of the campus, over several phases of construction. Each cluster consists of two one-bedroom homes with den patio, joined as a duplex, and two two-bedroom homes with a patio. The homes reflect a high level of thoughtfulness and detailing in a relatively small square footage at a modest price point. Aimed at residents who require less space, but prefer living in a house rather than an apartment, the Houses on Bayberry feature efficient, marketable floor plans.

Virtually every provider strives to provide affordable, low-cost housing options for their constituents. Few are able to achieve this goal without sacrificing aesthetics. At $113/square foot, the project achieves the owner's affordability goals without compromising design integrity. Despite their small size and affordability, the Houses on Bayberry deliver handicap accessibility, sheltering porches, adjacent parking, walk-in closets, cathedral ceilings generously lit from above with dormer skylights, and covered connections to common areas. The Bayberry

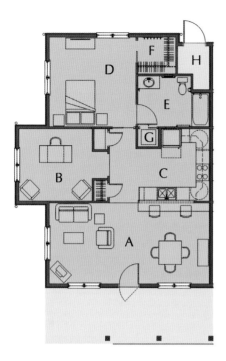

One-bedroom unit floor plan

A   Living/dining room
B   Den
C   Kitchen
D   Master bedroom
E   Bathroom
F   Walk-in closet
G   Laundry
H   Mechanical

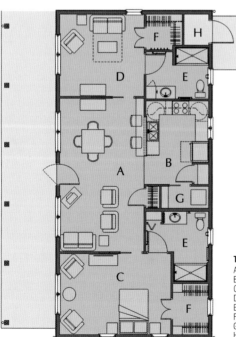

Two-bedroom unit floor plan

A   Living/dining room
B   Kitchen
C   Master bedroom
D   Bedroom
E   Bathroom
F   Walk-in closet
G   Laundry
H   Mechanical

Ultimately, the design team managed costs by controlling building complexity while maximizing visual impact through creative use of color and familiar materials. A distinctive color palette, appropriate to the regional vernacular, is used for each housing cluster to provide a unique sense of identity, and visual interest.

Challenges: What were the greatest design challenges faced by the project?

Disciplining the team to "stay small" to control costs. The tendency to increase square footage was a constant challenge. The final plans reflect a high level of thoughtfulness and detailing to ultimately deliver an open floor plan incorporating marketable amenities in a compact footprint. The design solution reflects traditional detailing

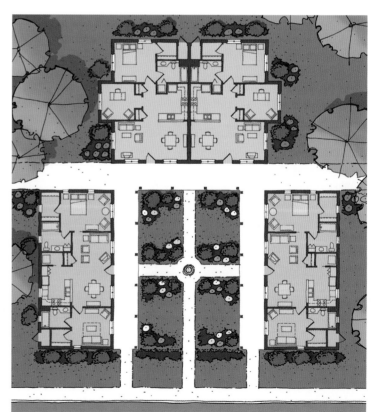

Site plan for single Bayberry cluster

evident elsewhere on campus and offers handicap accessibility, interconnectivity to commons areas, and highly valued courtyard gardens.

A second challenge was achieving sufficient resident acceptance to increase owner confidence in moving forward. The covered porches and courtyard flower gardens are a critical component of the new housing clusters. The plan layout and façades highlight the courtyards, while providing equal appeal in a more supportive, marketable setting.

A third challenge is that the phase I cluster is the most aggressive of the site allocations, because its location did not require removal of any existing homes. The owner paid a premium for site development costs associated with an aggressive terrain.

Innovations: What innovations/unique features were incorporated into the design of the project?

The housing clusters allow seniors with similar interests – gardening, traveling, learning in retirement – to live together in a community environment. The garden space between the buildings gives the structures a sense of freedom and independence, while deep porches and a system of covered walkways offer residents a safe, weather-protected connection to the commons areas at the heart of the community. The covered front porches serve as a catalyst for neighbors to connect with each other, and the shared gardens encourage community among the residents living around them. Each Bayberry cluster features its own color palette and small-scale garden commons to promote a sense of identity and commonality between residents.

Features/Services/Amenities: What are the most important features/services/amenities that were incorporated into the project specifically to attract the targeted market?

The design turns limited room size into an advantage, and compensates for the shading of porches through the use of cathedral ceilings and dormer skylights for abundant natural light, as well as to reinforce volume and spaciousness in a small house.

Below right: View from kitchen looking toward the front door in the one-bedroom unit
Below left: One-bedroom great room has cathedral ceilings and dormer windows for natural light

The project elaborates on an existing concept of courtyard gardens with a new interpretation of building placement and wraparound porches, which expand a sense of ownership while providing community connectivity.

Providing residents with access to affordable, yet appealing homes in a continuing care community upholds choice, dignity and control, all of which are critical to quality of life and wellbeing. Discreetly supportive features, such as shower grab rails, pocket doors, elevated commodes and vanities, and wheelchair accessible doorways and bathrooms facilitate aging-in-place.

Green/Sustainable Features: What are the green/sustainable features that had the greatest impact on the project's design?

Conscientious choice of materials, energy efficiency, and maximizing daylight.

What are the primary motivations for including green/sustainable design features in the project?

To promote good public relations, and to support the mission and values of the client/provider.

What challenges have you faced when trying to incorporate green/sustainable design features?

Actual first cost premium.

Aesthetic: Identify which aesthetic your project embraces, why it was chosen and how it was achieved.

The Houses on Bayberry focus on a residential appearance. The design is inspired by the human scale and traditional architectural forms and detailing of historic Winston-Salem, North Carolina. The resulting small neighborhood and unique color palette of each grouping fosters community, strengthens identity, and improves way-finding.

For the residential component, what was critical to the success of the project?

Improving units/private spaces.

Common Spaces: What common spaces are included in the project?

Courtyard garden for each housing cluster.

Design Process: Who did the design team work with to gather information that could be applied to the design of the project?

Current/existing residents, market analysts, and provider administrators.

Which techniques were used with non-design team members to gather information that could be applied to the design of the project?

Charrette/working session, focus group/interview, and a presentation to a review board.

In addition to the client and designers, who had a key decision-making role?

Provider administrators, and provider board of directors.

Perkins Eastman

Saint John's on the Lake

Milwaukee, Wisconsin // Saint John's Communities

Facility type: Independent Living, Town Center with Gallery, Café Bistro, Wellness/Fitness, Pool, Classrooms, Outdoor Spaces and Gardens, Outdoor Exercise and Dining Patios. Apartments are designed to meet state regulations to be converted to Assisted Living apartments.
Target market: Middle/Upper Middle
Site location: Urban; Brownfield site
Project site area (square feet): 98,000

Gross square footage of the new construction involved in the project: 290,000
Gross square footage of the renovation(s)/ modernization(s) involved in the project: 16,500 – includes common spaces in existing Independent Living.
Purpose of the renovation/modernization: Upgrade the environment
Number of parking spaces added by the project: 165

The site is within 1000 feet of public transportation and everyday shopping and/or medical services. The project offers transport to nearby shopping, medical, and/or cultural services/amenities.
Provider type: Faith-based non-profit
Completion date: June 2011

Opposite: The entry drive ends at a residential *porte-cochère* on a bluff overlooking the lakefront.
Left: A view from the marina shows the new tower's connection to Milwaukee's recreational lakefront.

The new Independent Living tower offers larger apartments with multiple layout options, open and spacious floor plans and outdoor space. The public amenities offer choice in dining options, a comprehensive wellness program, and outdoor terraces. Since Saint John's is in an urban area, they were able to take advantage of a trend of seniors wanting to be a part of an urban environment. The new building improves the community's connection to the city, providing residents with an urban lifestyle, shopping, restaurants, and public transportation at their door.

Overall Project Description

Saint John's on the Lake initiated a campus repositioning to respond to changing market demands. A master plan of the entire campus was completed assessing the existing Independent Living tower, Assisted Living facility, and Skilled Care, along with the town center and supporting spaces. Their existing Independent Living apartments were deemed too small, and they wished to open up their campus and integrate it with the surrounding community. Wellness and sustainability were underlying factors in the programming and design of the new campus components.

The new 21-story, 87-unit tower energizes Milwaukee's Prospect Avenue at street level. The project's urban location puts dining, shopping, and activities within walking distance.

The building offers a hospitality-branded street-side café, art gallery, spa and wellness center, classroom, and community performance space.

Another primary focus of the project was to enhance staff and resident quality of life through sustainable building design, with LEED-NC Certification or equivalence as a goal.

The existing facilities were not part of the scope of work, other than the renovation of the existing Independent Living building's corridors.

Project Goals

What three project goals had the greatest impact on the project?

Integrating with the surrounding neighborhood/ greater community, including hosting programs and/or sharing amenities with non-residents; promoting holistic wellness; and repositioning to appeal to the market.

- Repositioning to appeal to the market. The driving force behind this project was to appeal to the shift in the marketplace and address demands of the new consumer, including greater choice in living options and amenities.

- Integrating with the surrounding neighborhood/ greater community. Saint John's aimed to break down the perceived barriers between their campus and the surrounding community. The design team used the new tower to connect the campus with the surrounding community. The large windows and mainly glass façade create a transparency. The bistro is open to the public and it activates the building at street level, welcoming residents and visitors. The new gallery, wrapping around the first floor, exhibits a broad range of artwork, drawing residents, visitors, and members of the surrounding community.

- Promoting holistic wellness. The Independent Living tower provides an environment promoting health and caters to the six dimensions of wellness: physical, intellectual, social, vocational, spiritual, and emotional. All of the spaces within the existing building and the new building are designed to be flexible in addressing these six

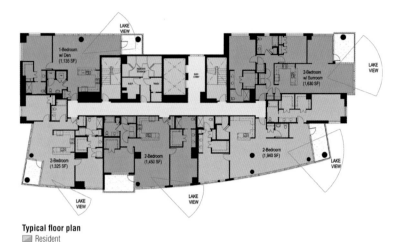

Typical floor plan
- ▨ Resident
- ☐ Circulation
- ☐ Service
- ▨ Parking

1-Bedroom
w/ Den
(1,135 SF)

2-Bedroom
w/ Sunroom
(1,630 SF)

2-Bedroom
(1,325 SF)

2-Bedroom
(1,450 SF)

2-Bedroom
(1,940 SF)

LAKE VIEW

LAKE VIEW

LAKE VIEW

LAKE VIEW

LAKE VIEW

SCULPTURE GARDEN &
CULTURAL ARTS TERRACE

CULTURAL
ARTS CENTER

CAFE
BISTRO

LIFESTREAMS

ENTRY
MOTOR
COURT &
OUTDOOR
EVENT
SPACE

GALLERY

CIRCULATION CONNECTS NEW & EXISTING
PROGRAMS AND OFFERS BOTH PASSIVE &
ACTIVE INTERACTION W/ EVENTS & PROGRAMS

OFFICE

WELLNESS
CLASSROOM

LAP / THERAPY POOL

SPA
POOL

OFFICE

FITNESS
AREA

MEN'S
LOCKER ROOM

WOMEN'S
LOCKER
ROOM

WELLNESS
LOBBY

MASSAGE
ROOM

FITNESS
STORAGE

A/V
ROOM

STORAGE

MAIL
ROOM

RECEP.

WORK
ROOM

FIRE
COMMAND
CENTER

SERVING
ROOM

RESIDENT LOBBY

MOB.
CART
STO.

STORAGE

MARKETING
OFFICE

First floor plan
- ☐ Circulation
- ▨ Common areas
- ▨ Support
- ☐ Service
- ▨ Pool

dimensions. The circulation path is central to this goal, providing a loop for walking during any season and encouraging residents to participate in various wellness-based programs.

Challenges: What were the greatest design challenges faced by the project?

A key challenge was designing for a tight urban site. The design team worked with the owner to add programmatically-rich components to a dense urban campus with limited space to expand. A main focus of the plan was how to address the entry sequence and service areas based on setback requirements.

Exisiting entries were utilized and expanded upon. One way the design team met this challenge was by working closely with the owner's Head of Facilities in an effort to minimize duplications of service areas. For example the new garage was designed to connect with the existing garage, so there was no need for a new receiving area.

Access to the building via the side-street was also a challenge. Sufficient building setbacks to allow for bus and senior dropoffs could not be achieved on this city street. By placing the entry sequence of the new building on the back-side of the building facing Lake Michigan, arrivals are not only greeted with views, but zoning requirements are also met.

A second challenge was maintaining an ease of connection between existing buildings and the new building. An internal loop connects the new building with the existing pieces of the campus, making it accessible to the entire campus. An existing chapel that occupied part of the site for the new project became the heart and soul of the new Independent Living tower. A courtyard was designed around the chapel while the new building wraps around it, making it a focal point in the views to the courtyard. The new tower is also pushed back to make sure residents to the south and west maintain their views of the lake.

A third challenge was designing new components for the campus. In addition to the new Independent Living tower, Saint John's has an existing Independent Living building. There was not a large change as one walked through the campus between the new and the old, to keep the existing residents of this building connected to the new building, and also to provide them with appealing amenities of their own. Corridors with views and functional indoor/outdoor space connect the new spaces with the old. A new library was created at the connection point where the new and old buildings meet. A new rooftop garden on top of the parking garage of the North Tower provides outdoor gathering spaces and a putting green. Open to all residents, the North Tower has direct access to this spot. The existing restaurant was also left in the North Tower. In addition, the lobby and corridors of the existing tower were remodeled.

Innovations: What innovations/unique features were incorporated into the design of the project?

- Customizable and marketable units. The process to design the units included in-depth interviews with existing and future residents. The design team met with potential residents in their current homes to ensure that the new Independent Living apartments would meet their lifestyles. The client set up teams and systems to allow each residence to be customized by prospective buyers, thereby helping in retention.

  Each apartment includes a balcony designed as an outdoor room with a view of Lake Michigan. Balconies are a minimum of eight feet deep and have at least two full walls to provide additional security and comfort.

Right: The entry motor court offers a variety of large event opportunities.

- Intergenerational activity. The street-side bistro and art gallery act as a storefront, bringing the outside street-level energy in and promoting intergenerational activity within the project.

- Programming. To achieve comprehensive, innovative programming that supports holistic wellness, the design team met with the Universtiy of Wisconsin at Milwaukee, local churches, marketing consultants, food service consultants, community organizations, and local businesses.

Features/Services/Amenities: What are the most important features/services/amenities that were incorporated into the project specifically to attract the targeted market?

- Highly marketable units. The new Independent Living tower offers larger apartments with

Opposite left: The reclaimed-wood ceiling provides warmth while articulating the art wall and circulation throughout the space.
Opposite right: The café, with outdoor terrace, provides a connection to the street integrating Saint John's with the surrounding community.
Left: A street-side grab-and-go style bistro café provides a new vibrant dining venue for residents, staff, and the surrounding community.

The public spaces are more open and transparent, reflecting the hospitality-based programs. Each space is designed to reflect the program use. Overall, the project connects to both the lakefront and the energy of the city.

LifeStreams embraces a 'day spa' feel and borrows soothing colors and materials found on the lakefront: gold tones from the beaches, blues from the water and sky, and warm earth tones from the landscape and rock formations. Patterns and textures represent elements found in nature.

In contrast, the bistro café is full of life and energy. Bolder earth tones and textures echo the excitement of the city, the street life beyond, and the orange in the setting sun. The adjoining terrace space is slightly elevated from the street, providing a distinction between public and semi-public space, and a sense of security for the residents. Between LifeStreams and the bistro café is the Cultural Arts Center and Gallery. Within these spaces the colors, materials, and patterns become a simple backdrop to the art, performances, and other events that occur within the spaces. The reclaimed-wood ceiling warms the space and articulates the circulation throughout the gallery. The elevator lobby to the tower residences' floors echoes a more residential characteristic as one travels from semi-public space to semi-private space. Here lower ceilings, familiar furniture pieces, antiques, and accessories embrace a residential scale and aesthetic.

multiple layout options, with open and spacious floor plans and outdoor space.

- Wellness features. All of the spaces within the existing building and the new building are designed to be flexible to address the six dimensions of wellness. Amenities include a spa, pool, classrooms, art gallery, and bistro.

- Urban connectivity. The new tower connects to the urban street, providing transportation, shopping, and dining opportunities.

Green/Sustainable Features: What are the green/sustainable features that had the greatest impact on the project's design?

Conscientious choice of materials, energy efficiency, and maximizing daylighting.

What are the primary motivations for including green/sustainable design features in the project?

Lower operational costs, to make a contribution to the greater community, and to support the mission and values of the client/provider.

What challenges have you faced when trying to incorporate green/sustainable design features?

Actual first cost premium.

Aesthetic: Identify which aesthetic your project embraces, why it was chosen and how it was achieved.

The site and building embrace a contemporary urban environment, addressing residential characteristics within the tower defined by the fenestration, punched openings, and balconies.

For the residential component, what was critical to the success of the project?

Improving units/private spaces.

Common Spaces: What common spaces are included in the project?

Art studio/craft room, bistro/casual dining, dedicated classroom/learning space, dedicated exercise classroom, dedicated fitness equipment room, large multipurpose room, library/ information resource center, marketplace/ convenience store, massage/aromatherapy room, gallery space, outdoor dining patio, outdoor exercise patio, resident-maintained gardening space, and swimming pool/aquatics facility.

Describe the largest interior common space in the project (excluding dining).

The Cultural Arts Center and Gallery is a highlight of the project and comprises 3000 square feet, 180 seat banquet/lecture/presentation space with stage, and theatrical audiovisual and lighting systems.

Supporting Saint John's connection to the arts within Milwaukee, the Center provides space to host art exhibits, performances, lectures, banquets, and various social events. The events are open to residents, staff, and the greater community.

Within the Cultural Arts Center, the lighting and audiovisual systems are designed to allow for flexibility for various events. A mobile stage can be moved to the center of the room for in-the-round performances, allowing audience members to enjoy performances such as a ballet from a close distance that allows them to experience the detail of the dance.

The entire first floor is designed to support the Cultural Arts Center and can be activated to host a large event or art exhibit, with room for activity to spill into the bistro, connecting corridors and even outdoors into the sculpture garden, terraces, and/or the motor court. The surrounding spaces are designed to be used as pre-function spaces,

offering areas for cocktails, coat collection, mobility device storage, and even dining in the bistro or the Cultural Arts Center.

Describe each dining venue incorporated in the project.

Saint John's already included a formal dining option facing the lakefront and offering views. A new bistro, with a marketplace, is designed to connect the community to its urban surroundings, energizing the campus with the neighboring street activity. Located on the street edge, this casual dining spot includes indoor and outdoor dining options.

The bistro is a fully functioning market offering diverse menu options including made-to-order salads, rotating entrée specials, prepackaged foods, beer, wine, and cocktails. A full display kitchen allows residents to see their food being prepared and is also set up to host special cooking events with guest chefs and wine tastings.

The support spaces of the bistro also serve as the catering kitchen for the Cultural Arts Center/multipurpose room with 65 chairs.

Design Process: Who did the design team work with to gather information that could be applied to the design of the project?

Affiliated yet independent agencies, care team staff, city planners/code officials, contractor/construction team, current/existing residents, design consultants, family or friends of residents, market analysts, neighbors/members of the greater community, non-care team staff, potential/future residents, and provider administrators.

Which techniques were used with non-design team members to gather information that could be applied to the design of the project?

Charrette/working session, focus group/interview, in situ observations, computer graphics to depict spaces, a built model of the project to be used for marketing, and a survey.

In addition to the client and designers, who had a key decision-making role?

Provider administrators, and provider board of directors.

Off-site Outreach Services: What off-site outreach services are offered to the greater community?

Art gallery, bistro, lectures, concerts, and wellness facilities with classes.

Opposite left: LifeStreams embraces the six dimensions of wellness – physical, intellectual, social, vocational, spiritual, and emotional.
Opposite right: Frosted glass connects the pool to the fitness room and main circulation spine, while the large glass windows provide a connection to the outdoors in any season.
Below: All residences enjoy unparalleled views of Milwaukee's lakefront.
Photography: Chris Barrett

Gund Partnership

South Franklin Circle

Chagrin Falls, Ohio // Judson Services, Inc.

Facility type: Assisted Living, Independent Living, Senior Community Center, Wellness/Fitness Center
Target market: Middle/Upper Middle
Site location: Suburban; Greenfield site
Project site area (square feet): 3,833,280
Gross square footage of the new construction involved in the project: 798,634

Number of parking spaces added by the project: 393
The project offers transport to nearby shopping, medical, and/or cultural services/amenities.
Provider type: For profit
Completion date: September 2009, phase 1

Below: Sloped roofs, gabled wings and large windows recall the estate architecture of Cleveland's Western Reserve.

Photography: Frank Salle

Opposite: Creative siting strategies limited impact of existing wetlands and preserved major tree areas on the 82-acre site.

Photography: Brad Feinknopf

Overall Project Description

South Franklin Circle was envisioned as a new type of retirement community that offers a unique approach to senior living. The master plan is based on new urbanist principles for livable communities and comprises a village square with outlying parcels to promote an active adult lifestyle that emphasizes personal responsibility, community engagement, connection to nature, and comprehensive physical and mental wellness. Specialized services within the community provide the framework for an independent lifestyle that allows residents to retain their individuality and engage in an active lifestyle.

Project Goals

What three project goals had the greatest impact on the project?

Offering choice through a diversity of housing options and alternatives in skilled care; offering daily choice through extensive amenities; and promoting holistic wellness.

- Creating a community that promotes comprehensive physical and mental wellness is at the heart of the design approach. The village square with outlying parcels allows residents to retain their individuality and lifestyle in their residences, while providing a vibrant social hub at the Community Center where residents can connect and engage in a wide range of social, fitness, intellectual, and cultural activities. The richly landscaped grounds – with walking and biking trails – invite residents to engage in physical activity and nature. Enclosed bridges connecting the various Independent Living Apartment buildings surrounding the Community Center allow residents to circulate during inclement weather.

- South Franklin Circle is about choice. A variety of housing options are focused around a Community Center and landscape amenities. Housing styles range from Independent Living apartments to Assisted Living facilities, townhouses, cottages, and garden duplexes. This mix is designed to appeal to a range of age groups and support the development of a diverse community of residents planning to age-in-place. Residents choose from 30 individual floor plans and customize their units with a variety of finishes.

- Extensive amenities provide daily choice and promote a sense of community among residents, staff, and visitors. The 80,000-square foot Community Center is the hub for residents. A soaring lobby and communal room creates a welcoming and active environment in which to see and be seen. The Community Center houses three restaurants that are all scaled to provide residents with an intimate dining experience regardless of the number of patrons. The center also includes fitness facilities with an indoor heated swimming pool, distance learning classrooms, art and woodworking studios, guest suites, bank, storefronts, spa and pet grooming.

Challenges: What were the greatest design challenges faced by the project?

Unlike a typical flat development site, the South Franklin Circle site features varied terrain and wetlands. Zoning and environmental restrictions limited the amount of land that could be impacted by the new community development and required creative siting to preserve the existing wetlands and major tree areas. Only 20 percent of the site was developed, and only a quarter-acre of the original wetlands was impacted. The resulting site layout benefits the community design by maintaining the landscape's natural character and framing views with the built environment.

Another significant challenge was designing a new community that appealed to both today's seniors and the next generation of seniors. Unlike typical senior-living communities that are interior-focused, South Franklin Circle is more

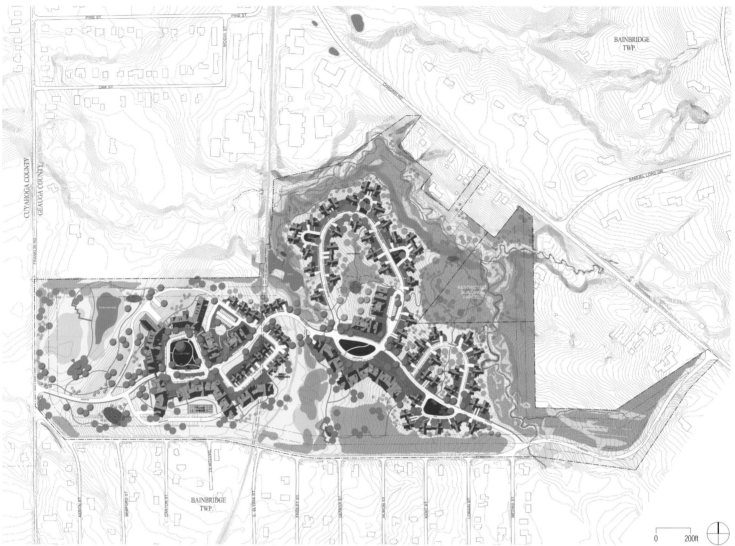

Site plan

like a typical village, with a focus on the exterior landscape. The assortment of housing options are designed to appeal to a range of age groups and support a variety of living preferences. Recognizing that the needs of the older residents may be different from their younger counterparts, enclosed bridges between the apartments and the Community Center provide residents the option to circulate either inside or outside.

A third challenge was that designing this new community within the established budget required creative design solutions. The structural design for each of the building is varied to achieve the most cost-effective solutions. The Community Center is designed with a steel structure, while the residential buildings are designed with a wood structure. Because the Assisted Living Unit layouts are more repetitious, a concrete plank

block structure was determined most efficient. In addition, several of the building floor plans are repeated or mirrored, however the façades are finished with different skins for variety.

Innovations: What innovations/unique features were incorporated into the design of the project?

South Franklin Circle includes a variety of housing styles that contribute to a rich community. The

home styles include many features and amenities not commonly found in traditional senior-living communities, including double-height living spaces in the townhouses, cottages, and garden duplexes. Additionally, the site design preserves the distinct natural features with wetlands and major tree areas. Walking and biking trails encourage residents to engage in outdoor activities.

Features/Services/Amenities: What are the most important features/services/amenities that were incorporated into the project specifically to attract the targeted market?

The targeted market is most interested in maintaining their current lifestyle and individuality. The Community Center, with its formal restaurant dining, fitness center and indoor swimming pool, in addition to the community's intellectual and cultural programming, provide residents the opportunity to continue engaging in an active lifestyle and pursue new interests.

Green/Sustainable Features: What are the green/sustainable features that had the greatest impact on the project's design?

Improved indoor air quality, maximizing daylighting, and site design considerations.

What are the primary motivations for including green/sustainable design features in the project?

Lower operational costs, to support the mission and values of the client/provider, and to support the mission and values of the design team.

What challenges have you faced when trying to incorporate green/sustainable design features?

Actual and perceived first cost premium.

Aesthetic: Identify which aesthetic your project embraces, why it was chosen and how it was achieved.

A homelike environment was favored to appeal to residents who want to maintain their current lifestyles and individuality. The range of housing types includes Independent Living apartments, townhouses, cottages, and garden duplexes – all have been designed to fit into the Chagrin Falls

suburban context. Buildings located on the village green are a mix of stone and white clapboard siding. Sloped roofs, gabled wings, and large windows evoke the estate architecture of the Western Reserve. Cottages and garden duplexes with white clapboard siding and mahogany doors are clustered around common green spaces to create small neighborhoods. Generous living spaces are provided in townhouses, cottages, and garden duplexes.

For the residential component, what was critical to the success of the project?

Improving units/private spaces.

Households: Describe the role households had in the project.

Assisted Living facilities are designed in a household model, encouraging residents to dine

Above: Buildings located around the village green are connected by enclosed pedestrian bridges on the second floor.

Photography: Brad Feinknopf

and socialize collectively. Living and dining rooms anchor the households. Assisted Living units include a small refrigerator and desk that could be used as a table, if needed.

Common Spaces: What common spaces are included in the project?

Art studio/craft room, bistro/casual dining, coffee shop/grab-and-go, dedicated classroom/ learning space, dedicated conference/meeting space, dedicated exercise classroom (for example for aerobics and pilates,) dedicated fitness equipment room, dedicated rehabilitation/therapy gym, formal dining, a large multipurpose room, library/information resource center, massage/ aromatherapy room, pet grooming facility, resident-maintained gardening space, salon, and swimming pool/aquatics facility.

For a typical household wing/facility, describe the common spaces.

Common dining and living rooms anchor the Assisted Living facilities. Dining rooms include 22 seats. The living room includes 17 seats in the main area and an additional six seats in an adjoining space. The main area includes a television and a variety of seating options. The adjoining area includes books and magazines with a variety of seating options.

Describe the largest interior common space in the project (excluding dining).

The great room is a 2318-square foot grand space adjacent to the formal dining area. It includes casual seating for 20, a fireplace and piano, and can be reconfigured to support large events accommodating 100 people.

Describe each dining venue incorporated in the project.

The main formal dining area seats 60, with an adjoining bar seating 20, and a private dining area seating 25. The formal dining is designed

with several seating environments to provide an intimate dining experience regardless of the number of patrons. An informal bistro, which includes a grab-and-go, seats 20.

Design Process: Who did the design team work with to gather information that could be applied to the design of the project?

Care team staff, market analysts, non-care team staff, potential/future residents, and provider administrators.

Which techniques were used with non-design team members to gather information that could be applied to the design of the project?

Charrette/working session, focus group/interview, presentation to a review board, and a reduced-scale mock-up.

In addition to the client and designers, who had a key decision-making role?

Provider administrators, and provider board of directors.

Off-site Outreach Services: What off-site outreach services are offered to the greater community?

Many of the Community Center amenities are open to the greater community, including the fitness facilities, restaurants, and cultural programming.

Opposite: The great room is a flexible space that accommodates large communal events as well as intimate gatherings.
Above left: The 50-meter indoor heated swimming pool is a popular amenity for residents.
Above right: The main restaurant is divided into three distinct areas to provide an intimate dining experience to all members.

Photography: Brad Feinknopf

Solomon Cordwell Buenz

The Mather South

Evanston, Illinois // Mather LifeWays

Facility type: Independent Living, Wellness/Fitness Center
Target market: Middle/Upper Middle
Site location: Urban; Brownfield site
Project site area (square feet): 56,105
Gross square footage of the new construction involved in the project: 204,068

Number of parking spaces added by the project: 34
The site is within 1000 feet of public transportation and everyday shopping and/or medical services.
Provider type: Non sectarian non-profit
Completion date: 2011

Below: View looking northeast – The Mather South on right
Opposite: View looking west – The Mather South on left

Illustrations: SCB

Overall Project Description

The Mather is a Continuing Care Retirement Community (CCRC) formed in response to its context and location near downtown Evanston, Illinois. The project replaces two existing seniors' residences that had become functionally obsolete. The Mather was born of the need for a modern CCRC that could fulfill the many goals of Mather LifeWays, as embodied in their mission of creating "Ways to Age Well."

The 3.2-acre urban infill site encompassed two lots separated by a street and adjacent to a beautiful residential historic district north of Chicago. From the inception of the phased project, the goal was to capitalize on the advantages of the location – a walkable community on the edge of a vibrant and diverse downtown anchored by Northwestern University, with views of Lake Michigan and the historic lakefront district. With close proximity to mass transit options traversing greater Chicago, residents could take advantage of the versatility of the total building program within the limitations of a small urban site.

This second phase of The Mather will be an 11-story building providing 99 Independent Living units, a bistro and rooftop café, a wellness/fitness center with massage/aromatherapy rooms and a rehabilitation-hydrotherapy pool, as well as a hair salon, art studio, a cinema/media room, a multi-purpose room, and an expansive garden. This phase will take the total number of Independent Living units in the complex to 240 in total.

With the first phase of The Mather (Mather North, completed in October 2009) the entire development will be a 601,315 gross square feet CCRC of 297 homes, comprising 40 different floor plans and providing a continuum of living options. The first phase provides 141 Independent Living units, plus 10 Assisted Living units, 12 Memory Support units and 35 Skilled Nursing suites located in five distinct neighborhoods.

Project Goals

What three project goals had the greatest impact on the project?

Promoting holistic wellness; repositioning to appeal to the market; and responding to local conditions.

- A truly unique feature of The Mather is the availability of a rooftop terrace with expansive views, as well as ground level walking paths in an informal, multifaceted garden with climbing roses, quiet sitting enclaves, and resident planting beds.
- The development provides a complete program – tight urban sites impose limitations on physical area and dictate stacking of program elements. As a result, it was critical to study a variety of planning options that would provide a complete community replete with dining options, entertainment, health/fitness facilities, access to the outdoors, and housing options including Independent Living, Assisted Living, and Skilled Nursing, ranging from one-bedroom units to two-bedroom and den units; with ample room for entertaining.
- Sandwiched between the historic lakefront district of single-family homes and the edge of the downtown commercial district, the project had to strike a balance by providing the scale and character consistent with a historic area and the street presence to frame the entry to the downtown business area occupied by many larger buildings.

Challenges: What were the greatest design challenges faced by the project?

Square footage – the project faced severe development constraints due to its diminutive site at the edge of a multi-family and single-family district and the resultant building setback/height restrictions. To fit within the 1.2-acre buildable footprint, and to encourage residents to remain active and engaged in the greater community, certain CCRC amenities were excluded that are made redundant by neighborhood retail offerings, as well as amenities that are often underutilized in many retirement communities. The compact urban site dictated a vertical community with its footprint in the multi-family district and the two acres of open space in the single-family district, with parking below ground.

Providing parking underground was another design challenge. While it is expensive, it is also essential to provide residents and guests with convenient, on-site parking in a busy urban neighborhood. Creative planning was required to accommodate parking below the complex programs of the towers above.

A third design challenge involved a tunnel 35 feet below the city streets to connect both buildings. This tunnel is fully finished with an elevator service, providing an all-weather connection between the first and second phases of the project. A major feat of engineering was the sequencing of construction, allowing the team to complete the tunnel in two phases while maintaining significant city infrastructure (sewerage, power lines, and water mains). Also, the tunnel and the buildings' deep and significant foundation system required waterproofing; being so close to Lake Michigan, the tunnel and the building foundations are below the water table.

Innovations: What innovations/unique features were incorporated into the design of the project?

Technological innovations, such as a computerized wine dispensing system located in the ground-floor bistro, will allow residents to purchase individual servings using a pre-paid smart card.

Unique features, such as maximizing the rooftop area to provide an expansive outdoor terrace with food service and unobstructed views of Chicago, Lake Michigan, and the mature trees of the historic residential district, will provide a valuable amenity for The Mather residents.

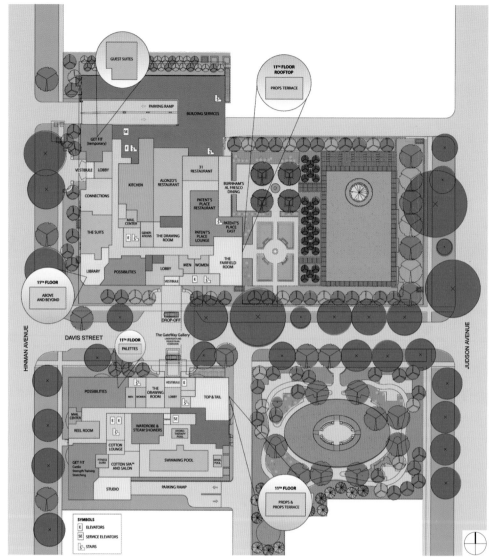

Space utilization plan (The Mather North on the north side of Davis Street, The Mather South on the south side of Davis Street)

Features/Services/Amenities: What are the most important features/services/amenities that were incorporated into the project specifically to attract the targeted market?

A pre-development survey yielded insight into the wishes of older adults, which led to the community's creation of Repriorment™: a forward-thinking approach to providing the lifestyle priorities and desires of today's emerging older adults. These insights inspired The Mather South, resulting in spaces and amenities that support and encourage wellness.

For this market, The Mather South will provide dining options, entertainment, and fitness. There will be an informal café/coffee shop/bistro, movie theatre, rooftop terrace, spa, and salon. The residents at The Mather will also enjoy a 20-meter, infinity-edge lap pool, warm water therapy pool, sauna, spa treatment rooms, a group exercise studio and a cardio/weight training room with all necessary modern equipment, a 'brain gym,' and personal training options.

Green/Sustainable Features: What are the green/sustainable features that had the greatest impact on the project's design?

Energy efficiency, reducing overall energy consumption by a targeted 20 percent, and water efficiency.

What are the primary motivations for including green/sustainable design features in the project?

Lower operational costs, to make a contribution to the greater community, and to support the mission and values of the client/provider.

What challenges have you faced when trying to incorporate green/sustainable design features?

Actual and perceived first cost premium.

Above: Overall site perspective – The Mather South on left

Illustration: Bondy Studio

Aesthetic: Identify which aesthetic your project embraces, why it was chosen and how it was achieved.

The Mather LifeWays opted for a transitional/ modern feel for the interiors, with each building having a unique identity.

The well-appointed common areas of The Mather South will feature a different color palette than those in the occupied Mather North. Interior finishes will be soothing blue and green tones, allowing colors from selected artwork with custom commissions to invigorate the spaces. All carpets in the common areas and residential corridors will be custom designs. Furnishings will be simple yet sophisticated, functional, and have clean lines. The interior decorative light fixtures are custom-designed companion fixtures to those used in The Mather North, using a combination of polished and satin nickel finishes with faux alabaster and amber-acrylic shades.

Artifacts from the original building will be repurposed in The Mather South. This includes carved mahogany pilasters for the lobby and main corridors, plaster of Paris lily pads for the granite fountain at the indoor pool, terracotta griffins

for the feature wall behind the lily pad fountain, decorative ironwork for the outer side of the granite fountain, a terracotta lion fountain at the entrance to the community, and ornate stairway spindles for the theater.

Aging-in-place features will include community commons that provide a variety of lounge, activity, dining, and wellness venues; midrise residential floors that facilitate shorter walking distances; large expanses of windows that allow natural light in; and wide corridors for easy passage and egress.

For the residential component, what was critical to the success of the project?

Improving common spaces/amenities.

Common Spaces: What common spaces are included in the project?

Bistro/casual dining, coffee shop/grab-and-go, dedicated conference/meeting space, dedicated exercise classroom, dedicated fitness equipment room, large multipurpose room, library/information resource center, marketplace/convenience store, massage/aromatherapy room, a rooftop terrace café and rooftop party room, men's and women's locker rooms in the wellness center, whirlpool, steam

showers, sauna, computerized wine bar, brain gym, mail center and concierge desk, resident-maintained gardening space, salon, small-scale cinema/media room, and swimming pool/aquatics facility.

Describe the largest interior common space in the project (excluding dining).

Get Fit, the fitness and wellness center, is 7533 square feet. Get Fit was designed with an emphasis on healthy living. Complete with fitness, spa, and aquatic activities, Get Fit will stimulate socialization and wellbeing. The fitness component consists of strength/weight training, cardio equipment, a stretching area, a group exercise room with a Wii station, a wellness assessment office, and a 'brain gym.' Spa services in the Cotton Spa™ and Salon will include salon, manicure, pedicure, massage, and a quiet room for tranquil meditation. The indoor lap pool and hydrotherapy pool with built in treadmill will offer low-impact exercise and rehabilitation. Locker rooms, sauna, steam showers, and whirlpool complete Get Fit.

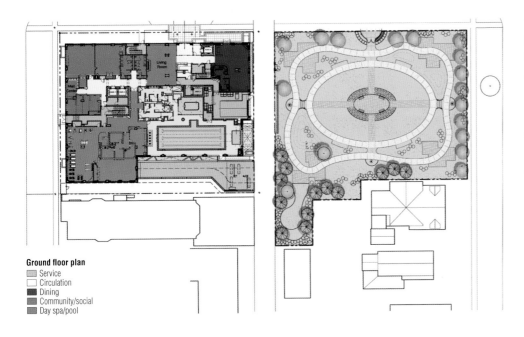

Ground floor plan
- ☐ Service
- ☐ Circulation
- ■ Dining
- ■ Community/social
- ■ Day spa/pool

Describe each dining venue incorporated in the project.

One casual bistro lounge with 38 seats indoors and 16 seats on the outdoor terrace. The rooftop party room has seating for 13.

Design Process: Who did the design team work with to gather information that could be applied to the design of the project?

City planners/code officials, contractor/construction team, design consultants, market analysts, neighbors/members of the greater community, potential/future residents, and provider administrators.

Which techniques were used with non-design team members to gather information that could be applied to the design of the project?

Charrette/working session, focus group/interview, presentation to a review board, and a survey.

In addition to the client and designers, who had a key decision-making role?

City planners/code officials, and provider administrators.

Opposite top left: The Mather South – perspective of typical living space in one-bedroom unit
Opposite top right: The Mather South – north elevation
Illustrations: SCB

Left: The Mather South – pools and spa environment
Illustrations: Bondy Studio

RLPS Architects

The Townhomes on Hendricks Place

Lititz, Pennsylvania // Townhomes on Hendricks Place at Moravian Manor

Facility type: Independent Living
Target Market: Middle/Upper Middle
Site Location: Urban (City or Town)
Project site area (square feet): 152,460
Gross square footage of the new construction involved in the project: 42,584

Number of parking spaces added by the project: 7
The site is within 1000 feet of everyday shopping and/or medical services.
Provider type: Faith-based non-profit
Completion date: June 2012

Below: Perspective rendering of courtyard townhomes

Illustration: RLPS Architects

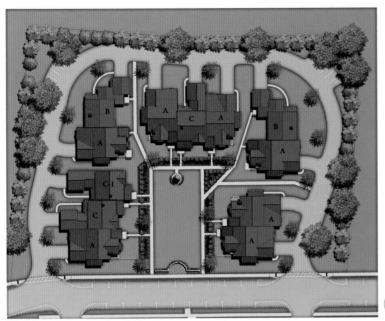
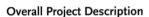
Site plan

Overall Project Description

The Townhomes on Hendricks Place provide a new Independent Living option for residents of Moravian Manor, a Continuing Care Retirement Community (CCRC) located in Lititz, Pennsylvania. This new neighborhood of 12 attached, two-story cottage-style units offers residents the opportunity to live, work, and play within blocks of their new homes. These upscale townhomes, configured around a central green, offer two-story living with amenities on the first floor. They are built to accommodate active adults who prefer to maintain a house-sized residence and maintenance-free living within a retirement community. Three different models, ranging from 2609 up to 2833 square feet, all include two bedrooms plus a den and rear-loaded two-car garage. Other features include nine-foot ceilings, walk-in closets, an eat-in kitchen, covered porch, gas fireplace, laundry room, and an optional sunroom with patio.

Located on 3.5 acres in downtown Lititz, the Townhomes on Hendricks Place are designed to architecturally emulate the character of their surroundings. An interconnecting sidewalk network provides residents with direct pedestrian access to the center green and to Lititz Borough's sidewalk and trail network. Hendricks Place is in close proximity to the Main Street shops and restaurants, nearby recreation facilities, parks, farmers' markets, and other amenities.

Project Goals

What three project goals had the greatest impact on the project?

Aging-in-place; responding to local conditions; and taking advantage of existing infrastructure and amenities found in the surrounding neighborhood.

- A challenge was to design marketable units that provide desirable living amenities and flexibility to allow for aging-in-place. The two-story townhomes were planned so that, if necessary, a resident could live comfortably on the first floor, with the second floor functioning as a bonus area for a guest bedroom, game room, office or hobby area. All homes were designed with the option for a residential elevator to access the second floor loft. Other more discreetly supportive features for accessibility, ranging from wider door clearances and higher countertops to lower shower thresholds, are designed into all of the townhomes as well.

- A design priority was creating a traditional neighborhood development that complements the historical context of the surrounding downtown. The character of the townhomes was developed with reference to the Lititz/Warwick joint Strategic Comprehensive Plan, designed to preserve and enhance the predominant characteristics of the region. To reinforce the residential scale, the building façades take on the appearance of attached buildings along the town's streetscape. The varied color palette and building materials reflect the local vernacular to blend in with the existing community.

- This infill site in downtown Lititz is located across from the Moravian Manor main campus, and within walking distance to a wide range of services and amenities, ranging from the Wilbur Chocolate Factory to an English-style pub. Targeting active adults, the new townhomes overlook a common green and are interconnected via a sidewalk system that leads to the adjacent retirement campus and the town's sidewalk network. Hendricks Place residents will not only have easy access to Moravian Manor's services and amenities, but are also just steps away from a thriving small town environment with a vibrant network of shops and unique events, such as the annual Chocolate Walk.

Unit A first floor plan

Unit A second floor plan

Unit B first floor plan

Unit B second floor plan

Unit C first floor plan

Unit C second floor plan

Challenges: What were the greatest design challenges faced by the project?

Implementing the necessary stormwater quantity and quality control measures without compromising the design concept of interconnected townhomes arranged around a common green challenged the design team to explore a non-traditional approach. A combination of rain gardens to define the boundaries between the private and public green spaces and underground stormwater storage allowed for the desired building configuration within the constraints of a tight infill site.

Another challenge for the design team was obtaining variances from traditional zoning and planning regulations to a unique, higher-density design solution on the site zoned for residential use. A series of meetings utilizing concept images and a street-view rendering to illustrate the primary concept of clustering traditional townhomes around a center green helped to secure the allowances to proceed with the project.

The target market for the townhomes is active adults who wish to live in a spacious home within a pedestrian-friendly town. While one of the primary design goals was to accommodate aging-in-place, those accommodations could not be at the expense of the residential aesthetic. Prospective residents were clear that they did not wish to live in a home where accessibility features were apparent. Wide doorways and similar measures, such as extra blocking in showers, allow for future accommodations when needed by the residents living in the home.

Innovations: What innovations/unique features were incorporated into the design of the project?

The façades for the townhomes at Hendricks Place are designed to provide dual front doors for both the street side – to provide visitor and vehicle access and views – as well as the courtyard side facing the common green, to provide sidewalk access and views from Second Street, which runs in front of the townhomes.

Features/Services/Amenities: What are the most important features/services/amenities that were incorporated into the project specifically to attract the targeted market?

Moravian Manor wished to utilize the available infill site to provide a new Independent Living housing option on its campus for active seniors. The most important feature for the townhomes was creating spacious, open-plan residences that allow for first-floor living, and provide ample space for amenities found in traditional residences. This includes the second-floor bonus space that is accessed via a residential elevator. A secondary feature is providing ample outdoor connections through covered porches and optional sunrooms. Each townhome has a covered porch leading to the sidewalk network connecting the homes around the central green. Finally, although the design tucks them behind the street façade, the two-car, attached garages are a priority to attract the senior target market.

Green/Sustainable Features: What are the green/sustainable features that had the greatest impact on the project's design?

Maximizing daylighting, relocation of an existing home on the site rather than demolition, and site design considerations.

What are the primary motivations for including green/sustainable design features in the project?

To make a contribution to the greater community, stay competitive against other similar/local facilities, and to support the mission and values of the client/provider.

What challenges have you faced when trying to incorporate green/sustainable design features?

Lack of knowledge about green/sustainability.

Aesthetic: Identify which aesthetic your project embraces, why it was chosen and how it was achieved.

The townhomes at Hendricks Place needed a residential appearance that would blend with the surrounding downtown. This necessitated traditional materials and layouts that were in keeping with the historical context of Lititz.

For the residential component, what was critical to the success of the project?

Improving units/private spaces.

Common Spaces: What common spaces are included in the project?

The center-green courtyard space, walking paths, and a gazebo for gatherings and events.

Design Process: Who did the design team work with to gather information that could be applied to the design of the project?

City planners/code officials, current/existing residents, design consultants, neighbors/members of the greater community, potential/future residents, and provider administrators.

Which techniques were used with non-design team members to gather information that could be applied to the design of the project?

Focus group/interview, and presentation to a review board.

In addition to the client and designers, who had a key decision-making role?

City planners/code officials, provider administrators, and provider board of directors.

Top: Elevation showing varied exterior elements used to blend with surrounding townscape
Illustration: RLPS Architects

Perkins Eastman

Jewish Home Lifecare

New York, New York // Jewish Home Lifecare

Facility type: Long-Term Skilled Nursing, Short-Term Rehabilitation, Green House®
Target market: Mixed income – the project is long-term care and will accommodate Medicaid, Medicare and private pay.
Site location: Urban; Brownfield site

Project site area (square feet): 31,804
Gross square footage of the new construction involved in the project: 469,218
Number of parking spaces added by the project: 0
The site is within 1000 feet of public transportation and everyday shopping and/or medical services.

The project offers transport to nearby shopping, medical, and/or cultural services/amenities.
Provider type: Faith-based non-profit
Completion date: August 2016 (estimated)

Overall Project Description

The project was undertaken to replace an existing Long-Term Care campus that was built over a period of several years in the 1960s. The existing campus was physically and programmatically obsolete, with small shared-head-wall semi-private rooms and very little program space for dining or activities on the nursing units.

In searching for a site, the client wanted a location in a vibrant neighborhood where residents could conduct commerce, meet friends, and watch passersby. The new campus, a single 24-story building on Manhattan's Upper West Side will integrate into a neighborhood with a variety of experiences and conveniences, including grocery stores, laundries, banks, pharmacies, restaurants, fitness clubs, movie theaters, places of worship, and parks.

A total of 408 residents will be accommodated in a Green House® model of care: 288 in long-term care and 120 in short-term rehabilitation. Aging adults

in need of long-term care will live in one of the 24 apartments, which will be located on the upper 12 floors. Each apartment will contain private rooms for 12 residents along with the kitchen, dining, and living spaces. Older adults in need of short-term transitional care will be accommodated on the short-term rehabilitation floors, where each floor contains complete rehabilitation programs.

The lower floors of the building house common spaces for residents with an auditorium, kosher bistro and coffee shop, library, wellness spa, and outdoor terrace. Additional spaces include an adult day care program, offices for Home Health Care, and corporate offices for the community.

Project Goals

What three project goals had the greatest impact on the project?

Creating a homelike environment; integrating with the surrounding neighborhood/greater community; and offering daily choice through extensive amenities.

- Creating a new campus that is integrated into the Upper West Side neighborhood, and adapting the Green House® model to an urban context. The site was selected because of its close proximity to many commercial and cultural amenities. The program and design of the first floor (and its garden) and the second floor were created to draw the public into the community.

- Maximizing elders' privacy, dignity, and independence. All of the elders living in long-term care live in private rooms that are equipped with private baths. Each house is equipped with all the elements needed by elders on a day-to-day basis and the walking distances within the houses are short.

- Building strong relationships between elders, and between elders and caregivers. The intimate size of the houses fosters strong relationships.

Challenges: What were the greatest design challenges faced by the project?

Addressing the New York City zoning law was the largest programmatic and architectural challenge. The requirement for open space on the ground floor significantly limited the amount of enclosed space that could be built there. The zoning approach forced larger garden spaces on the ground floor, which was a benefit but limited the enclosed space that could be provided for elders there.

Another challenge was planning the ground floor to accommodate pedestrian and vehicular entrances, loading docks, and elders' access to the gardens.

A third key challenge was finding the right mix of public amenity spaces on the second floor and connecting the most active of these spaces to the street below.

Innovations: What innovations/unique features were incorporated into the design of the project?

Solving the challenges of cooking within the houses and responding to the technical and life safety ramifications.

Creating a life safety approach to allow the long-term care residents to lock their individual doors at night.

Inserting a dense program into a high-rise building with the limitations of structure, mechanical and plumbing shafts, and construction cost limitations.

Features/Services/Amenities: What are the most important features/services/amenities that were incorporated into the project specifically to attract the targeted market?

One of the benefits of developing the independent household model is that each house can respond to the needs and desires of its unique residents.

The large common program on the second floor creates the ability for residents who live in separate houses to interact with residents from other houses and to make choices about where they eat or spend their time. This space also provides neighborhood amenities.

Green/Sustainable Features: What are the green/sustainable features that had the greatest impact on the project's design?

Energy efficiency, maximizing daylight, and site design considerations.

What are the primary motivations for including green/sustainable design features in the project?

Good public relations, lower operational costs, and to support the mission and values of the client/provider.

What challenges have you faced when trying to incorporate green/sustainable design features?

Actual first cost premium.

Aesthetic: Identify which aesthetic your project embraces, why it was chosen and how it was achieved.

From the beginning, the design team acknowledged that the non-resident floors would have a more public or commercial feel to them,

Opposite left: Location map
Opposite right: Actual view of neighborhood
Left: Typical resident room
Below: Green House® interior view

Illustrations: Perkins Eastman

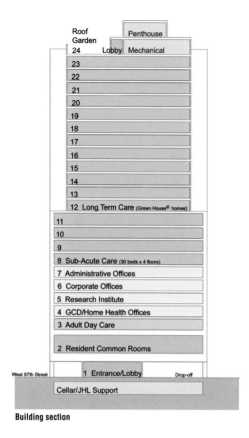

Building section

Roof Garden 24	Penthouse
	Lobby Mechanical
23	
22	
21	
20	
19	
18	
17	
16	
15	
14	
13	
12 Long Term Care (Green House® homes)	
11	
10	
9	
8 Sub-Acute Care (30 beds x 4 floors)	
7 Administrative Offices	
6 Corporate Offices	
5 Research Institute	
4 GCD/Home Health Offices	
3 Adult Day Care	
2 Resident Common Rooms	
West 97th Street 1 Entrance/Lobby Drop-off	
Cellar/JHL Support	

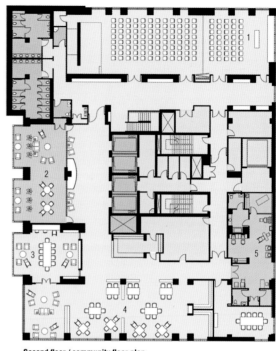

Second floor / community floor plan
1 Synagogue / multipurpose room
2 Porch
3 Library
4 Café
5 Spa / salon

making them spaces where residents from various houses could mingle with the public. The design of the houses is intended to be residential.

For the residential component, what was critical to the success of the project?

Improving units/private spaces.

Households: Describe the role households had in the project.

The household model is at the core of this development, and adapting the Green House® model to an urban context is integral to the project design and planning.

Common Spaces: What common spaces are included in the project?

Bistro/casual dining, coffee shop/grab-and-go, dedicated classroom/learning space, dedicated conference/meeting space, dedicated rehabilitation/therapy gym, formal dining, large multipurpose room, library/information resource center, marketplace/convenience store, massage/aromatherapy room, religious/spiritual/meditative space, and a salon.

For a typical household wing/facility, describe the common spaces.

- Formal living room with fireplace; 320 square feet.

- Dining room with a single dining table to seat 14 people; 240 square feet.

- Den – an enclosed room for television watching, crafts, and games; 320 square feet.

Describe the largest interior common space in the project (excluding dining).

The largest common space in the project is the auditorium/chapel. These two rooms are separated by a moveable partition that allows the rooms to be combined into one 2750-square foot room that will accommodate 175 people for large formal events.

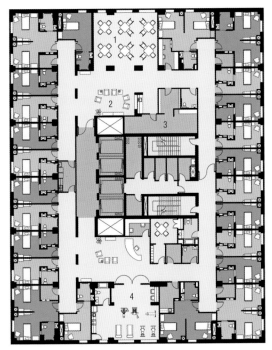

Typical short-term rehabilitation floor plan
1 Dining
2 Living room
3 Kitchen
4 Rehabilitation

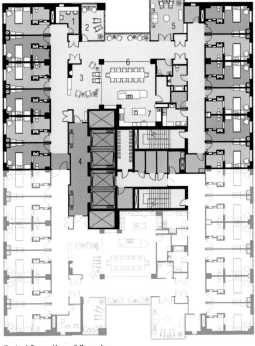

Typical Green House® floor plan
1 Office
2 Screened porch
3 Hearth
4 Entry lobby
5 Den
6 Dining
7 Kitchen

Describe each dining venue incorporated in the project.

- Long-term care house dining room: a residential/family-style dining room in each of the 24 houses; each dining room will accommodate 14 people.

- Short-term rehabilitation: a small restaurant-style dining room on each of the four short-term rehabilitation floors; each dining room will accommodate 24 people.

- Coffee shop: coffee and kosher/dairy foods; this is an informal retail outlet with no seating.

- Bistro: kosher/meat foods; this is a retail outlet with seating for 50 people.

- Family/private dining: formal dining with seating for 12.

Design Process: Who did the design team work with to gather information that could be applied to the design of the project?

Affiliated yet independent agencies, care team staff, city planners/code officials, contractor/construction team, current/existing residents, design consultants, family or friends of residents, market analysts, neighbors/members of the greater community, non-care team staff, potential/future residents, and provider administrators.

Which techniques were used with non-design team members to gather information that could be applied to the design of the project?

Charrette/working session, focus group/interview, full-scale mock-up, in situ observations, and a presentation to a review board.

In addition to the client and designers, who had a key decision-making role?

Affiliated yet independent agencies, care team staff, city planners/code officials, contractor/construction team, current/existing residents, non-care team staff, potential/future residents, provider administrators, and provider board of directors.

BAR Architects

Sun City Palace Showa Kinen Koen

Tokyo, Japan // Half Century More

Facility type: Independent Living, Other Medical Services Care Facility, Short-term Skilled Nursing, Short-Term Rehabilitation, Wellness/Fitness Center
Target market: Upper
Site location: Urban; Brownfield site
Project site area (square feet): 400,000
Gross square footage of the new construction involved in the project: 560,000

Number of parking spaces added by the project: 192
The site is within 1000 feet of public transportation. The project offers transport to nearby shopping, medical, and/or cultural services/amenities.
Provider type: For profit
Completion date: September 2014 (estimated)

Below and opposite: Exterior rendering of overall community

Illustrations: BAR Architects

Overall Project Description

The site for this project has been in the developer's family for many years. It is part of a larger holding in an affluent suburb of Tokyo, and immediately north of a large public park, Showa Kinen Koen, which contains large and mature gardens. The design team was given several directions:

- South or southerly facing units are prized in Tokyo. The aim was to capitalize on the site's overlook of the park to the south and the park's landscape.

- The developed facility was to have an air of exclusivity.

- The project contains around 645 units in total, with a full complement of public spaces and recreational amenities, including Assisted Living and Nursing facilities.

- The project was to develop in such a way as to enable a future phase on the adjacent site area.

- Included in the scope of work is a full development of the landscape design in the tradition of Japanese garden design, but with a modern sensibility.

- Height limits on the property are strict. Building siting and massing would have to conform to these while maintaining density, operational efficiency, and program.

- Design and develop world-class architecture, interior design, and landcape design as a total concept that capitalizes on the assets of the site, and operational program of the developer.

Project Goals

What three project goals had the greatest impact on the project?

Collaboration during design development; providing a hospitality/resort feel; and responding to local conditions.

- The primary goal of the project was to respond to local conditions. In any high-density urban setting, the presence of a park immediately adjacent to the property is an asset. In addition, the property faces south over the park, affording an uncommon opportunity to maximize solar access to all units.

The project was conceived as a series of four fan-capped elements, all linked at their lower floors, and shaped around a series of courtyard spaces, each with its own character. Each fan shape gestures southeasterly or southwesterly towards the park, Showa Kinen Koen, with the link buildings gaining southeasterly and southwesterly views. Buildings were placed with gaps to allow views through to the park from the more northerly locations. The Nursing and Care Center was conceived around a U-shaped courtyard garden of its own along the southwest side of the site. Buildings were carefully massed to conform to the regional planning guidelines.

From a site-planning perspective, the entrance was placed as far north as possible, towards the point of access – the main access road runs along park space. Also central to this concept is the idea of structuring the residents' and visitors' experience to gradually reveal all the interior public areas and exterior open spaces. This would heighten the experience of residents living there every day, provide for convenient way-finding, visual variety, and spatial richness.

- The second goal was to provide a hospitality/ resort feel. This goal was addressed concurrently with goal number one above. It contains both interior and exterior components. Entering the site from the north, one drives southeast and then south along the main tree-lined entry road adjacent to

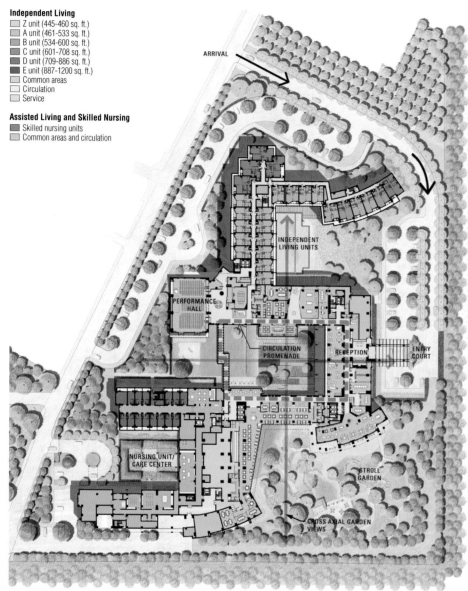

Independent Living

- ▢ Z unit (445-460 sq. ft.)
- ▢ A unit (461-533 sq. ft.)
- ▢ B unit (534-600 sq. ft.)
- ▢ C unit (601-708 sq. ft.)
- ▢ D unit (709-886 sq. ft.)
- ▢ E unit (887-1200 sq. ft.)
- ▢ Common areas
- ▢ Circulation
- ▢ Service

Assisted Living and Skilled Nursing

- ▢ Skilled nursing units
- ▢ Common areas and circulation

ARRIVAL

INDEPENDENT
LIVING UNITS

PERFORMANCE
HALL

CIRCULATION
PROMENADE

RECEPTION

ENTRY
COURT

NURSING UNIT/
CARE CENTER

STROLL
GARDEN

CROSS AXIAL GARDEN
VIEWS

Overall building floor plan

park space. All visual information provided to a visitor or resident arriving on the property is designed from the point of entry. The road terminates at a contemporary *porte-cochère*, and from this point one sees due south to the gardens beyond. Entering the building one finds a reception/concierge desk, the main lobby and a gracious lounge space, and beyond it the primary courtyard, which is bounded by outdoor loggia adjacent to the lobby, a reflecting pond, and a "floating bridge" across the water, enclosing the court in the distance.

Primary circulation is placed around this central court, as are the main public spaces. All spaces are proportioned and have access to light and air. A main access corridor terminates at the library space, opening onto the south garden and borrowing the landscape of Showa Kinen Koen. Another corridor ends at the two dining rooms, which share the views of the south garden and park. Activity rooms and assembly spaces are placed strategically along the circulation path, and similarly afford views of the assembled courtyards and gardens.

Interior design, furnishing, and finishes were developed in conjunction with goal number three, below.

- The third goal was collaboration during design development. This project was awarded as the result of a limited design competition. The effort began by collectively visiting the site with the client, listening to his goals, and carefully documenting all the on- and off-site opportunities. Then design teams of all three primary disciplines – architects, landscape architects, and interior designers – worked together over a period of weeks and collaboratively developed the design. The multidisciplinary team presented to the client at regular intervals throughout the process.

Challenges: What were the greatest design challenges faced by the project?

Developing the required number of units on the site while maintaining their southerly facing aspect and maximizing views to the park, while providing a gracious and functional public space layout, was the greatest design challenge the project faced. This challenge was met through the collaborative design process. The decision to break the design into separate buildings linked on their lower floors, with surrounding varied courtyard and garden spaces, was the first breakthrough in this challenge. This move enabled the team to break down the massing of a very dense project, and simultaneously respect solar access, maximize views, and create value for the client. The other breakthrough was the proposal to enter the project site at the end, rather than in the middle of the project, which enhanced the "site experience" and allowed for a central, efficient entry.

Another challenge facing the project was the rigorous height limits governing development on the property. This challenge was met by modeling the various building "pieces" and studying their height/shadow impacts on their adjacent outdoor space, and molding the building mass into conformance in ways that would not adversely affect light and views.

Another design challenge was to provide a secondary entrance and identity for the Care Center of the project. By placing the Care Center spaces in a U-shaped configuration around its own courtyard and backing this up to the central kitchen and service areas of the project, this challenge was addressed in a simple and direct way, and make more identifiable and controllable outdoor space for the Care Center.

Innovations: What innovations/unique features were incorporated into the design of the project?

The "fan-shaped" wings and the tightly knit system of public space and outdoor courts and gardens are representative of unique features of this project.

Features/Services/Amenities: What are the most important features/services/amenities that were incorporated into the project specifically to attract the targeted market?

Japan is a country that, like many, has a rapidly aging population. Many services, features, and amenities address the aspirations of this new generation and its thinking. One component of this is in the food service area. While the idea of multiple dining destinations is not new, this innovation provides it in a setting that affords great light and amenity in a contemporary and non-traditional space. Another component is the fully functioning library/lounge, which in addition to being a space to accommodate books is a social and learning center, with programming incorporating the other multi-function spaces. A third is the ofuro/spa/wellness and pool component. Public bathing is a ritual in Japanese culture; incorporating this with a wellness component and social awareness affords a new opportunity in a centuries-old tradition.

Above left: Interior renderings of Common Facilities; lobby lounge (top), dining (bottom)
Illustrations: BAMO, Inc.

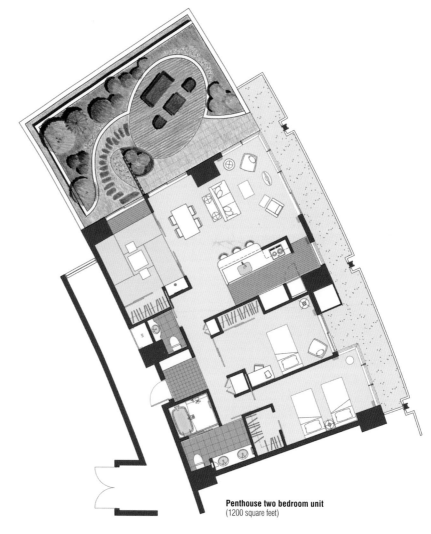

One bedroom unit
(445 square feet)

Penthouse two bedroom unit
(1200 square feet)

Smallest and largest living unit plans

Opposite: Interior renderings of Common Facilities;
reception lobby (top), library (bottom)
Illustrations: BAMO, Inc.

Green/Sustainable Features: What are the green/sustainable features that had the greatest impact on the project's design?

Energy efficiency, maximizing daylighting, and site design considerations.

What are the primary motivations for including green/sustainable design features in the project?

Lower operational costs, to support the mission and values of the client/provider, and to support the mission and values of the design team.

What challenges have you faced when trying to incorporate green/sustainable design features?

Actual and perceived first cost premium; and lack of knowledge about green/sustainability.

Aesthetic: Identify which aesthetic your project embraces, why it was chosen and how it was achieved.

This project can definitely be described as having a "contemporary, modern feel, couched in a hospitality approach," but with a twist. It was

incumbent on the design team to develop an aesthetic and feel that was distinctly Western in orientation, but just as Japanese in influence. The exterior approach was fairly straightforward, but the garden design and interior design required more study and experimentation to achieve the desired "mix and blend" of cultures and design influence. The architecture, interiors, and landscaping are contemporary and meant to instill a residential feeling – purposefully non-institutional and non-commercial – for residents, their families and guests. The interior material palette of warm wood, light-colored stone, creamy-white surfaces, woven raffia, and decorative glass is subdued and elemental, providing a container for the fresh, clean colors of the furnishings, fabrics, artwork, and accessories. Furnishings, light fixtures and accessories are an eclectic mix of Western and Asian pieces, contemporary and traditional in craft. Many artworks are commissioned specifically for this project.

For the residential component, what was critical to the success of the project?

Improving common spaces/amenities.

Common Spaces: What common spaces are included in the project?

Coffee shop/grab-and-go, dedicated conference/meeting space, dedicated exercise classroom, dedicated fitness equipment room, dedicated rehabilitation/therapy gym, formal dining, large multipurpose room, library/information resource center, massage/aromatherapy room, a salon, small-scale cinema/media room, and swimming pool/aquatics facility.

Describe the largest interior common space in the project (excluding dining).

The Sun City Hall is a 3300-square foot multipurpose room for meetings, concerts, ceremonies, and fitness, with 481 regular and 66 overflow seats.

Describe each dining venue incorporated in the project.

In the main dining room, there are 270 seats. For private dining, there are four rooms with flexible partitions and 56 seats in total.

Design Process: Who did the design team work with to gather information that could be applied to the design of the project?

Care team staff, city planners/code officials, current/existing residents, design consultants, neighbors/members of the greater community, non-care team staff, and provider administrators.

Which techniques were used with non-design team members to gather information that could be applied to the design of the project?

In situ observations, presentation to a review board, and a survey.

Design For Aging Review 11

International Projects Supplement

AIA Introduction to International Projects Supplement

IAHSA Introduction to International Projects Supplement

IAHSA Projects

AIA Introduction to International Projects Supplement

The *Design for Aging Review 11* (DFAR 11) offers an exciting opportunity – the addition of international projects. In keeping with the global times and to address the challenges of our aging society, we are including a supplement to highlight noteworthy international senior living projects. Their inclusion provides an opportunity to share ideas across borders, see how providers in other countries address the design of their environments, and examine the trends shaping their housing and service options. The projects came to us through the International Association of Homes and Services for the Ageing (IAHSA). Although they were not reviewed in an extensive juried competition like the DFAR submissions, these projects represent creative solutions that the DFAR Jury thought worthy of sharing. In selecting the projects to publish, the DFAR Jury felt strongly about sticking to the criteria of innovation, choosing only six projects that they felt were inspirational in the ideas they represent.

The AIA Design for Aging (DFA) Knowledge Community actively works with LeadingAge to review and promote projects to educate architects, designers, and providers about designing for aging adults. As the goal of the DFAR is to represent excellence in design and quality operations, we are hopeful that we will continue to share innovations from throughout the world in future DFAR publications.

Joyce Polhamus, AIA
2012 DFA Chair

IAHSA Introduction to International Projects Supplement

While the global economic downturn has left no country untouched, demand for elder care and services remains strong. This is largely due to the undeniable demographic shift that the world is experiencing. The exponential growth of the older population is unprecedented in human history and will have a profound impact on governments, civil society, and families throughout the world.

As people age, their preferences and needs for living arrangements and environments change. Architects are responding to these needs with innovative approaches. Designs allow residents to connect to nature, engage in physical activity, and create communities during shared meals and other social occasions. Because preferences among the elderly are far from homogeneous, the designs that are included in this supplement have a strong focus on maximizing resident

independence and autonomy in decision-making. Wellness and social programs for residents include opportunities for reflection and spirituality, as well as self-expression through the arts.

Active aging is increasingly acknowledged as a way for seniors to enjoy their lives, continue to contribute to society, and stay healthy. The communities featured in this supplement promote resident engagement by providing areas for familial visitation, group activities, and community interaction. There are examples of integrated communities that allow residents to mix across care levels while ensuring safety and security.

The designs presented in this supplement also have a particular focus on affordability and sustainability. The designs support cost-effective delivery models and structures that are

versatile, adaptable, and environmentally-friendly. Innovative systems for heating and cooling allow organizations to manage energy costs and also provide for resident needs through features such as radiant floor heat.

Innovative design to meet the changing needs of our aging society is a global concern. The designs included in this supplement confirm that architects throughout the world are singularly focused on creative solutions to address the many dimensions of the aging process through effective design. The International Association of Homes and Services for the Ageing (IAHSA) is pleased to be part of the 11th cycle of the *Design for Aging Review*. As a broad network of providers, architects, researchers, and others, the IAHSA is committed to enhancing the quality of life for people as they age, regardless of where they live.

Katie Smith Sloan
Executive Director, International Association of
Homes and Services for the Ageing

Pozzoni LLP

Belong Wigan Care Village

Wigan, Greater Manchester, UK // Belong

Facility type: Active Senior/Independent Living Residence, Subsidized Affordable Independent Living, Special Care Residence (for those with dementia), Skilled Nursing Care Residence
Site location: Urban
Site size: 2.46 acres

Building footprint: 2845 square meters
Building area: 5743 square meters
Total building cost: £9,487,858
Building cost per square unit: £1652/ square meter
Date of completion: May 2011

Below: Belong Wigan is contemporary architecture with a human scale
Opposite: Independent Living Apartments

Owner's Statement

Belong Wigan Care Village is a lifestyle concept for older people that aims to prevent isolation and to protect, promote, and uphold a person's autonomy and independence. The village is a two-phase development that incorporates innovative design concepts and details and is the result of an evolving brief and design process. Phase one of the scheme was a 66-bed Care Home. Phase two was the completion of 54 Independent Living apartments, which completed the village.

Belong Wigan Care Village provides 11 private ensuite rooms located within six small, self-contained, open plan, contemporary households that provide individuals with 24-hour access to support and rehabilitation opportunities. Each house is safe and secure and has access to a garden or balcony. The 54 Independent Living apartments allow for an independent lifestyle within easy reach of the full facilities the community can offer.

Architect's Statement

There are four key themes to the design:

- To create a homely, non-institutionalized environment: six self-contained households of 11 residents each enable a lifestyle of an "extended family" to be realized. A domestic, human ratio to space, details, fixtures, and fittings creates a homely feeling throughout. Each household has its own kitchen, lounge, dining and activity areas in an open plan configuration so that residents can find their way around easily and staff can discreetly monitor residents – some residents report feeling safer because they can see staff around. The 54 Independent Living apartments are also domestic in nature to maximize independence, with easy access to the communal facilities.

- To design with flexibility for current and future use: in both the Care and Independent Living facilities, the floor areas and communal spaces exceed the national minimum standards. Older people have and will continue to have a high expectation of design and service. Large floor areas allow space for residents' personal possessions to be brought in if they wish and for additional equipment to be used if a resident's needs change. The layout of the ensuite bedrooms allows for the combining of two bedrooms to create a single one-bedroom apartment in the future, if this is required. The principles of designing for people with dementia have been adopted throughout the design.

- To provide facilities for the use of the community within the home and the wider neighborhood: the central 'hub' provides a bistro, hair and beauty salon, community room, visiting doctor room, gym and internet café. These are designed and fitted-out as if they were independent businesses, reinforcing the non-institutional theme. These spaces allow for contact between residents, families and the wider neighborhood.

- To achieve this while balancing staffing and cost issues: an excellent working environment has been created for the staff, incorporating technology to assist staff and enable them to spend quality time with residents. Staff multi-task and spend their day with the residents living and working as a large family. Value-engineering sessions throughout the design and construction process have eliminated waste and promoted value.

Client Goals and Design Team Solutions

- To provide a contemporary living experience for an ageing client group, where people feel secure and experience a sense of belonging.

People are helped to live a lifestyle that is familiar, comfortable and safe, with home and family involvement. It is thought of as a change of address – not a change of lifestyle.

Therapeutic activity is valued, companionship with pets is encouraged, and intergenerational activity is promoted within the community.

- To create smaller living environments that meet the intimate, private needs of individuals, while providing larger spaces to accommodate the more public needs of the community.

There is an increasing need to support people with dementia through the provision of specialist services within familiar environments, while providing facilities that will meet the needs of more physically frail people. Villagers will have access to health care specialists without needing to leave the building.

- To create environments where life revolves around purposeful activity and each day has meaning.

Belong Village is a place where individuals have made an active choice to live in the village. Every day is different and not governed by tasks and time constraints. Opportunities will be created for the older person to give care and support to others, as well as receive it.

Major Design Objectives and/or Project Challenges

- The concept of open plan living areas is a departure from conventional thinking about fire safety. The lessons learnt from the previous Belong Villages have been incorporated and confirmed that the building design and the management of the fire evacuation strategy are interlinked.

- Maximizing the potential of the site area without over-development: the economics of high land values and building costs required a high-density scheme. The design process arrived at a three-story building to achieve the economic solution while retaining the project's goals and objectives.

- To reinforce the idea of independent living, these apartments have been constructed in two blocks; each block has its own front door. Residents and visitors can come and go without passing through a central reception area. Security is maintained by secure access points to the village, intercom entry and natural surveillance from overlooking windows.

Unique Context

In the UK, government policy is to encourage people to remain in their own homes for as long as possible. Consequently, when people do move to a care environment, they are more likely to have higher dependency requirements. The principles of designing for people with dementia and other cognitive or physical impairments have been used throughout to accommodate these needs while avoiding an institutional environment.

The scarcity of sites and high land values require a high-density scheme to work financially. High-density schemes are likely to be more commonplace as land values increase, despite the current economic downturn.

The Independent Living Apartments provide the option for people to maintain an independent lifestyle while having specific care packages to suit individual needs. There will be a degree of cross-subsidizing the community and Care

Opposite top: The bistro is open to the public and is very popular with the neighbourhood.
Opposite bottom: Open-plan spaces within the households allow for flexibility in use.
Above: An easily accessible kitchen allows residents to participate in kitchen activities, acts as a focal point and memory cue and is the heart of the home.

Home facilities by the revenue generated by the Independent Living Apartments.

Conventional design to accommodate UK Building Regulations would require fire-risk areas to be enclosed behind fire-resistant construction. With a fire-suppression system, compartmentalization and a robust fire evacuation strategy, the open-plan households have been created to meet safety regulations.

Environmental Sustainability and Energy Conservation

A dynamic thermal model was produced, allowing for an in-depth energy appraisal of the building design. High levels of thermal insulation, low-energy light fittings and appliances, and individual room heating controls reduce the demand for energy.

Balcony and roof overhangs prevent glare and overheating and, where possible, building materials have been sourced locally and local tradesmen have been used, reducing the embodied energy in transport. Building materials have been obtained from sustainable sources.

Advanced Technology

The Belong Wigan Care Village is fitted with a nurse call system that covers the entire village. Each bedroom has the specialist dementia network that provides:

- Automatic light guidance for ensuite and bed head

- 16 behavior profiles
- Falls or illness notification
- Bed-exit and ensuite activity sensor
- Server that recalls all nurse call activity.

Each room has a call unit that uses speech, call lead and pull cord for individual users' requirements. Residents' calls are made through a call button or neck pendant. There are up to 29 Radio frequency (RF) sensors in each room for inactivity and falls, which are included in each individual's life plan. All calls go to a Digital Enhanced Cordless Telecommunications (DECT) phone carried by staff, which has cascade programming for security. Doors are monitored for security purposes.

Design and Philosophy of Care

The physical layout of each household is simple, orienting and understandable to maximize independence. Personal cues such as color-coding and memorabilia help individuals to identify each room. Décor and furnishing are homely and welcoming, with minimal use of patterns that may cause confusion.

Within the households, the private bedrooms are visible and accessible from the lounge areas. There are facilities that promote privacy for people who have physical or sensory disabilities. An open and accessible kitchen is central to the household to enable residents to participate in daily living tasks.

Support is taken to the person, rather than the person to the support, thereby reducing the need for a room or house move as a person's condition changes.

Integration of Residents with the Broader Community

"Belong" has an intergenerational approach and encourages the local community to use the village facilities. The bistro is situated on the ground floor, welcoming people in for meals and refreshments throughout the day. Also, themed events are run by volunteers and staff to provide opportunities for the residents to socialize.

The hair and beauty salon provides services to residents, staff and visitors, and welcomes the local community.

The village center is available for groups, such as the Alzheimer's Café, Slimmer's World and Steps to Health, to use for functions and entertainment. Movie evenings and dance events are hosted for the local community. The gym suite is available for older people to use with the aim of improving wellbeing and is supported by local health improvement initiatives.

Opposite top left: Independent Living Apartments are spacious and comfortable.
Opposite top right: The community room can be used by visitors from the wider neighbourhood.
Opposite bottom: Communal gardens include a children's playground, raised flower beds, greenhouse, walking paths and sitting areas.

Photography: James White

Comcorp Architects

The Pines Lodge

Adelaide, South Australia, Australia // Southern Cross Care (SA & NT) Incorporated

Facility type: Assisted Living/Hostel Residence,
Special Care Residence (for those with dementia),
Skilled Nursing Care Residence
Site location: Suburban
Site size: 13,500 square meters

Building footprint: 5130 square meters
Building area: 10,080 square meters
Total building cost: AUD$21.5 million
Building cost per square unit: AUD$2133/square meter
Date of completion: August 2010

Below: Entrance to residential care building
Opposite: Entrance to memory support building

Owner's Statement

The owner's overall objective was to replace an existing outdated residential aged care facility on the site with a new 144-bed facility surpassing current aged-care standards. The new facility aimed to lift community expectations for aged care accommodation to a new level.

In providing this new facility, Southern Cross Care (a not-for-profit charitable institution) aimed to move away from long-held, stereotyped modes of aged care accommodation, with the associated stigmas and the institutionalized feel that these often represent, aspiring to a more enlightened, person-centered paradigm. A facility was envisioned that better supports the delivery of care and simultaneously presents a desirable ambience and enhances lifestyle opportunity for the residents.

The facility was to provide for "Aging in Place," meaning that as the care needs of the residents move from low to high, the residents can remain within the facility and as long as possible within the same room – with all of their care needs met – as they transition through increasing degrees of frailty.

As the resident population was already housed on site, the project required construction staging during the development process. This was a major challenge requiring staged resident decanting and the balancing of contractor requirements with resident safety and amenity. Access was segregated between construction traffic and the home's servicing and general running requirements.

Another significant challenge and a landscape design opportunity presented itself in the form of magnificent old conifer and Moreton Bay Fig trees located along the northern boundary of the site. These were to be protected and their presence to be integrated into the ambience and outlook of the new facility.

Architect's Statement

The response to the client's objectives involved a collaborative team effort. The response began with both the client and the architects undertaking field research into the latest aged care trends in the US and Scandinavia. Alzheimer's Australia was consulted as were other Australian aged care providers. A project control group was set up to meet regularly throughout the research, design and construction phases of the project and guide the procurement process from start to finish.

The result is the delivery of a light, bright and colorful two-story, twin-building solution of striking architectural design and eye-catching street presence, distinctive yet integrating into its environment. The twin buildings utilize plan forms responding to the needs of the residents and maximizing efficiencies, ambience and functionality. The scale and atmosphere is domestic. The interior is airy, spacious and welcoming with comfortable, amenable, home-like accommodation. Integrated state-of-the-art technology enhances functionality and resident support.

The Pines Lodge has equally been acknowledged by its residents, by the families of residents, and by staff and visitors alike for its exceptional ambience and its uplifting, resort-like feel and great facilities. Residents are often overheard saying words to the effect of, "I just love it here" or "How did I get to live out my life in such a beautiful place?" There is a resident waiting list, which stands at around 100 at any point in time; staff walk-ins seeking employment at the facility are commonplace; a significant staff waiting list is also maintained, hugely reducing reliance on agency staff, which in turn increases efficiency and effectiveness of deliverable care.

The suburban site was very restricted. The design solution saw the implementation a twin-building arrangement. The eastern building, known as

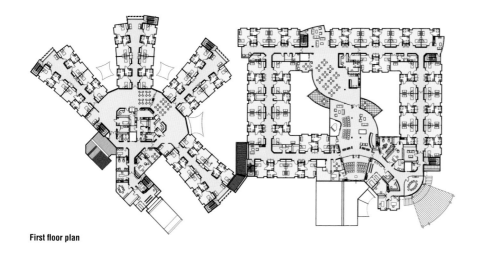

First floor plan

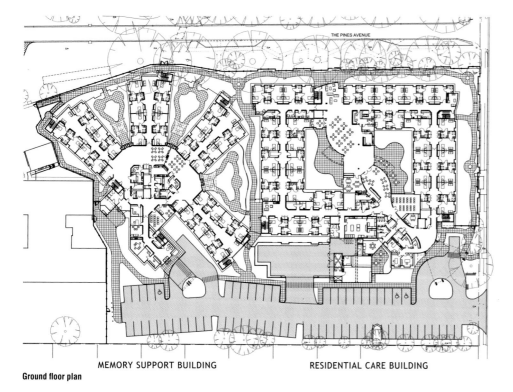

THE PINES AVENUE

MEMORY SUPPORT BUILDING   **RESIDENTIAL CARE BUILDING**

Ground floor plan

Moreton Bay House, is home to 80 low-care and high-care residents on two levels. The 80 individual rooms with ensuite facilities are 15 percent larger than what may be typical and are laid out around two internal courtyards and central communal facilities. All rooms are open to light and air and have an outlook onto landscaped gardens. On the north side, the view encompasses stately conifer and Moreton Bay Fig trees, which line the adjacent historic Pines Avenue.

The western building, known as Conifer House, is a stand-alone, 64-bed memory-support wing on two levels designed as a series of fingers radiating out from a central communal and service area. The innovative layout is designed to support spatial orientation for memory-challenged residents and to facilitate effective care, interaction and supervision by carers and staff, both inside the facility and outside in the courtyard garden areas. Each of the color-coded corridors expands into a destination nodal space that looks out onto nature, avoiding the occurrence of dead-end passages. The residents are calmer in their new, more open living arrangement than in their previous, more restricted environment. An operable wall within the central communal area allows the flexibility of operating the unit as either two 16-bed groups or one 32-bed group per floor. Quiet areas off the communal spaces use music and aromatherapy to help calm and relax residents. The provider indicates that their ability to deliver quality dementia care has gone ahead by "quantum" leaps with the opening of the new facility.

A well-planned, integrated overall development process saw a sequence of coordinated steps, which provided the safe and secure retention on site of the resident community throughout the demolition and construction phase. This was achieved by strategic site planning and construction staging, which maintained functionality, services and personal and vehicular access throughout, including safe construction access for all contractors.

Client Goals and Design Team Solutions

To maximize residents' chances of healthy aging in line with the World Health Organization's definition of health, the client goals are:

- To maximize resident "physical wellbeing" by maximizing enjoyment and lifestyle opportunity through provision of individual room accommodation with maximized access to sun, natural light, fresh air and outlook to nature; provide state-of-the-art functionality, advanced communication and care support technology; provide communal or in-room dining capability; provide exceptional, resort-style communal areas and recreation facilities.

Functional and efficient planning facilitating care delivery has been achieved. Every resident is afforded an individual room complete with ensuite. The provision for a couple to enjoy connected rooms is made with interconnecting doors creating a suite arrangement where one room can be used as a bedroom with ensuite and the other as a living room. All rooms have generous windows that open to admit light, fresh air and a view to a garden or trees, and facilitate connection with nature. All rooms have individually controlled heating and cooling, allowing room temperatures to be set to personal preference.

Nurse-call, internet, telephone and television facilities are provided as standard, with resident movement monitoring capability built in for activation if and as required for resident safety and convenience in accordance with individual resident profiling.

Above: Sunlight and shadow play on colorful forms and landscaped walkways

Communal and activities spaces and facilities are spacious and resort-like, encouraging ongoing participation in life and lifestyle. Wellness facilities such as physiotherapy, medical, dental and podiatry services are all provided. Access to both the garden courtyards and to landscaped paths with external seating around the buildings is available from the communal areas for resident recreation and exercise.

- To maximize resident "social wellbeing" by maximizing resident to resident, resident to family, resident to staff and resident to community connection and interaction through provision of socializing and lifestyle support opportunities.

A fully functional commercial café has been integrated into the communal space, providing a successful and popular social hub for residents, families, staff and members of the broader community. This has proven to be an effective social integration factor.

A consecrated chapel, as well as a dedicated prayer room, provide for the spiritual needs of the residents and staff. The chapel services are attended by the wider retirement village community. This provides an enriching depth of social connection for the residents. The chapel is designed with operable walls, which enables seating to expand to include the adjacent communal function room on significant religious occasions.

Other socializing and recreational opportunities are provided by state-of the-art cinema and audio-visual facilities, well-equipped and dedicated recreational, social and performance spaces, and a commercial-feel hairdressing salon. Private dining areas enable residents to enjoy private time and celebrate special

occasions with families and friends. Intimate nooks with tea and coffee-making facilities in quiet corners with pleasant outlooks enable families to enjoy private moments with their loved ones, as well as provide residents with quiet spaces for personal contemplation.

Lifestyle opportunities provided on site are complemented by off-site outings and events organized by the Southern Cross Care.

- To maximize "mental wellbeing" by fostering meaningful engagement with the physical and social environment; by elevating the ambience and appearance of a residential aged care facility to a new paradigm; helping to break down the less than positive preconceptions and stigma long associated with aged care accommodation.

The integration of the aforementioned lifestyle opportunities helps to create a fresh welcoming atmosphere around the facility. This is enhanced by the spacious and resort-like feel of the interiors, the deft use of color and architectural form to capture the ambience of the existing major trees along the northern side, and relating their impact to the internal spaces of the building. The result is a building that affirms life, lifestyle, and a relationship with nature. It has succeeded in helping to transform the face of aged care to the community and gives residents every opportunity to enhance their engagement with life.

The internet library sees residents "skype" or "email" residents and loved ones far and wide. Such new life experiences in the latter years of the residents' lives are a typical example of the gratifying outcomes achieved in terms of the client's goals and objectives.

Major Design Objectives and/or Project Challenges

- To be at the forefront of the field of aged care delivery in Australia.

  Create a home that: fulfills residents' physical as well as intangible needs and aspirations; delivers maximum functionality; facilitates the easy delivery of quality care to residents; and speaks to the community of the new model of aged care accommodation through surpassing governmental regulatory standards.

- Identify a dementia-friendly building design to become a center of excellence in relation to dementia care in South Australia and Australia.

  While this ambition is necessarily a constant work in progress, the distinctive planning arrangement of the west building (the memory support unit) provides a backdrop for the development of care models and strategies for the memory-impaired.

- Maintain residents on-site during development.

  A sequence of development stages on a restricted site began with the residents of a pre-existing nursing home on the site being moved to a newly built facility off-site. The vacated nursing home was then demolished, enabling the construction of the first stage of the new Pines Lodge facility, while the hostel residents remained on-site occupying an existing hostel building. Construction of the new facility came virtually to within arm's length of the existing buildings. Upon completion of the first stage of the new facility, the residents were moved into their new accommodation, allowing the demolition of the old premises and completion of the second stage of the development. Construction access to the

building site was coordinated with service and personnel access to the functioning facility. A series of orchestrated steps allowed the building project to proceed essentially unimpeded while full functionality and safety of access was maintained for the home. This achievement is testimony to the cooperation and teamwork between all of the stakeholders in the process, including the coordination provided by the building contractor.

Above: The café – invites social interaction for residents, staff, families and visitors.

Unique Context

The site of this development is located in suburban Adelaide on a bus route at 342 Marion Road, North Plympton, South Australia. The site is situated within a broader independent living retirement village estate owned by Southern Cross Care and holds significant heritage value for the Southern Cross Care organization, as well as for the broader community. The pre-existing buildings on the site, which were demolished to make way for the development, were the first aged care accommodation buildings built by Southern Cross Care in this state. The demolition of these buildings, which no longer met community expectations or the latest legislated standards for aged care, was a sensitive issue requiring adherence to due protocols appropriate to the process. The building of The Pines Lodge is part of the ongoing strategic development of the broader site, which will see an integrated mix of retirement village accommodation ranging from residential low-care and high-care hostel accommodation – which The Pines Lodge represents – through to surrounding independent living cottages and apartments.

The avenue of conifers and Moreton Bay Fig trees that line the historic Pines Avenue on the northern boundary of the site is also of significant heritage value. This avenue was originally the entrance to an estate owned by one of the state's major pioneer retailers, and the original home still stands at the end of the avenue. In addition to the heritage value attaching to the trees, local statutory authorities required their protection by virtue of their size alone. Protective measures included fencing off the trees during construction, excavation by "air spade" (high-pressure air) of any trenches within the drip line of the trees, and the laying of railway sleepers over the root systems during construction to prevent soil compaction around the roots by construction traffic and operations. No trees were lost or damaged during the development and today they stand majestically, lending their magnificent character to the ambience of the site.

Environmental Sustainability and Energy Conservation

- Gas-boosted solar hot water heating with thermostatic mixing valves to all resident areas.
- Electronic control of hot water temperatures. By periodically shutting down the pump and therefore the water flow through the unit, the continuous flow unit is able to shut down and the electronics to reset.
- Use of refrigerants with zero ozone-depletion potential.
- Use of insulation products manufactured with zero ozone-depletion potential agents.
- R1.0 wall and R2.5 roof insulation.
- High-performance heat-resistant glass ("ComfortPlus").
- Sun-shading of external windows.
- Variable speed drive (VSD) fans to air-conditioning.
- Inverter driven air-conditioning plant.
- Opening windows throughout, maximizing fresh air exchange and minimizing need for air-conditioning.
- Generous windows throughout maximizing access to daylight and minimizing need for artificial lighting.

Above left: Internal courtyards and balconies afford ambience and lifestyle for residents, staff and families.
Above right: Secure courtyards provide outdoor recreation space for residents.

Photography: courtesy of Comcorp Architects

- High-efficiency T5 lighting where applicable.
- C-Bus lighting system coupled with movement sensors to power down communal lighting when it is not in use.
- Minimum 3.5 star house energy rating using NatHERS or First Rate indices.
- 5 stars house energy rating by Accurate.
- WELS 3 stars ensuite hand shower.
- WELS 4 stars ensuite basin mixer in the east building.
- WELS 5 stars ensuite basin mixer in the west building.
- Use of AAA-rated sanitary fixtures.
- Rationalization of water efficiency through native planting and sub-soil irrigation.
- Stormwater detention prior to discharge from site in accordance with local regulations.

- Preservation of significant trees on site and protection of trees during construction activities.

Advanced Technology

A state-of-the-art digital nurse-call system is installed for maximum resident safety, security and care, and maximum facility for staff to deliver care.

The buildings are fully fitted out with sprinklers for fire safety with full monitoring by local fire fighting authorities. Electric strikes to security doors are cabled for release upon a fire signal from the fire indicator panel. The air conditioning system is cabled for shutdown on a fire signal with activation of fire dampers as required.

A state-of-the-art digital movement sensor system is built in and activated on an as-required basis in accordance with individual resident profiling to enhance resident safety, security and care.

A state-of-the-art digital access control and security monitoring system operates internally and externally site-wide with video intercom and remote release function for the front doors of both buildings for after hours access by visitors or family.

A state-of-the-art digital telephone and IT communication system is linked to the site security, fire safety and computer and telephone system, and to the organization's broader intranet communications network. State-of-the-art audio-visual capacity is built into communal function areas, audio-visual facilities, meeting rooms and training rooms. A C-Bus lighting system, coupled with movement sensors, powers down communal lighting when it is not in use.

Design and Philosophy of Care

The program's philosophy of care revolves around person-centered care with the wellbeing of the individual being paramount.

This is achieved through provision of technology and facilities set against a backdrop that engages a person's senses in terms of space, materials, color, their contact with nature and contact with the elements.

The floor plans of both buildings are statements of efficiency and functionality, and create spatial experiences that are pleasant and establish good contact with the outdoors – with sun, light, air, nature, the sky, and the movement of the diurnal and seasonal cycles.

Integration of Residents with the Broader Community

The integration of a commercial café open to the public into the design has been mentioned. This sets a new standard for integration of an aged care facility within the broader community and, based on feedback and responses to date, is likely to remain a benchmark requirement for future developments.

The chapel at The Pines Lodge caters for communal worship or private prayer and contemplation among the wider retirement community on the surrounding estate, which is also owned by Southern Cross Care. This provides another opening for residents to have contact with a broader community.

The more open and attractive ambience and general atmosphere created in this development, along with the specific facilities mentioned above, creates a new opportunity for the families of the residents, especially younger children, to visit and spend time with their elderly relatives. Consistent feedback indicates that the once-apparent wide gap between aged care accommodation and mainstream community is being bridged in quantum leaps.

Scurr Architects Ltd

The Royal Star & Garter Home, Solihull

Solihull, West Midlands, UK // The Royal Star & Garter Homes

Facility type: Special Care Residence (for those with dementia), Skilled Nursing Care Residence
Site location: Suburban
Site size: 1.75 acres
Building footprint: 2276 square meters

Building area: 4462 square meters
Total building cost: £7.3million
Building cost per square unit: £1636/square meter
Date of completion: August 2008

Below and right: External View

Owner's Statement

The Royal Star & Garter Home is a registered charity caring for ex-servicemen and women. The home in Solihull is only a few minutes from the town centre and provides accommodation on two floors for 60 residents, in four clusters of 15. The building is fully compliant with the Commission for Social Care Inspection standards and passed the CSCI registration inspection on its first application with no requirements or recommendations made.

Construction and fit-out is at typical market value standards and was completed within budget. The home provides exceptional standards throughout the building, maximizing the space within corridors by incorporating them into the communal living areas.

The design objectives were achieved through an intensive briefing process – this occurred between the client and the design team and involved the residents and staff of the existing home. Ceiling-mounted hoist systems in residents' rooms and communal bathrooms provide assistance for those unable to independently mobilize themselves, and a nurse call system is in place in all resident areas for reassurance and staff access and support when required.

Good space standards in all the communal areas make alternative furniture layouts simple to achieve, allow residents in wheelchairs plenty of manoeuvrability, and staff access to utilize mobile hoists when required. The dementia garden is fully accessible for the residents living in this wing. However, it also has the benefit of being a safe environment in light of the care needs of those individuals.

Architect's Statement

The Royal Star & Garter Home wanted to create an exemplary care environment. They are passionate about providing a home that is filled with natural light and is not defined by its corridors; a home that marries domestic architecture with a sense of arrival, the internal community with the local community, and a sense of the comradery of life in the services coupled with independence and individuality. The building is formed by two curved arms – one on either side of the central communal spaces. These arms wrap around to hug the entrance and provide a protective enclosure in the form of the courtyard gardens at the front of the home. The roofs in turn sweep down to the landscaped gardens, which open out towards the local community.

The wide, curving corridors and 45-foot splayed walls make movement around the home easy to navigate, especially in a wheelchair. The break-out areas form part of the circulation space and are a fundamental part of the design. They flood the corridors with natural light, provide access and views to the patios and gardens, make orientation easier and the outside world more accessible. The gardens are carefully designed for accessibility and use by the residents with dementia – they contain a residents' gardening club with raised flower beds and a sensory garden with meandering paths – to promote the sense of going on a journey through the grounds.

Client Goals and Design Team Solutions

- The building must sit comfortably within the local-domestic vernacular, using a similar palette of materials and architectural motifs.

  The building forms two curved arms that are positioned either side of the central communal spaces – they wrap around the entrance and courtyard gardens at the front of the home. The roof sweeps down to the landscaped gardens that open outwards into the local community. The elevations are dominated by a rhythmic series of gable walls and steeply pitched roofs. The building uses a similar palette of materials to the adjacent housing, which forms part of the same development. A warm domestic appearance is achieved with red-brick walls and feature bays clad in self-colored render and stone. The roof is covered in brindle-plain tiles, giving the home a warm, soft appearance matching the quality and warmth of the interiors, which are enhanced by oak doors, frames and joinery.

- All areas are to be well lit with lots of natural light and outside views.

There are no straight corridors or long straight walls. Wide, well lit circulation spaces break out into communal sun-lit seating areas with large oak-framed areas of glass overlooking the gardens. The glazing to the communal seating area fills the entire wall and is made from large-section oak framing, creating the feel of an orangery, with lots of natural daylight and fantastic views into the gardens.

- To provide residents' rooms that have the appearance of a quality environment with a defined seating area and fully assisted ensuite wet rooms.

Each room has two splayed windows that reveal the maximum amount of natural light, and a projecting bay window provides each resident with their own personal seating area. The color scheme is restful and domestic, and the furnishings are high quality.

Entrances to all the rooms are set back from the corridor with plenty of space for furniture and features to personalize both the entrances and the rooms – memory boxes, door knockers, framed pictures and furniture – promoting privacy, choice, independence and respect.

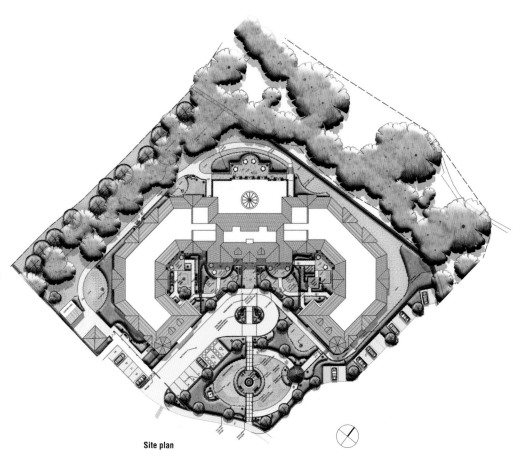

Site plan

Major Design Objectives and/or Project Challenges

- Create a 'Wow' factor for residents and visitors to the home by blending a grand but homely style with simple and elegant interiors.

The interiors are clean and uncluttered with a separation between the simple domestic clusters of residents' rooms and the central communal rooms, which are dominated by the double- and treble-height spaces that form the centrepiece of the dining room, bar and lounge.

- Provide an internal environment that is easy to navigate, easy to understand, and allows residents to see and be seen by staff.

Wide, undulating corridors avoid dead-end routes and open out to form the main seating and activity areas within the residential wings, which in turn look out over the gardens or into the communal rooms. This ensures that the residents have good visual communication and the reassurance of seeing a carer most of the time, and that the layout assists with orientation and way-finding.

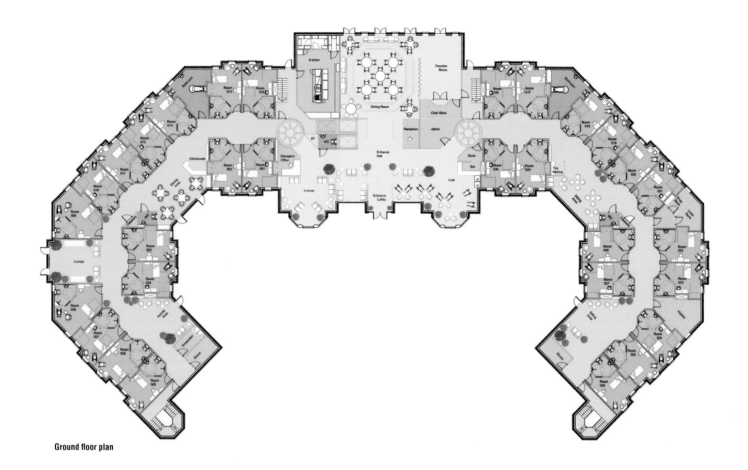

Ground floor plan

- Provide gardens or terraces on all floors that are readily accessible, integrate with the building, are overlooked by the communal spaces and provide a stimulating environment and choice of setting.

The gardens provide a mix of formal and informal spaces and include raised planters within the residents' gardening club; a sensory garden; a wooded copse; private and public seating overlooking the ornamental planting areas; a formal footpath entrance promenade beneath a planted pergola; and a large patio for garden parties, military bands and other activities or events.

Environmental Sustainability and Energy Conservation

The home utilizes low-tech sustainable design solutions to reduce energy consumption and minimize its carbon footprint. The provision of a central void passing up through the building enables stack-effect ventilation to cool the communal spaces, totally eliminating the need to use mechanical cooling.

High levels of insulation reduce heat loss from the building and reduce the energy consumption of the building.

Advanced Technology

All residents will receive fully assisted personal and nursing care and have a fully assisted ensuite shower room suitable for independent or assisted use. The health, safety, and wellbeing of staff will be paramount in all activities and operational duties.

The residents' rooms are fitted with overhead ceiling tracks that provide full room coverage. This enables lifting hoists to be fitted to any room, making the transfer of residents simpler and nursing or caring roles easier for staff and residents alike. Fully adjustable Presalit shower room sanitaryware enables each ensuite to be

laid out to suit independent or assisted use and fittings to be adjusted to suit different heights for ambulant or wheelchair users.

Design and Philosophy of Care

All residents will be encouraged to furnish their room with their own furniture and personal possessions, receive fully assisted personal and nursing care, and have a fully assisted ensuite shower room, suitable for independent or assisted use.

The residents' rooms are fitted with knockers and keyed locks, fostering a sense of respect and personal privacy. The rooms are 215 square feet and provide ample space to individualize the room and receive personal or nursing care. The ensuite wet rooms are 70 square feet and are laid out to enable them to be used independently or with full assistance from one or two carers.

Integration of Residents with the Broader Community

There is an extensive program of activities that often involve family, friends and the local community. These are created to provide an active and fulfilling life for residents, and to ensure the home becomes a vibrant part of the local community.

Large windows with low window sills provide excellent views out of the building to the gardens and beyond. The rear terrace is used for summer parties and barbecues, and a large paved area at the front of the home is used for external activities and events, such as military bands, garden parties, outdoor performances and community events.

Above: Entrance reception
Opposite top right and left: Bedroom
Opposite: Lounge

Photography: © Scurr Architects

KWL Architects Limited

Sandford Station Care Village

Sandford, North Somerset, UK // St Monica Trust

Facility type: Active Senior/Independent Living Residence, Subsidized Affordable Independent Living, Special Care Residence (for those with dementia)
Site location: Rural
Site size: 8.03 acres
Building footprint: 10,317 square meters

Building area: 15,598 square meters
Total building cost: £23.8 million
Building cost per square unit: £1525/square meter
Date of completion: Dementia Home – March 2009, Residual Site – August 2009

Below: Sherwood Care Home
Opposite: Sherwood Care Home family dining room

Owner's Statement

In March 2009 the St Monica Trust opened its development at Sandford Station, a retirement care village, 15 miles southwest of Bristol on a historic railway site. It addresses all of the Trust's overall goals, offering: a range of accommodation for older people in the form of 108 units and houses; care for those who require it; partnership with statutory services including 20 extra care apartments; and facilities to address wellbeing such as an impressive restaurant, a well-appointed atrium housing a gym with pool, and meeting rooms.

At Sandford Station however, there is one significant difference: The Russets nursing home includes five, large interlinked open plan bungalows situated in a circle around a central garden and clubhouse, facilitating larger group activities and gatherings. Detailed consideration has been given to every internal and external aspect to address the objective of creating a homely environment, where space and sensory stimulation offer a positive environment to residents with a wide range of needs.

Developed to the highest standard, this service design "squares the circle" for the organisation as it offers an opportunity to respond to individuals with a range of complex dementias.

Architect's Statement

The Sandford Station site contained a number of railway buildings, namely the railway station, baggage shed and platform, engine shed and stationmaster's house. All of the buildings were listed and were to be retained within the scheme. The existing farmhouse and barn were also to be retained and incorporated into the facility.

To provide the range of accommodation and facilities required by the client, various building sizes and their functions were to juxstapose with the retained buildings and provide a harmonious architecture at ease with its rural setting. The scheme was to be contained within the "brown field" area. The opportunity to have the railway station and associated buildings refurbished and integrated into the new development provided both the focus and some constraints for the layout, assisting in the development of the final design solution.

The rural location of the site provided an opportunity to have views from all dwellings to the surrounding open countryside and to design rustic buildings with a colorful palette of material for an exciting and vibrant care village.

Client Goals and Design Team Solutions

- To provide a range of accommodation and facilities that address wellbeing.

  Opportunities for designing a range of accommodation existed across the site, allowing each group of residents to experience a high quality of life and environment on this rural site (formerly only occupied by the railway facilities).

- To provide a unique single storey dementia home modelled on a successful service in Australia.

  The facility at Brightwater, Perth was visited and its design heavily influenced this smaller site at Sandford. With the climate that England enjoys, this layout offers residents the ability to take long walks while staying dry, while in summer allowing for exploration of the enclosed garden and communal facility.

- To provide a Care Village of a size that could financially support a wide range of communal facilities for all residents to enjoy.

  The single-story dementia unit naturally limited the possible density of accommodation on this part of the site. The residual land is dotted with railway buildings and barns that require high-density solutions, while retaining a rustic and rural design vernacular.

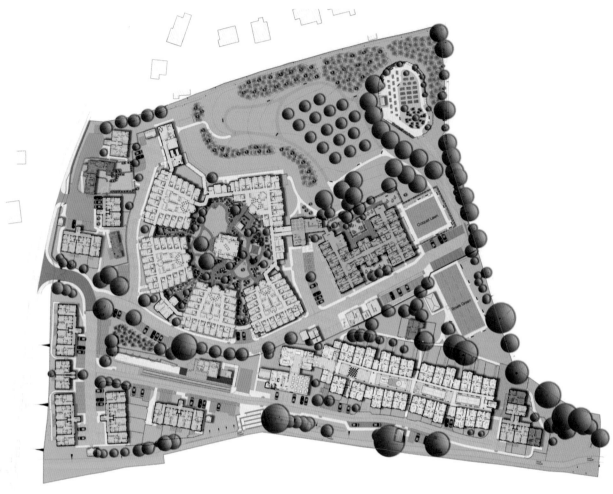

Site plan

Major Design Objectives and/or Project Challenges

• The integration and refurbishment of the Railway Building and other listed buildings into cohesive care scheme.

The railway station and platform have been refurbished back to their original condition. Upon completion they were handed over to the Railway Society and are now used as a museum. The engine shed is the focus of the Atrium Building, which houses the restaurant and galley kitchen. Other retained buildings have been refurbished and used for dwellings.

• To phase the construction, enabling the Care Home to be built and occupied within 12 months from receipt of planning permission.

To enable St Monica Trust to establish themselves on site at the earliest opportunity, work commenced immediately after receiving planning consent. Within 11 months the first residents were moved into The Russets. On the same completion date of The Russets,

a number of dwellings were completed for the sales team. The residual units were completed in August 2009.

• To deliver a cohesive design and style for the differing size, function and facility demanded by each building/building group.

Constraints of the site included its rural location, the site lying outside of settlement boundaries, existing railway buildings and other listed buildings, planning and conservation officer views, and the client's desire to provide

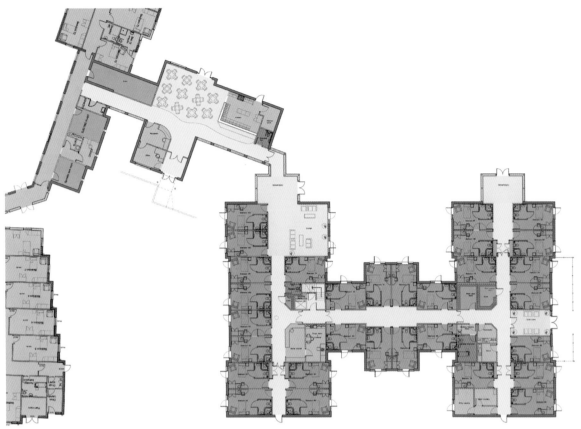

Sherwood Care Home and link to The Russets—ground floor plan

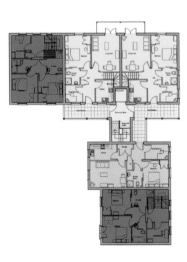

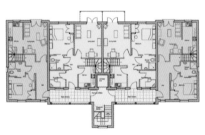

Typical Independent Living units—first floor plan

Typical Independent Living units—first floor plan

Typical Independent Living units—ground floor plan

Typical Independent Living units—ground floor plan

a high-quality and attractive care environment. A traditional English farmhouse/cottage/village style of architecture was used, with a palette of traditional stone, timber, render, and clay roof tiles with rural detailing.

Unique Context

Ownership of homes is prevalent in the UK; it is estimated that 75 percent of retired people owned their own homes in 2010. Accommodation on the site is available through a mixture of tenure, with rent, lease purchase, and shared equity with the Trust.

The land was originally used by the Great Western Railway (GWR) servicing the railway station and supporting buildings. More recently, the site was used by a stone and concrete business, the cement clearly visible in the original aerial photograph. When the business went into receivership St Monica Trust purchased the site on the open market.

Encouraging elderly people to lead exciting and invigorating lives is promoted by the leisure and recreational facilities on the site. The British climate is often cold and wet, and therefore many facilities and buildings are linked by covered areas with activities provided inside these spaces.

The development will increase the size of Sandford Village's population quite dramatically. To assist with its integration both physically and visually, care has been taken to provide a well-designed traditional rural English architectural style. Facilities within the development are accessible by locals in the village, and all the previously abandoned and damaged railway buildings have been saved and refurbished.

Environmental Sustainability and Energy Conservation

- All railway buildings, part of Sandford and GWR's heritage, have been saved, refurbished and have new life.

- The Strawberry line (public footpath) has access to the site.

- Most meals are prepared off-site at the St Monica Trust central kitchen in Bristol then distributed to the site for reheating and finishing, saving energy and overheads.

- The buildings are designed to make use of natural daylight wherever feasible.

- The Atrium provides a controlled environment with a zero energy rating – passive stack ventilation system.

- A biomass wood chip boiler system is used to provide heating and hot water to the Care Home.

Advanced Technology

St Monica Trust utilizes the latest care technologies, including motorized, ceiling-mounted hoists to facilitate care provision, as well as an Eclipse Nurse Call System, decked handsets across the site, electric buggy points outside all front doors, and CCTV covering all areas and boundaries of the site.

The Russets Dementia Home facility provides an advanced layout for resident care and wellbeing, creating a homely and positive environment for residents with a wide range of needs.

Design and Philosophy of Care

The Russets design is unique in the UK to date, modeled on a successful service in Australia. Its open-plan, colorful and light design supports individuals by emphasizing opportunities to participate in homely activities and offering sensory and spatial cues to maximize orientation and minimize anxiety. For ambulant residents it offers the opportunity to walk freely and explore in safety. Overhead hoisting equipment and nursing paraphernalia discreetly tucked away support individuals needing maximum physical assistance. The discreet "study" in each bungalow enables sensitive observation and appropriate supervision by staff. Residents and staff benefit from its sense of peaceful purpose.

Integration of Residents with the Broader Community

The refurbishment of the railway station and platform, together with their designation as a museum, welcomes the community into the heart of the village. St Monica Trust also handed over the ownership of the Strawberry line footpath to North Somerset Council and constructed an access ramp and stairs to the museum, as part of a Planning Section 106 Agreement.

Short-term care and physiotherapy are available to non-residents. The licensed restaurant and lounges will be open to older people from the local community to socialize and enjoy the village atmosphere. They may also use the gym, swimming pool, hairdressing salon and conference facilities.

Left: Independent Living flat, typical master bedroom
Bottom left: Typical care bedroom and ensuite

Photography: courtesy of KWL Architects Limited

Scurr Architects Ltd

Sunrise of Chorleywood

Chorleywood, Hertfordshire, UK // Sunrise Senior Living

Facility type: Assisted Living/Hostel Residence,
Special Care Residence (for those with dementia)
Site location: Suburban
Site size: 8283 square meters

Building footprint: 1995 square meters
Building area: 6475 square meters
Date of completion: March 2007

Below: External view

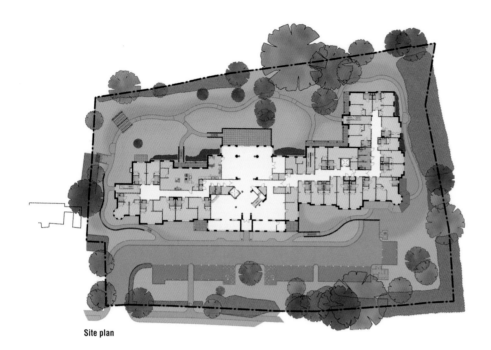

Site plan

Owner's Statement

A major theme for Sunrise's Assisted Living Care Homes in the UK is to create an environment and atmosphere reminiscent of a large traditional house that relates back to many residents' aspirations to live in the architectural style of the large country or town houses of the Georgian and Victorian eras, which had large Arts and Crafts movements. In aspects of both the internal and external design of the building, references to an inspirational grand house that maybe the resident once visited as a child and dreamt of living in are key to the sense of home, splendor and comfort.

The overall shape and mass of a Sunrise home is often broken down into a series of interconnected buildings that are designed to create the environment and atmosphere of a group of linked houses. The plan layout, the elevation of its form and its roofscape are varied to break down massing: this reduces the impact and scale, and provides local interest and variation to parts of the building. Materials used are chosen to enhance and reflect the high-quality domestic environment.

Sunrise Assisted Living Care homes are designed to exceed current and anticipated future UK legislation. Accommodation and service standards continue to be set well above the current National Minimum Care Standards.

In addition to Assisted Living, Reminiscence Care is also provided for residents with Alzheimer's disease and other forms of dementia. In association with experts in the treatment and management of Alzheimer's and related memory disorders, Sunrise's own highly acclaimed Reminiscence Program is provided, which specifically addresses the needs of these residents through the provision of dedicated facilities and a patient-centered program of care.

Architect's Statement

Due to the residential location of the proposed site, the property was designed with three building elements. The west element was kept with a lower roof line at two and a half stories, to reflect the lower scale development to the west along Rickmansworth Road and to provide variation with the adjacent central building element. The central building element provides the focal point for the home, being the communal center, and is therefore designed to be three stories in height with a pair of central feature gables. These large gables with associated chimneys emphasize the different elevated form. This building also provides the central entry point for residents and visitors, which is covered by the extended porch to reinforce this focal statement. The eastern building element uses the natural gradient of the site to provide additional accommodation at a lower level while continuing to use the half-story accommodation in the roof space to provide variation with the central building element. In effect, this end of the building will continue to be read as two and a half stories when viewed from Rickmansworth Road.

Client Goals and Design Team Solutions

• To obtain planning permission for a new build in a desirable location.

This was achieved by thorough research of the area, landscape, and buildings and by using key elements from the Arts and Crafts Architectural movement such as turrets, gables and bays, and low-level porches in a bid to meet the aspirations of the clients and a solution acceptable to the local planning authority.

• The inclusion of a Reminiscence Neighborhood.

Sunrise provides a registered environment for residents suffering from mental frailty and dementia. The Reminiscence Neighborhood is a self-contained, secure and care-managed area that provides a safe and stimulating environment for residents inside and outside the home. There is generous provision of communal space throughout: living rooms

Ground floor plan

and activity spaces are supplemented by the neighborhood's own dining room and kitchen server – the latter is used by both staff for serving main meals and residents for activities.

- To remove any feeling of institutionalization.

Breakout spaces have been created to remove the feeling of long corridors. Seating is available in these spaces so that they become places of relaxation, diversion and interest where residents can sit informally and chat. Residents' rooms are provided to the same size and standards as elsewhere in the home; however, residents' bathrooms and communal toilets are provided with memory-jogging facilities, including automatic light sensors (the light will come on as the resident passes the bathroom) and strong color association (at least one prominent wall is painted green).

Major Design Objectives and/or Project Challenges

- The location of site – adjacent to a public highway, sandwiched between the M25 motorway and residential areas – affected the final design of the building.

  All existing trees on the boundary were retained to limit noise. A terrace was created to reduce any overlooking of the site – this was lined with trees. The lower two-and-a-half-story element on the west of the property is in keeping with the adjacent properties.

- Local residential concerns of a new build in a strongly influenced Arts and Crafts designed property area.

  This building was designed to make strong reference to older buildings in the area and also historical references to the Arts and Crafts Architectural movement. Consequently, it provides sympathetic local and historical reference points for the elderly residents of the home.

- To ensure independent mobility for all residents wherever possible.

  This was achieved in many ways through the building circulation: two elevators provided for the residents' use ensure that even in the event of a mechanical breakdown access to the upper floors is still possible. These elevators are provided with large buttons and Braille signage. The grand staircase that links the ground and first floor is designed to standards in excess of current regulations, with low risers and handrails to both sides. All corridors used by residents are provided to a minimum width

of 71 inches, with local lounges increasing this dimension. All doors are installed to a minimum clear opening of 35 inches.

Unique Context

This building was designed to make strong reference to older buildings in the area and also historical references to the Arts and Crafts Architectural movement, which has influenced the development in the area. Significantly there are two original Arts and Crafts Houses, designed by CFA Voysey, located in Chorleywood. The Orchard, designed in 1899, and Hollybank, designed in 1903, are both located on Shire Lane. The Orchard was designed for Voysey and his family and has been described as a quintessential country cottage.

Above and left: External views

Photography: © Scurr Architects

Scurr Architects Ltd

The Wohl Building

Wandsworth, London, UK // Nightingale Care Home

Facility type: Special Care Residence (for those with dementia)
Site location: Urban
Site size: 5.5 acres
Building footprint: 1330.8 square meters

Building area: 2639.7 square meters
Total building cost: £5.37 million
Building cost per square unit: £2034/square meter
Date of completion: May 2010

Below: External view
Opposite: Aerial photograph

Owner's Statement

The Wohl Building is a Nightingale Care Home and is dedicated to providing holistic quality care for life for older members of the Jewish community.

The existing facilities include an arts and crafts centre, concert room, garden café and terrace, landscaped gardens, physiotherapy and occupational therapy service, extensive cultural and leisure program, a synagogue, and a hairdresser and beauty salon.

Nightingale has become well-known for its extensive program of activities for residents, families and visitors. The highly experienced activities team strives daily to understand each resident's needs to help them to pursue their own diverse interests. The activities include discussion groups, French and German conversational groups, tai chi, keeping fit, a poetry group, music sessions, concerts, a monthly book club,

tea parties, garden therapy, bingo sessions, dances, arts and crafts, cookery club, art and drama therapy, reminiscence groups, music to communicate with people living with dementia, and numerous trips to a wide range of venues.

Always striving to provide care and opportunities for residents to pursue an active and rewarding life, the home intends to create a state-of-the-art dementia home, a day care centre, and extra care apartments to supplement the existing frail nursing accommodation.

Architect's Statement

Nightingale aims to provide a state-of-the-art building dedicated to the care of residents with dementia. The main house is "grade two" listed and provided the opportunity to develop a contemporary building, which would stand on its own within the historic context. Extensive research in dementia design and an intensive

client briefing process resulted in an integrated design solution between the architecture and interior design, the private and communal areas, and the gardens and terraces, which provide an environment for residents and staff alike.

Client Goals and Design Team Solutions

• Provide an environment that is simple and easy to understand, maximizes visual acuity and limits residents' accommodation to clusters of no more than 12 per wing.

Each wing has a varied design and avoids long, straight corridor walls. Entrances to rooms are set back providing an opportunity to personalize the space outside the room with personal effects. Communal areas form adjacencies, which allow residents to see and be seen by carers, providing reassurance for both staff and residents.

• Each area must be designed as a place, not a space – it should have a purpose and identity and the design should relate to its purpose.

Developing the brief from the outset with the specialist care team and the architectural and interior design teams has helped develop places that are defined by their use with a clear sense of purpose and clearly defined adjacencies.

• Avoid dead-end routes and long straight corridors and finishes, which can be confusing or frustrating to residents.

Fire separation doors and service doors are painted to match the walls to discourage use. Floor finishes are a similar color and tone thoughout, avoiding visual-threshold barriers. Corridors end with alternative routes or breakout spaces creating a natural turn-around or circular route.

Top left: Lounge
Top right: Dining Room
Above left: Activity Kitchen
Above right: Seating Area

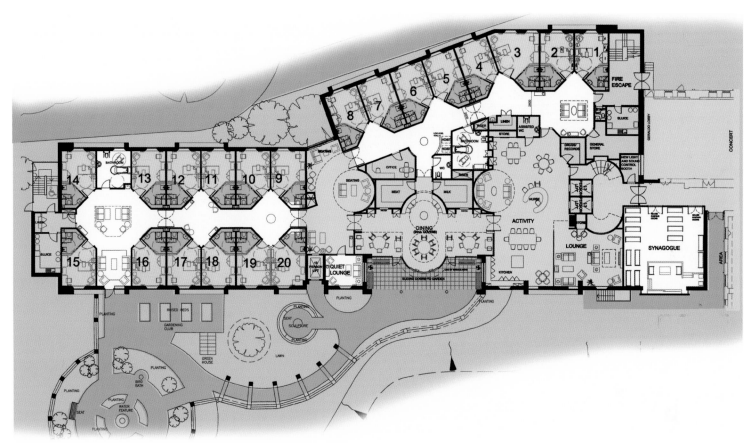

Ground floor plan

Major Design Objectives and/or Project Challenges

- The building must provide good views and a lot of natural daylight.

  Residents' corridors have breakout seating areas with large glazed windows overlooking the gardens or grounds. The dining room has full-height glazing and overlooks the access into the gardens. The first floor corridors are punctuated with rooflights, which flood the corridors with natural light.

- A clear hierarchy of spacial separation is required from communal space to private/communal to private.

The scheme design ensures that visitors enter the dementia wing in the communal areas and are not required to travel into or through the private communal areas (dining room and lounge) or private areas (residents' bedroom corridor). This maintains the dignity and respect of the residents and avoids visitors trooping through private areas to get to communal meeting rooms.

- Link the internal and external spaces and form dementia-friendly gardens, which do not dominate the existing grounds and provide alternative seating areas and activities.

The gardens provide walking paths and circular routes through and around a garden that is set predominantly away from the main garden terrace, maintaining the openess of the grounds for all the residents. There are an array of activities and routes to encourage residents to use the gardens, including seating in sunny or shady locations, a clothes line, a gardening club with raised planters, sculptures, water features, a greenhouse, and bird tables.

Unique Context

Nightingale provides holistic care for older members of the Jewish community. Physical, intellectual, emotional, cultural, religious, spiritual,

social, creative and artistic needs are catered for with sensitivity on an individual basis.

The food preparation areas include separate kitchen and storage facilities for the preparation and serving of meat and milk products.

A new Synagoue is provided as part of the scheme, enabling residents to maintain their religious beliefs and practices without having to leave the home.

Environmental Sustainability and Energy Conservation

- Significant use of passive energy conservation including high levels of thermal insulation and high-performance glazing.
- Renewable energy in excess of 20 percent including photovoltaic cells and CHP boiler.

Advanced Technology

An advanced nurse call system provides fall detection, and Passive Infrared (PIR) sensors provide automatic lighting to ensuite bathrooms.

Design and Philosophy of Care

Nightingale is committed to ensuring privacy, dignity, independence, respect and choice for residents in all aspects of their care in partnership with relatives and other stakeholders.

The home provides a range of communal spaces, allowing options and opportunities to integrate and socialize with other residents, take part in communal activities or sit quietly with a visitor or carer. Large bedrooms and ensuite facilities allow each resident to personalize their space or alter the layout to suit their own needs or preferences.

Extensive research within the area of dementia design has been applied to the briefing process to create a building that will assist residents and staff alike in creating an environment for the residents in pursuing a fullfilling life.

Integration of Residents with the Broader Community

Nightingale has an extensive program of activities for residents, families and visitors incorporating both the local community and the wider Jewish community. Numerous events, concerts activities and external trips help forge deep links with the community, inviting participation and interaction at every opportunity.

Opposite left: Lounge
Opposite right: Corridor
Left and Below left: Terrace
Below right: Garden

Photography: © Scurr Architects

Design For Aging Review 11

Appendix

Design for Aging Student Competition

New Urban Models for Aging: 'urban CARE'

College of Architecture, Texas A&M University // Austin, Texas

Akshay Sangolli
M.Architecture Candidate
College of Architecture
Texas A&M University
Certificate in Health Systems and Design

Professor: Mardelle M. Shepley, FAIA, DArch, ACHA;
College of Architecture, Texas A&M University

Below: The 'urban CARE' project is designed as a 'kit of parts' to promote maximum social interaction.
Opposite: Designed to provide home-like spaces, yet operate in the urban scale of downtown Austin.

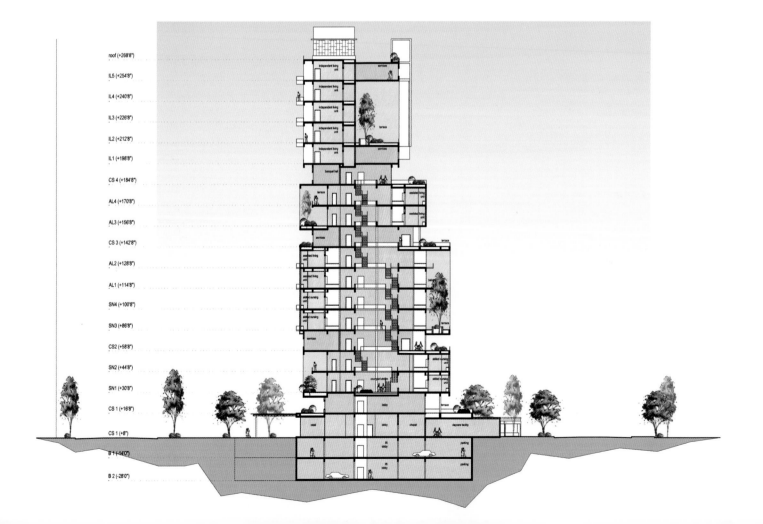

Master Plan Design

Briefly describe the site and the neighborhood you chose.

Austin is the 14th most populous city in the US and the cultural and economic center of the state of Texas. It is a vibrant city that offers a plethora of lifestyle opportunities that cater to youth as well as the elderly generation. Downtown Austin provides an opportunity for the creation of an elderly care facility that offers not only a historic connection with well-accepted landmarks, such as the Capitol Building and the Lady Bird Lake, but also an effervescent lifestyle to allow the elderly to be actively involved in the mainstream activities of downtown Austin. 'urban CARE' is located on the fringe of downtown Austin and offers easy walkable access to several public functions such as parks, libraries, post office, bus stops, theaters, dance schools, museums, and clinics, and yet is sufficiently removed so as not to be disturbed by the traffic and commotion of downtown. Thus

'urban CARE' not only satisfies the functional needs of an elderly care facility but also plays a unique part in offering the elderly an opportunity to participate in and help evolve the urban dynamics of the city.

How does your project integrate into the surrounding community?

'urban CARE' is basically conceptualized as a public space that offers 'the youth of today' an opportunity to acknowledge 'the youth of yesteryear.' It is designed so as to maximize interaction among the elderly, as well as to promote active involvement of the elderly into the day-to-day activities of the city, and vice-versa. Residents could become involved with the various libraries, museums, dance schools, and theaters in the vicinity. The contextual dynamics of downtown Austin have been advantageously used by enabling the residents to become integral members of the historic farmers' market that is held weekly on the very site that the project is proposed for. The

project also propels real estate development into the fringe areas of downtown Austin, which offer fantastic value in terms of proximity to public functions. The downtown fringe could possibly become a thriving and vibrant district that is sensitive to the 'urban ecology' around it. The project is conceptualized so that it actively interacts with the community around it, and therefore becomes an 'icon' in the city of Austin.

What inter-generational and community program elements invite the surrounding community into the project?

'urban CARE' offers as much to the community around it as it offers to the residents of the facility. A day care facility is integrated into the program to actively support the needs of working class families in downtown Austin. This also becomes an exciting activity for the elderly residents to participate in. The project also includes an 'adult day health center,' which would allow the elderly residents of adjoining areas who have no one to look after them during the day to receive genuine love and care from both medically trained professionals and also from fellow elderly residents. The building design incorporates a 'forecourt' that enables the retention of the farmers' market on the existing site. This is also an excellent incentive for the residents to grow organic vegetable and fruit produce in the courtyards and terrace gardens of the care facility. A 360-degree digital interactive screen is proposed in the congregational spaces within the project – this would become an exciting point of interest not only for the residents but also for the surrounding community. The project also includes an open air 'performance zone' in a well-shaded portion of the site that is segregated from heavy traffic corridors and lies in close proximity to the Ballet School of Austin. This zone would provide an excellent opportunity for creating a vibrant public space with kiosks and restaurants in Austin – the 'Live Music Capital of the World.'

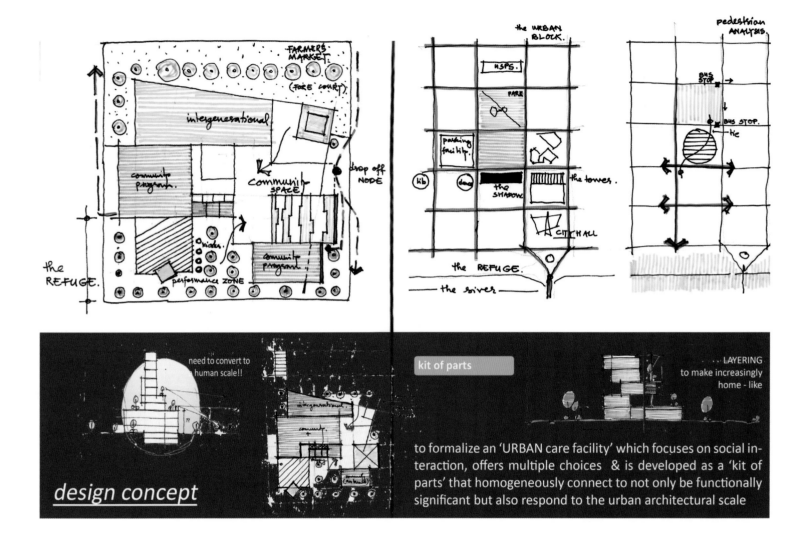

design concept

kit of parts

...LAYERING to make increasingly home - like

to formalize an 'URBAN care facility' which focuses on social interaction, offers multiple choices & is developed as a 'kit of parts' that homogeneously connect to not only be functionally significant but also respond to the urban architectural scale

How do the program elements interact with the various levels of housing within the project?

The 'urban CARE' project is essentially an amalgamation of the concepts of elderly 'healthcare' and 'urban housing.' The success of the project lies in enabling the dynamic interaction between the varied group of residents and the community around them. The project is envisioned so that the residents who live in Independent Living facilities could actively participate in easily walkable public activities

in the vicinity, which would give them not only physical exercise but also mental stimulus. Moreover, residents of the Independent Living and Assisted Living facilities can be actively involved in the day care facility and the adult day health center. They could collectively manage the organic produce gardens so as to actively participate in the farmers' market.

Another important feature of the design is the incorporation of several 'congregational

floors,' which act as buffer spaces that promote interaction between the various groups of residents, and also the residents with the community at large. All the intergenerational and community programs have been incorporated on these specifically designed floors. The floors are essentially transparent membranes that offer users options to interact in large or small groups and help them to feel at ease as they are visually and physically connected to the world around them.

How is the progression from Independent Living to Assisted Living and finally Skilled Nursing envisioned within the project?

Sensible thought has been applied in an attempt to decipher a method to ensure sequential progression between the various levels of care within the project. A review of past evidence poses a serious question as to whether it is advantageous to strategically stagger the various levels of care into individual modules, or to incorporate various levels of care within a single module.

'urban CARE' proposes a unique solution wherein the Independent Living units are accepted as being categorically different from the Assisted Living and Skilled Nursing units. These latter two unit types are designed so that they are very similar, so that residents feel a natural progression when they move from one level to another. Moreover, the similarity of these two unit types brings in the concept of 'acuity adaptability,' wherein the care giver is offered the flexibility to provide care to the residents while imposing the least physical and psychological hindrance to them.

The multitude of interaction and congregational spaces, as well as the vertical and horizontal visual connections between the three levels of care, ensures the least possible isolation of residents, and hence eases the process of progression between the various care levels.

What is your way-finding strategy for the project?

Way-finding is an extremely critical aspect of successful design. Inefficient way-finding causes 'spatial disorientation that is disruptive and causes stress' (Carpman and Grant). Sensible way-finding strategies were integrated into the design of 'urban CARE' that looked beyond signs, directions, and 'You Are Here' maps. Each module comprises units that are arranged in a 'race track' configuration that ensures easier way-finding.

Moreover, each floor plate is punctured by an atrium cut-out (double height) space, which ensures easier visual connection across the floor plate and also between two or more different floors. Double-height terraces and balconies offer choices for interaction spaces and also act as orientation mechanisms for residents.

It is also proposed that each congregational floor is developed around a different theme based on a variety of activities specific to that floor. The digital 360-degree screen could be the 'anchor activity' on one congregational floor, whereas a 'meditation cell' could be the anchor activity on another congregational floor. All the congregational floors have a green terrace garden, each with a different theme, such as the zen garden, the fruit and vegetable garden, and the flower garden – this would also assist in orientation and way finding.

Detailed Design of the Small Houses (Skilled Nursing level)

Describe which features of your small house design are typical of a home.

The Skilled Nursing module has been designed around the concept of 'community living.' The units are designed such that 10 units occur as a 'community.' Each community has its own terrace space, lounge area, recreational space, and service areas, all of which promote the concept of communal living.

In order to ensure that each unit has privacy and an individual identity, the units are designed so that each has its own foyer space in front of the entrance, and also its own private balcony where residents could look out over the park and towards downtown Austin. Moreover, each unit is self-contained and has its own kitchen, washing, lounge, and sleep areas within the compact layout of merely 450 square feet.

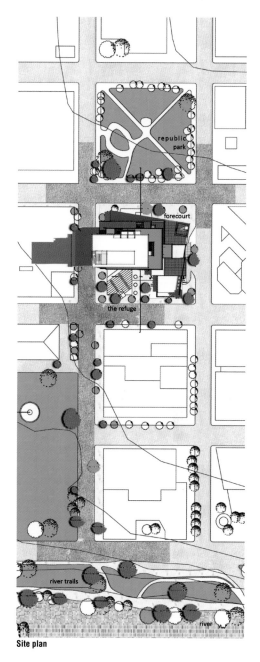

Site plan

Opposite: The 'urban CARE' project is designed as a 'kit of parts' to promote maximum social interaction

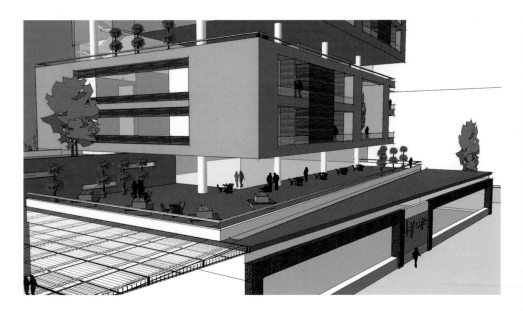

What accessible outdoor spaces did you include that encourage engagement and stimulate interest?

'urban Care' is punctuated by a multitude of outdoor spaces that offer residents choices based on the type of interaction they want to engage in. The individual balconies attached to each unit offer residents the opportunity to gaze out towards downtown, and the space and solitude for reflection and imagination. Next, the residents could use the larger terraces on each floor that offer them the opportunity to interact with fellow residents, particularly – but not limited to – those within their particular level of care.

The residents could also go to the congregational floors where several community programs exist in which they could interact with fellow residents of different care levels, and also possibly members of the larger community. The activity on each congregational floor is specifically programmed so that the digital 360-degree screen could stimulate residents' brains on one floor, and the meditation cells could act as soul-searching spaces on another. All the congregational floors have a green terrace garden, each with a different theme such as the zen garden, the fruit and vegetable garden, and the flower garden, which would engage and stimulate interest in the residents.

Overall Building Imagery

Describe your overall building design concept and composition.

The basic design simply evolved out of the contextual dynamics associated with the program and the site. A detailed study of the traffic patterns, figure ground study, proximity analysis, pedestrian analysis, noise analysis, and the urban activity clearly revealed that 'urban CARE' had to be able to successfully create a strong sense of place – it had to be an icon that could stand tall and holds its own against the random and rampant development in downtown Austin. 'urban CARE' is an attempt

What universal and accessible design considerations did you include for frail residents?

The building is designed to be ADA-friendly. All floor plates are horizontal and have wide corridors for ease of movement. Unit designs are universal, which means that the repetitive nature of the units is easy for both the resident and the care giver. The elevator core comprises two passenger elevators, and one hospital and one service elevator. They run through the building and offer easy vertical circulation. Lounge, dining, and kitchen facilities are provided on each level to ensure easy access to every resident, irrespective of the severity of their physical ailment. Stairs also

occur between floors through an atrium space, which offers a livelier atmosphere for walking than using a vertical stairwell.

Within an individual resident unit of your small house, what accommodations did you design to support the frailty of residents?

The units are designed so that residents feel at home while in the Skilled Nursing facility. Each unit is provided with a foyer space outside the unit, which accommodates a decentralized nurses station where a nurse can easily monitor the resident. Adequate storage space is provided outside the unit, part of which acts as storage for medicines and medical supplies for the nurses, and another part of which enables the residents to store umbrellas, footwear, and so on. Each unit is provided with easily accessible pantry space and study space. The wash rooms are designed so that they could be accessed using a wheelchair. Also, the wet and dry areas are clearly segregated – this would minimize accidents.

Above: The 'congregational floor' with its ADA-friendly terraces that promote social interaction
Opposite top left: 'urban CARE' as a 'celebrative space' in the high-rise urban context of downtown Austin
Opposite top right: Clearly layered functions identifiable in the elevation that shows a vibrant building imagery

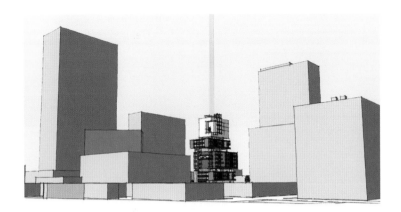

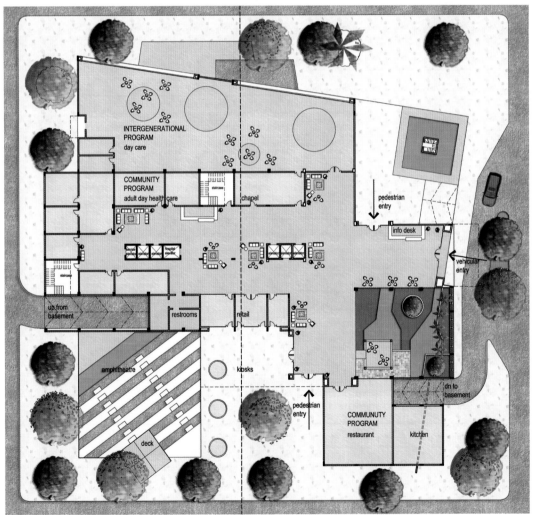

Ground floor plan

Within the plan, the following labels appear:

INTERGENERATIONAL PROGRAM
day care

COMMUNITY PROGRAM
adult day health care

chapel

staircase

pedestrian entry

info desk

vehicular entry

staircase

up from basement

restrooms

retail

amphitheatre

deck

kiosks

pedestrian entry

dn to basement

COMMUNUTY PROGRAM
restaurant

kitchen

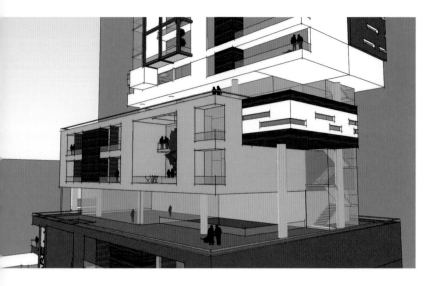

to not only satisfy all the functional requirements of a senior living facility, but also to develop it as an avant-garde model for offering senior residents an opportunity to be involved in day-to-day cosmopolitan activities. 'urban CARE' offers not only healthcare facilities for the residents but also acts as a public forum where community and elderly residents could interact. The various elements, such as community programs, intergenerational programs, farmers' market, Skilled Nursing facility, Assisted Living facility, Independent Living facility, and interaction spaces, act together to create a dynamic model wherein all the individual parts successfully function to create a vibrant and active care facility for downtown Austin.

What about the front door is welcoming and provides a unique image for the building in its context?

The facility is designed so that it does not necessarily have a single front door. Rather, the building is designed so that it creates a 'mall-like' space that is open to the public and offers several intergenerational and community activities arranged close to a strong public court, which

acts as a lobby space for the various functions. It ensures adequate security through the creation of smaller foyers and buffer spaces for each activity. The main vehicular and pedestrian entrance is well-accentuated by means of a mast tower that acts as an landmark to designate the active access zone of the project and channel movement from that corner to the diagonally opposite one where a refuge is located – the performance zone of the project, which is one of the most important community areas of 'urban CARE.'

Describe your architectural style and vocabulary that is site and context specific.

The building is essentially envisioned as a 'kit of parts' that ensures the layering of various activities and programs so as to successfully break down scale of the building into smaller fragments suitable for an elderly care facility and yet be able to respond to the architectural scale of downtown Austin.

The vibrant imagery of the building is in tune with the unofficial slogan of Austin – "keep Austin weird." The 'kit of parts' is designed using a rectilinear theme since it may be easier for elderly

adults to associate themselves with cleaner forms and spaces. 'urban CARE' is intended to function in the context of Austin's downtown, not only as a functional home for the aged, but also to symbolize the vibrancy of the city's culture and the people who have helped to form it.

The 'beacon of light' symbolizes the spirit of 'urban CARE' and announces that this celebrative space is a significant destination in the city of Austin, Texas.

Above left: Multiple social activities proposed on the 'congregational floors' to maximize interaction
Above right: Multiple opportunities for both private & public interaction made available to the residents

Illustration: Akshay Arvind Sangolli

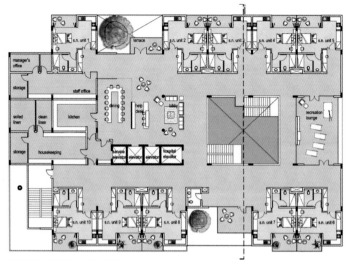

Skilled Nursing second level plan

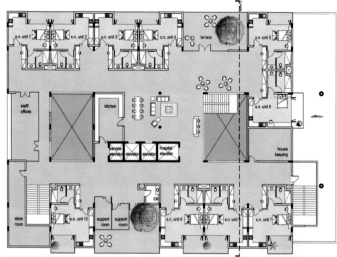

Skilled Nursing third level plan

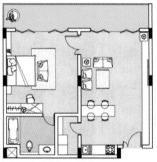

Independent Living unit plan

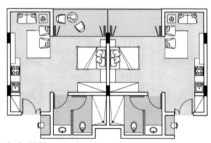

Assited Living unit plan

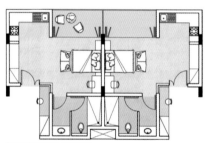

Skilled Nursing unit plan

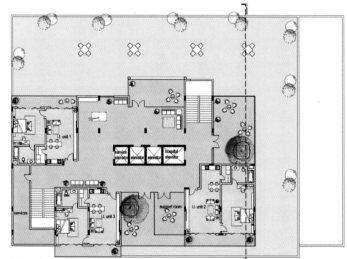

Independent Living second level plan

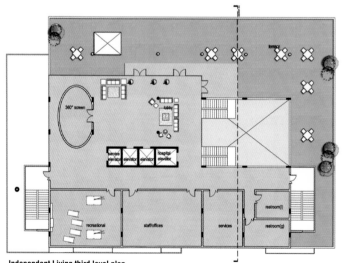

Independent Living third level plan

The 10-Year Award

The 10-Year Award was established in 2007 by the AIA Design for Aging (DFA) Knowledge Community to recognize projects that:

- have been completed and occupied for more than 10 years
- incorporate innovative, high-quality designs
- have survived the test of time
- offer lessons still valuable to today's consumers and competitive environment.

The award started by offering jurors, made up of Emeriti Chairs of DFA, the ability to reflect upon and recognize those timeless projects that set new standards and became the catalyst for change in seniors' housing and care environments. These projects would not only be aesthetically beautiful, but also programmatically and functionally innovative, which has been the premise behind the *Design for Aging Review* for more than 20 years.

In its short history, the 10-Year Award has evolved and expanded to include more than just projects. In 2007, two projects – Meadow Lakes Retirement Community, an early CCRC with a strong connection to the natural environment, and Woodside Place, an early memory support household model – received the award for their innovative concepts and lasting impact.

In 2009, the jury chose to recognize not a project, but two individuals, Paul and Teresa Klaassen, whose foresight and vision significantly impacted the design direction for seniors and the Assisted Living market with their Sunrise Communities.

In 2011, the jury – consisting of Jeffrey Anderzhon, Leslie Moldow, Ingrid Fraley, Jim Warner and Eric McRoberts – again chose not a project, but an organization, "LeadingAge," as the recipient of the 10-Year Award. Coincidentally, this is the same year that LeadingAge (formerly AAHA and AAHSA) celebrated its 50 year anniversary. The organization's long-standing and continuing emphasis on leadership, education, collaboration, technology advancements, and advocacy has dramatically shaped and improved the built environment for our ever-expanding senior population.

'Change' has been the only constant in the seniors' housing and care industry, perhaps more so than for any other building type. From the early days of the "old folks" and "convalescent" homes, which were often grim and clinical, LeadingAge has worked tirelessly to promote a change in attitude towards a warmer, friendlier, more residential design approach that addresses the specific needs of the aging process and promotes the highest possible quality of life.

LeadingAge has accomplished much in 50 years.

50 years of building a community of 5400 not-for-profit organizations in the United States, 38 state partners, and hundreds of businesses, research partners, consumer organizations, and foundations that speak with one voice for seniors' needs and rights; there is truly strength in numbers.

50 years of providing and promoting education that expands our minds and provides new ways of thinking that challenge care providers and design professionals to be always improving seniors' environments for housing and care.

50 years that have encompassed a philosophical design shift, from institutional settings to environments that are residential in scale and décor, offer privacy and dignity, and allow for resident-centered care and choice as the new standard – environments where a resident's quality of life is the true measure of a project's worth.

50 years of advocacy, working to promote changes to antiquated codes and regulations that fail to meet the needs of seniors, and making sure that community leaders and politicians are aware of the necessity for regulatory change.

50 years of collaboration, providing a platform of State and National conferences where care providers, educators, consultants, product vendors, and design professionals can come together to share experiences and information.

50 years of supporting and speaking for the not-for-profit care providers, where nurturing and caring environments complete the equation of what truly makes a great project.

30 years of promoting "aging-in-place" through universal design principles that allow environments to adapt and be flexible to meet the changing needs of residents through the aging process.

20 years of partnering with the AIA Design for Aging Knowledge Community on the *Design for Aging Review* competition, now in its 11th cycle, which has become a key resource in recognizing innovative seniors' housing and care environments.

15 years of supporting and collaborating with the AIA Design for Aging Knowledge Community on Post Occupancy Evaluations of seniors' communities, recognizing that evidence-based research will provide the knowledge and tools to improve future project outcomes.

Architects are taught how to design a *house*, but it takes an organization like LeadingAge to turn that house into a *home*, a place of comfort and beauty that offers a nurturing environment that promotes a true sense of "family."

We congratulate LeadingAge on its 50-year anniversary and, more specifically, the organization's support, knowledge, and guidance in working with design professionals on the built environment for seniors.

As history has shown, change is ever-present, and LeadingAge will be there at every step to lead the way, promote the good, identify the needs, and celebrate the fact that we are all getting older – they show us that what lies ahead can truly be life's golden years!

Eric S. McRoberts, AIA
2010 DFA Chair

Insights and Innovations from DFAR11

By Emily Chmielewski, Perkins Eastman Research Collaborative

In the summer of 2011, the American Institute of Architects' Design for Aging Knowledge Community conducted its eleventh biennial Design for Aging Review design competition (DFAR11). Using data submitted by the design competition applicants, the DFAR11 Insights Study provides a more comprehensive look at statistics, patterns, and innovations impacting today's senior living industry and design community—helping designers and providers improve the quality of design and the industry as a whole.

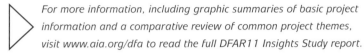

For more information, including graphic summaries of basic project information and a comparative review of common project themes, visit www.aia.org/dfa to read the full DFAR11 Insights Study report.

Below: The common spaces and programming at AgeSong at Bayside Park help residents be more engaged with the neighborhood and also invite members of the greater community inside.

Photography: Bruce Damonte Photography

The DFAR11 Insights Study identifies commonalities that reflect larger-scale trends and unique features that challenge those trends. Several of the DFAR-recognized projects stand out as leadership projects, reflecting the changes in and evolution of the senior living industry today. From filling gaps in the continuum of care to increasing the options from which residents can choose, the following are some examples of how innovative thinkers are using the built environment to address ongoing, new, or emerging issues for designers, providers, and building occupants.

Below: Armstrong Place Senior Housing enhances resident independence and connectivity to the greater community through its ground floor retail and adjacency to the city's newest mass transit rail line.

Photography: Brian Rose

Urban Resources: Siting and Program to Promote Connectivity

At AgeSong at Bayside Park (designed by Kava Massih Architects and owned by AgeSong, Inc. and Long Wharf Real Estate Partners, LP), the provider believes that "aging is a resource not a liability, and their goal is to re-establish the role of eldership in the community." Accordingly, this facility in Emeryville, California uses its common spaces and programming to affirm the presence of the residents in the neighborhood and also to invite members of the greater community in. This reportedly promotes a greater sense of community, as well as "develops a synergy with the surrounding community."

Jewish Home Lifecare (designed by Perkins Eastman and owned by Jewish Home Lifecare) is an urban adaptation of the Green House® model of care. A site in Manhattan's Upper West Side was selected to integrate the facility into an existing, thriving neighborhood. Residents can enjoy a variety of

experiences and conveniences right outside their door, including grocery stores, laundries, banks, pharmacies, restaurants, fitness clubs, movie theaters, places of worship, and parks. In addition to common spaces for residents (which are designed and located to encourage public access), the building also houses offices for home health care services as well as corporate offices for the greater community.

Similarly, The Mather South (designed by Solomon Cordwell Buenz and owned by Mather LifeWays) takes advantage of its location in downtown Chicago, with views of Lake Michigan, proximity to public transit, and access to nearby urban amenities, such as walkable connections to the lakefront historic district.

On a less urban scale, the Townhomes on Hendricks Place (designed by RLPS Architects and owned by Moravian Manor) provides the opportunity for residents to be within blocks of Lititz, Pennsylvania, a thriving small town that boasts "a vibrant network of shops and unique events." In addition, the residents of the townhouses are able to take advantage of the services and amenities offered by nearby Moravian Manor. An interconnecting sidewalk system links the housing to both the town and the retirement community.

The combined benefits of neighborhood amenities and a senior living provider can also be found at Armstrong Place Senior Housing (designed by David Baker + Partners Architects and owned by BRIDGE Housing). This intergenerational, mixed-use development is a resource to the greater community, providing services and amenities to senior residents while opening up opportunities for intergenerational relationships and partnerships with other, non-senior living service providers. Located in San Francisco, the facility offers apartments for seniors adjacent to market-rate residential units. With its ground floor retail, this project is acting as a catalyst for neighborhood revitalization. In addition, Armstrong Place Senior Housing's adjacency to the city's newest mass transit rail line further enhances resident independence and connectivity to the greater community.

Sense of community now goes beyond residents relations: Facilities are promoting resident connections to the surrounding neighborhood and also inviting the greater community in.

Opposite top: Seen here at dusk, the glazed façade of Saint John's on the Lake showcases the literal and figurate transparency of the semi-public ground floor spaces, which welcome visitors in addition to serving the residents.
Photography: Chris Barrett

Opposite bottom: Willson Hospice House was developed as a demonstration of ecological sustainability and is a resource for the greater community.
Photography: Jim Roof Creative, Inc

On-Site Resources: Serving the Greater Community to Promote Connectivity

Saint John's on the Lake (designed by Perkins Eastman and owned by Saint John's Communities) underwent an extensive renovation with the goal of improving the community's connection to the city. The facility, located in Milwaukee, Wisconsin, not only allows residents to maintain an urban lifestyle (through easy access to neighborhood shopping, restaurants, and public transportation), but also was redesigned to invite the local community into the building. The glazed façade connects residents to the streets beyond, enabling residents to feel part of the surrounding urban life and inviting visitors from the city into the facility. The ground floor bistro and Uihlein-Peters Gallery (which exhibits art through a partnership with the Museum of Wisconsin Art, creating a satellite gallery) are open to the public; and activates the building at street level, welcoming residents and visitors.

Another community resource can be found at Willson Hospice House (designed by Perkins + Will and owned by Phoebe Putney Memorial Hospital/Albany Community Hospice). This project was designed to be an ecological oasis for the local community of Albany, Georgia, as well as an amenity for the project's residents. It is currently the only healthcare facility in the world recognized as a Certified Silver Audubon International Signature Sanctuary. In addition to the hospice care offered and the publicly accessed natural preserve designed into the site, this facility also includes 15,000 square feet of administrative space, allowing 50 home care staff to travel to patients in eleven nearby counties. Space for meetings, education/training, and counseling is also provided for volunteers and community groups, allowing the building to serve the greater community.

Mabuhay Court Senior Housing and Northside Community Center (designed by David Baker + Partners Architects and owned by BRIDGE Housing) also supports an interesting mixed-use, public-private partnership. This project offers nearly 100 low-income senior housing units alongside a new intergenerational community center in San Jose, California. Designed for both capacity and flexibility, the community center serves the senior and youth populations of the area; and provides a large space for community events, such as weddings or concerts.

Another DFAR-recognized project that pairs senior housing with an intergenerational community center—though on a much larger scale—is the Moldaw Family Residences at the Taube-Koret Campus for Jewish Life (designed by Steinberg Architects and owned by Moldaw Family Residences at the Taube-Koret Campus for Jewish Life). Co-planned and built alongside low-income housing, this project offers nearly 300,000 square feet of senior living residences and over 134,000 square feet of publicly accessed commons. The community center is said to attract thousands of people daily from the Palo Alto, California area by offering spaces for events and meetings; fitness programs (with a

Opposite: Moldaw Family Residences at the Taube-Koret Campus for Jewish Life not only provide senior residences, but are also a resource for the greater community, with a publicly accessed civic center, fitness facilities, and a school for young children.

Photography: Tim Griffith

Below left: At the Leonard Florence Center for Living, supportive adaptations like the use of eye-gaze computer technology and resident command centers enable residents with MS or ALS to turn on/off lights, open and close doors, adjust temperature settings, and even order a drink at the café via email.

Photography: Robert Benson Photography

Below right: The new dining room at the Skilled Nursing facility at the Read Cloister Nursing Community offers a dining experience akin to that found in a restaurant that serves a younger population.

Photography: W. Baker and GMK

gymnasium, three swimming pools, weight training and fitness equipment, and classroom space); an early childhood education center; a major cultural arts and performance center (the Schultz Cultural Arts Hall); and the Stanford Hospital Health Library, which "is a free, public consumer health information library with scientifically-based medical information, empowering people to make informed decisions about all aspects of their health and healthcare."

Designing For Capability, Not Disability

At the new 100-bed Skilled Nursing Green House® project at the Leonard Florence Center for Living in Chelsea, Massachusetts (designed by DiMella Shaffer and owned by Chelsea Jewish Foundation), two households are dedicated to the care of people living with Multiple Sclerosis (MS) or Amyotrophic Lateral Sclerosis (ALS), more commonly known as "Lou Gehrig's Disease." Through supportive adaptations, like the use of eye-gaze computer technology and resident command centers, people's everyday lives are made easier and richer. Without staff assistance, residents can turn on/off lights, open and close doors, adjust temperature settings, and even order a drink at the café via email. Tasks that should be simple now are, again.

The goals of culture change and resident empowerment also guided the renovation and expansion of the dining room in the Skilled Nursing facility at the Read Cloister Nursing Community (designed by Cummings & McCrady, Inc. and owned by Bishop Gadsden Retirement Community). This Charleston, South Carolina project offers a restaurant-quality dining experience with high-end, hospitality finishes and furnishings and a servery that allows residents to see and smell the food being prepared and to converse with the chef and other dining staff. Residents can serve themselves, get assistance moving through the servery line, or may be seated and have their order taken by wait staff. The design offers a resident-centered dining experience and supports independence through choices and flexibility. This renovation has also served the purpose of improving sense of community and mitigating transition resistance since families feel more welcome and members from other parts of the community (i.e. Independent Living and Assisted Living) are now dining more frequently with the Skilled Nursing residents.

Community-wide participation is sometimes an important part of the design process as well as for the finished project. For example, during the renovation and expansion of Foulkeways Community Center (designed by RLPS Architects and owned by Foulkeways at Gwynedd), the design team received 246 letters from existing residents that "challenged every aspect of the initial design." The designers used this feedback to completely revise their plans for the new community center at the Gwynedd, Pennsylvania facility. The existing residents were considered active collaborators during the design process, resulting in a savings of $2 million and much greater resident buy-in.

Affordability-Driven Innovations

Project costs are always a driving factor in the design and success of a project, and some projects have responded by reinventing the product they create. For instance, two DFAR-recognized projects described a hybrid building that crosses the independence of cottages with the density (and therefore cost savings) of an apartment building. This innovative housing type was presented by Landis Homes: Hybrid Homes in Lititz, Pennsylvania (designed by RLPS Architects and owned by Landis Homes Retirement Community), as well as Air Force Villages in San Antonio, Texas (designed by Perkins Eastman and owned by Air Force Villages).

Both projects offer 10 to 14 residences, with ground level covered parking. All apartments are corner units with large balconies, providing opportunities for extensive glazing, great views, and daylight. Landis Homes' Hybrid Homes also incorporate several common areas within the building, or that are shared between paired buildings. "Particularly well suited to heavily populated suburban areas," Landis Homes states that the "hybrid homes offer a higher-

density model than patio homes, but are smaller than a typical apartment building allowing providers to incrementally expand housing."

Another innovative housing option created to provide denser development is The Houses on Bayberry (designed by RLPS Architects and owned by Arbor Acres United Methodist Retirement Community). This project aims to create a new neighborhood of up to five affordable small houses clustered together near the center of the retirement community's campus in Winston-Salem, North Carolina. Each cluster includes four patio homes joined like duplexes, with a porch that wraps around the front of the building (connecting the

Above: The villa buildings at Air Force Villages are an example of the new cottage-apartment hybrid.

Photography: Casey Dunn

residents to the community's common building). This porch, along with a courtyard garden, promotes residents' sense of community and a connection to nature. Similar to the cottage-apartment hybrid, the Houses on Bayberry are said to be "aimed at residents who require less space, but prefer living in a house rather than an apartment."

Addressing affordability, however, is not just about the here and now. For instance, the building created for the Franciscan Sisters of St. Joseph (designed by Perkins Eastman and owned by the Franciscan Sisters of St. Joseph) recognizes the fact that the number of Sisters is dwindling. Once the Sisters have passed on, the

facility can be used for affordable senior housing for the greater Hamburg, New York community. The facility's eventual use is anticipated by the size and layout of the resident rooms as well as the inclusion of several amenities (e.g. a pool and fitness area, a full commercial kitchen, a multi-purpose space, two guest suites, a library, and various meeting rooms). These spaces are, in the meantime, being enjoyed by the Sisters, but were ultimately included to attract a future market.

Implementing cost savings not only affects operations today, but can also impact an organization's legacy.

Blurred Boundaries

Whether improving connectivity or creating innovative ways to achieve affordability, the projects submitted to the eleventh biennial cycle of the Design for Aging Review design competition were an interesting and informative group. From new housing types to improved dining experiences, today's designers and providers are beginning to challenge what it means to be and design environments for a "senior" population.

The current industry thinking recognizes that there are still gaps in today's senior living options; that people are being invited to take a more active role not only in their care but also in society at large; and that designing for wellness, rather than illness, has a great and far-reaching impact. Residents' day-to-day feelings of competence, relatedness, and autonomy influence one's emotional well-being (Reis, Sheldon, Gable, Roscoe, & Ryan, 2000). Operational and design decisions that empower people and that offer resident-centered care can influence building occupants' mental, social, emotional, and physical well-being—which, therefore, affects their quality of life (Gabriel & Bowling, 2004).

The most recognizable industry trend that has addressed the need for more resident-centered care is the (now common) household model and culture change shift that began in the early 1990s. The concept of culture change challenged designers and providers to create more emotionally and cognitively supportive environments for older adults (Koren, 2010). As the submission for Jewish Home Lifecare states, "the intimate size of the [households] creates better knowledge and understanding of elders and caregivers and fosters stronger relationships." Households not only promote resident participation, family involvement, and sense of community, but also create an environment where front-line staff are more attuned to resident needs and are empowered to make decisions to provide more personalized care.

Similarly, senior cohousing developments, which are becoming more widely known in the United States (though cohousing has a long history in places like Denmark), are engaging residents in meaningful social roles, which helps prevent loneliness, depression, and isolation (Jang, Haley, Small, & Mortimer, 2002; Reker, 1997; Pennix, van Tilburg, Kriegsman, Deeg, Boeke, & van Eijk, 1997; Lee & Ishii-Kuntz, 1987; Thoits, 1983). Residents of cohousing are not expected to become primary caregivers to their neighbors (as one might do for a family member), but they do develop neighborly relationships that support aging-in-place. Simple acts like checking in on or running an errand for a neighbor can mean the difference between staying at home and being forced by circumstance to move into a care facility.

The practice of aging-in-place, within an intentional community is becoming more common (Thomas & Blanchard, 2009). Aging-in-place is also blurring the boundaries along the continuum of care. For instance, in the previous awards cycle, we began to see some continuing care retirement communities (CCRCs) eliminate the Assisted Living component of their projects. Residents live in Independent Living (with in-home services provided, as needed) until their advanced needs require them to move to Skilled Nursing. Providers are now lengthening independence by offering in-home services. It's only a small step to envision a lifelong continuum, in which such services are available for people of any age: short-stay rehab, household services (like laundry, cleaning, and running errands) for busy professionals or overwhelmed new mothers, counseling and outreach for anyone in need.

Opportunities and innovations like these serve many purposes, including improvements to quality of life, but they often develop out of a need for affordability. Offering more in-home services to Independent Living residents developed out of a need to lower the costs of care and address a bigger market. The up-swing in organizations offering in-home services also stems from a broader public policy shift and shortage of tax revenue. Likewise, the previously described evolution in housing types evidenced by Landis Homes: Hybrid Homes, Air Force Villages, The Houses on Bayberry, and the Franciscan Sisters of St. Joseph all address issues of affordability.

Whether driven primarily by cost or by an organization's philosophy of care, today's innovators are redefining the traditional notion of the continuum of care. In fact, taking seniors out the continuum of care—and just letting them *continue*— is just one way the industry is blurring the line of what it means to be old. From neighbors supporting neighbors in cohousing developments to Montessori and other peer-support programs that are being adopted at senior living communities throughout the country, the concept of seniors solely as care recipients is being questioned, with more programs enabling seniors to play an active and meaningful role as care *givers*. A strong sense of meaning has been correlated to an extended number of years of life (Krause, 2009); and research has shown that social activities and productive engagement are as influential to elder survival as physical fitness activities (Glass, Mendes de Leon, Marottoli, & Berkman, 1999).

Whether driven primarily by cost or by an organization's philosophy of care, today's innovators are redefining the traditional notion of the continuum of care.

The senior living industry today continues to evolve in new ways away from custodial care towards a model that helps older adults maintain social and professional roles, stay engaged, and continue to live meaningful lives. This is evidenced by the popularity of programs for continued education; the introduction of Montessori-based activities to promote social, emotional, and cognitive engagement; and the number of projects submitted to DFAR11 that offer improved connections to the greater community (as seen by the previously described AgeSong at Bayside Park, Jewish Home Lifecare, The Mather South, Townhomes on Hendricks Place, Armstrong Place Senior Housing, Saint John's on the Lake, Willson Hospice House, Mabuhay Court Senior Housing and Northside Community Center, and the Moldaw Family Residences at the Taube-Koret Campus for Jewish Life).

The DFAR-recognized projects show that what it means to be an older adult in America today is changing, too. More people are staying active, whether through physical fitness or maintaining a career. These days, more residents of senior living facilities are still employed, or are only semi-retired. Others are continuing a professional role through volunteering, mentorships, or as board members. Older adults are no longer content to be segregated on "senior" campuses, but are engaged with the greater community.

The fact that senior living facilities are both more open to as well as opening themselves up to the greater community is seen not only in the spaces and services/programs being offered (or not offered, as the case may be when amenities in the surrounding neighborhood are used instead), but also in the interior design of the facilities. Senior housing is no longer a stereotypical, nostalgic interpretation of real life. The DFAR11 leadership projects are taking the industry beyond the "front porch" aesthetic with its indoor, mock-Main Streets. Seniors expect and designers are providing interior styles, finishes, and furnishings that are commonly found in market-rate housing or hospitality environments. Perhaps because today's seniors are a generation whose lives were shaped by the era of modernism, contemporary design is now received as a "home-like" option, in addition to the more traditional residential aesthetic that (up until now) was typically associated with senior living.

Simple and thoughtful design features enable older, frailer adults to continue to be active members of the larger senior living community. Easy access and shorter walking distances to common areas or special equipment (e.g. A/V provisions in multi-media theater spaces) and other newer technologies help

Above: Seniors today, like these residents of Moldaw Family Residences at the Taube-Koret Campus for Jewish Life, are maintaining their connections to the greater community, through continued education, the use of existing services/amenities, and on-going professional careers.

Photography: Tim Griffith

people stay engaged. Technology is also breaking down barriers and blurring spatial boundaries: from keeping in touch with family and friends through emails and video chats to signing up for services or activities online, residents are more tech-savvy. Facilities today are also more likely to offer adult day services in addition to live-in resident services, further integrating "senior" environments into urban and suburban neighborhoods.

Looking to the Future

A fundamental characteristic of the innovative DFAR11 projects is their recognition of the *strengths* of older people (such as the approaches taken by the previously described new 100-bed Skilled Nursing Green House® project at the Leonard Florence Center for Living, Read Cloister Nursing Community, and Foulkeways at Gwynedd). We saw a big difference between the projects that are designed to enhance people's capabilities, use their talents, and develop their interests, as opposed to designing to remediate people's disabilities and impairments. A defining theme of the DFAR11 leadership projects is the idea that the environment can enable older people, at any point in the continuum of aging, to grow and thrive and live a meaningful life.

Designing for wellness, rather than illness, has a great and far-reaching impact.

The innovative leadership projects submitted to DFAR11 framed older adults as strong and capable, as problem solvers, as people who want to be involved in their own care and personal growth. This fundamental perceptual shift, which is also at the heart of culture change, opens new possibilities for senior living and blurs boundaries that now limit seniors' quality of life. The "well-person" movement is out there and is gaining ground. Its implications for design are profound, and, as these projects show, it is leading to new design concepts that broaden opportunities, eliminate barriers, and enrich the experience of living.

Opposite: As evidenced by the new 100-bed Skilled Nursing Green House® at the Leonard Florence Center for Living, "homey" interiors are no longer limited to traditional aesthetics—contemporary design can be just as appealing, familiar, and comforting to today's seniors.

Photography: Robert Benson Photography

References

Gabriel, Z., & Bowling, A. (2004). Quality of life from the perspective of older people. *Aging & Society, 24*, 675-691.

Glass, T. A., Mendes de Leon, C., Marottoli, R. A., & Berkman, L. F. (1999). Population based study of social and productive activities as predictors of survival among elderly Americans. *BMJ, 319*, 478-483.

Jang, Y., Haley, W. E., Small, B. J., & Mortimer, J. A. (2002). The role of mastery and social resources in the associations between disability and depression in later life. *The Gerontologist, 42* (6), 807-813.

Koren, M. J. (2010). Person-centered care for nursing home residents: The culture-change movement. *Health Affairs, 29* (2), 1-6.

Krause, N. (2009). Meaning in life and mortality. *Journal of Gerontology: Social Sciences, 64B* (4), 517-527.

Lee, G. R., & Ishii-Kuntz, M. (1987). Social interaction, loneliness, and emotional well-being among the elderly. *Research on Aging, 9* (4), 459-482.

Pennix, B. W., van Tilburg, T., Kriegsman, D. M., Deeg, D. J., Boeke, A. J., & van Eijk, J. T. (1997). Effects of social support and personal coping resources on mortality in older age: The longitudinal aging study Amsterdam. *American Journal of Epidemiology, 146* (6), 510-519.

Reis, H. T., Sheldon, K. M., Gable, S. L., Roscoe, J., & Ryan, R. M. (2000). Daily well-being: The role of autonomy, competence, and relatedness. *Personality and Social Psychology Bulletin, 26* (4), 419-435.

Reker, G. T. (1997). Personal meaning, optimism, and choice: Existential predictors of depression in community and institutional elderly. *The Gerontologist, 37* (6), 709-716.

Thoits, P. A. (1983). Multiple identities and psychological well-being: A reformulation and test of the social isolation hypothesis. *American Sociological Review, 48*, 174-187.

Thomas, W. H., & Blanchard, J. M. (2009). Moving beyond place: Aging in community. *Generations - Journal of the American Society on Aging, 33* (2), 12-17.

Project Data
AIA Juried Projects

Armstrong Place Senior Housing

Developer/Owner: BRIDGE Housing
Architect: David Baker + Partners
Associate Architect: Full Circle Architecture
General Contractor: Nibbi Brothers General Construction
Landscape Architect: Adrienne Wong Associates

Building Data
Independent Living Total Building GSF: 130930
Independent Living Total NSF of Common Spaces: 7000
Independent Living Total NSF of Residential Spaces: 69849

Independent Living			
Unit type	Number of units	Size range (NSF)	Typical size (NSF)
Studio	12	575–575	575
One-bedroom	103	602–648	615
Two-bedroom	1	808–808	808
Total (all units)	116		

Accessible Independent Living Units (%): 5
Adaptable Independent Living Units (%): 95

Project costs, actual (or estimated, if the project has yet to be built)
Independent Living: Total cost for New Construction ($): 41200000
Independent Living: FF&E costs for New Construction ($): 170000
Independent Living: Site development costs for New Construction ($): 1179627
Independent Living: Soft costs for New Construction ($): 5974791

Project Funding Sources
Conventional/Private Funding %: 24
Public Sector Funding %: 73
Public-Private Sector Funding %: 3

Gender breakdown of the residents
Men %: 51
Women %: 49

Status of the residents
Living with an in-home caregiver (%): 1
Living with family/friend (%): 4
Married/domestic partner (%): 30
Single (%): 65

Source of resident payments
Government subsidy payment (%): 91
Private payment (%): 9

Age of residents
Independent Living: Average age designed to support: 65
Independent Living: Average entry age: 66
Independent Living: Average current age: 66

Occupancy
Independent Living occupancy date: 09 2010
Independent Living current occupancy (%): 95

Mabuhay Court Senior Housing and Northside Community Center

Developer/Owner: BRIDGE Housing
Developer/Owner: City of San Jose Department of Housing
Architect: David Baker + Partners
Contractor: L + D Construction
Landscape Architect: PGADesign
Interior Design: Design Mesh

Building Data
Independent Living: Total Building GSF: 110722
Independent Living: Total NSF of Common Spaces: 15418
Independent Living: Total NSF of Residential Spaces: 95304

Independent Living			
Unit type	Number of units	Size range (NSF)	Typical size (NSF)
Studio	20	416–416	416
One-bedroom	60	480–556	556
Two-bedroom	16	747	747
Total (all units)	96		

Accessible Independent Living Units (%): 5
Adaptable Independent Living Units (%): 95

Project costs, actual (or estimated, if the project has yet to be built)
Independent Living: Total cost for New Construction ($): 16983359
Independent Living: FF&E costs for New Construction ($): 344566
Independent Living: Site development costs for New Construction ($): 2194883
Independent Living: Soft costs for New Construction ($): 22324040
Senior Community Center: Total cost for New Construction ($): 5647797
Senior Community Center: FF&E costs for New Construction ($): 277976
Senior Community Center: Site development costs for New Construction ($): 201888
Senior Community Center: Soft costs for New Construction ($): 703660

Project Funding Sources
Conventional/Private Funding %: 42
Other Funding Source %: 13
Public Sector Funding %: 45

Gender breakdown of the residents
Men %: 41
Women %: 59

Status of the residents
Living with family/friend (%): 9
Married/domestic partner (%): 42
Single (%): 49

Source of resident payments
Government subsidy payment (%): 8
Private payment (%): 92

Average age of residents
Independent Living: Average age designed to support: 65
Independent Living: Average entry age: 73
Independent Living: Average current age: 73

Occupancy
Independent Living occupancy date: 11 2002
Independent Living current occupancy (%): 97

AgeSong at Bayside Park

Client/Owner: AgeSong, Inc. & Long Wharf Real Estate Partners, LP
Architect: Kava Massih Architects
General Contractor: James E. Roberts-Obayashi Corporation
Owner's Representative: Ventana Property Services
Interior Design: Kava Massih Architects
Interior Furnishings: Smith Group JJR
Structural Engineer: OLMM Consulting Engineers
Mechanical Engineer: FARD Engineers
Electrical Engineer: FARD Engineers
Landscape Architect: Miller Company
Civil Engineer: Luk and Associates
Acoustical Engineer: Rosen, Goldeberg, Der and Lewitz, Inc.
Food Service Consultant: Design West Partnership
Waterproofing Consultant: Wiss, Janey, Elstner Associates
Photography: Bruce Damonte Photography, Inc.

Building Data
Independent Living: Total Building GSF: 21559
Independent Living: Total NSF of Common Spaces: 8047
Independent Living: Total NSF of Residential Spaces: 13512
Assisted Living: Total Building GSF: 44827

Assisted Living: Total NSF of Common Spaces: 20306
Assisted Living: Total NSF of Residential Spaces: 24521
Assisted Living Dementia/Memory Support: Total Building GSF: 22175
Assisted Living Dementia/Memory Support: Total NSF of Common Spaces: 11537
Assisted Living Dementia/Memory Support: Total NSF of Residential Spaces: 10638

Independent Living			
Unit type	Number of units	Size range (NSF)	Typical size (NSF)
Studio	20	300-530	400
One-bedroom	10	515-660	550
Total (all units)	30		

Accessible Independent Living Units (%): 10
Adaptable Independent Living Units (%): 90

Assisted Living			
Unit type	Number of units	Size range (NSF)	Typical size (NSF)
Studio	53	250-520	300
One-bedroom	10	515-700	550
Total (all units)	63		

Accessible Assisted Living Units (%): 10
Adaptable Assisted Living Units (%): 90

Assisted Living Dementia/Memory Support			
Unit type	Number of units	Size range (NSF)	Typical size (NSF)
Private room*	10	230–260	250
Shared room**	23	310–470	400
Total (all units)	33		

*Single occupant
**Two occupants with a shared bed area and a shared bathroom

Project costs, actual (or estimated, if the project has yet to be built)
Assisted Living: Total cost for New Construction ($): 11357500
Assisted Living: FF&E costs for New Construction ($): 1232000
Assisted Living: Site development costs for New Construction ($): 781550
Assisted Living: Soft costs for New Construction ($): 2117500
Assisted Living: Soft costs for Renovation/Modernization ($): 2117500
Assisted Living Dementia/Memory Support: Total cost for New Construction ($): 5605000
Assisted Living Dementia/Memory Support: FF&E costs for New Construction ($): 608000
Assisted Living Dementia/Memory Support: Site development costs for New Construction ($): 835700
Assisted Living Dementia/Memory Support: Soft costs for New Construction ($): 1045000
Assisted Living Dementia/Memory Support: Soft costs for Renovation/Modernization ($): 1045000
Independent Living: Total cost for New Construction ($): 5310000
Independent Living: FF&E costs for New Construction ($): 576000
Independent Living: Site development costs for New Construction ($): 375000
Independent Living: Soft costs for New Construction ($): 999000
Independent Living: Soft costs for Renovation/Modernization ($): 990000
Wellness/Fitness Center: Total cost for New Construction ($): 590000
Wellness/Fitness Center: FF&E costs for New Construction ($): 108000
Wellness/Fitness Center: Site development costs for New Construction ($): 40600
Wellness/Fitness Center: Soft costs for New Construction ($): 110000
Wellness/Fitness Center: Soft costs for Renovation/Modernization ($): 110000

Project Funding Sources

Conventional/Private Funding %: 100

Gender breakdown of the residents

Men %: 21
Women %: 79

Status of the residents

Married/domestic partner (%): 10
Single (%): 90

Source of resident payments

Private payment (%): 100

Average age of residents

Assisted Living: Average age designed to support: 85
Assisted Living: Average entry age: 85
Assisted Living: Average current age: 85
Assisted Living Dementia/Memory Support: Average age designed to support: 85
Assisted Living Dementia/Memory Support: Average entry age: 84
Assisted Living Dementia/Memory Support: Average current age: 84
Independent Living: Average age designed to support: 80
Independent Living: Average entry age: 83
Independent Living: Average current age: 83

Occupancy

Assisted Living Dementia/Memory Support occupancy date: 01 2010
Assisted Living Dementia/Memory Support occupancy at opening (%): 12
Assisted Living Dementia/Memory Support current occupancy (%): 45
Assisted Living occupancy date: 01 2010
Assisted Living occupancy at opening (%): 6
Assisted Living current occupancy (%): 44
Independent Living occupancy date: 01 2011
Independent Living current occupancy (%): 33
Wellness/Fitness Center occupancy date: 01 2010

Air Force Villages

Client/Owner: Air Force Villages

Architect: Perkins Eastman

Landscape/Civil Engineer: Jacobs, Inc.

Structural: Jacobs, Inc.; Graef

MEP: Murray and Associates; Jacobs, Inc.

Food Service: Sodexo

Low Voltage: Jacobs, Inc; Combs Consulting Group

Program Manager: Jacobs, Inc.

General Contractor: Skanska

Building Data

Independent Living: Total Building GSF: 68805
Independent Living: Total NSF of Common Spaces: 13254
Independent Living: Total NSF of Residential Spaces: 5551
Long-Term Skilled Nursing: Total Building GSF: 41322
Long-Term Skilled Nursing: Total NSF of Common Spaces: 26982
Long-Term Skilled Nursing: Total NSF of Residential Spaces: 14340
Short-Term Rehab: Total Building GSF: 29833
Short-Term Rehab: Total NSF of Common Spaces: 22083
Short-Term Rehab: Total NSF of Residential Spaces: 7750

Independent Living			
Unit type	Number of units	Size range (NSF)	Typical size (NSF)
One-bedroom	3	918	918
Two-bedroom	27	1153–1404	1153
Two-bedroom plus den	6	1526	1526
Total (all units)	36		

Adaptable Independent Living Units (%): 100

Long-Term Skilled Nursing			
Unit type	Number of units	Size range (NSF)	Typical size (NSF)
Private room*	36	285–290	285
Semi-private room**	8	465–510	465
Total (all units)	44		

*Single occupant
**Two occupants with separate bed areas but a shared bathroom

Short-Term Rehab			
Unit type	Number of units	Size range (NSF)	Typical size (NSF)
Private room*	20	285–295	285
Shared room**	4	465–510	465
Total (all units)	24		

*Single occupant
**Two occupants with separate bed areas but a shared bathroom

Project costs, actual (or estimated, if the project has yet to be built)

Independent Living: Total cost for New Construction ($): 13624000
Independent Living: Site development costs for New Construction ($): 1008000
Long-Term Skilled Nursing: Total cost for New Construction ($): 21486000
Long-Term Skilled Nursing: FF&E costs for New Construction ($): 877313
Long-Term Skilled Nursing: Site development costs for New Construction ($): 1589964
Senior Community Center: Total Construction cost for Renovation/Modernization ($): 10175000
Senior Community Center: FF&E costs for Renovation/Modernization ($): 472525
Senior Community Center: Site development costs for Renovation/Modernization ($): 376475

Project Funding Sources

Conventional/Private Funding %: 56
Non-Taxable Bond Offering Funding %: 44

Gender breakdown of the residents

Men %: 33
Women %: 67

Status of the residents

Married/domestic partner (%): 57
Single (%): 43

Source of resident payments

Private payment (%): 77
Government subsidy payment (%): 2
Medicaid/Medicare payment (%): 21

Average age of residents

Independent Living: Average age designed to support: 81
Independent Living: Average entry age: 81
Independent Living: Average current age: 85
Long-Term Skilled Nursing: Average age designed to support: 90
Long-Term Skilled Nursing: Average entry age: 90
Long-Term Skilled Nursing: Average current age: 90
Short-Term Rehab: Average age designed to support: 90
Short-Term Rehab: Average entry age: 90
Short-Term Rehab: Average current age: 90

Occupancy

Independent Living occupancy date: 12 2010
Independent Living current occupancy (%): 25
Long-Term Skilled Nursing occupancy date: 06 2011
Long-Term Skilled Nursing occupancy at opening (%): 95
Long-Term Skilled Nursing current occupancy (%): 80
Short-Term Rehab occupancy date: 06 2011
Short-Term Rehab current occupancy (%): 80
Senior Community Center occupancy date: 07 2011

Atria Tamalpais Creek

Client/Owner: Atria Senior Living Group

Architect: GGLO

Interior Design: GGLO

Landscape Architecture: GGLO

Unit Contractor: Draeger Construction

Common Areas Contractor: Hearn Construction

Civil Engineer: KPFF

Structural Engineer: KPFF

Mechanical Engineer: Interface Engineering

Electrical Engineer: Interface Engineering

Building Data

Assisted Living: Total Building GSF: 73722
Assisted Living: Total NSF of Common Spaces: 21646
Assisted Living: Total NSF of Residential Spaces: 45635
Assisted Living Dementia/Memory Support: Total Building GSF: 8230
Assisted Living Dementia/Memory Support: Total NSF of Common Spaces: 2269
Assisted Living Dementia/Memory Support: Total NSF of Residential Spaces: 5520

Assisted Living			
Unit type	Number of units	Size range (NSF)	Typical size (NSF)
Studio	99	325-462	348
One-bedroom	6	651-682	661
Two-bedroom	1	692	692
Total (all units)	106		

Accessible Assisted Living Units (%): 29
Other Assisted Living Units (%): 71

Assisted Living Dementia/Memory Support			
Unit type	Number of units	Size range (NSF)	Typical size (NSF)
Private room*	6	332-342	334
Semi-private room**	5	530-683	563
Total (all units)	11		

*Single occupant
**Two occupants with separate bed areas but a shared bathroom

Project costs, actual (or estimated, if the project has yet to be built)

Assisted Living: Total Construction cost for Additions ($): 158000
Assisted Living: Total Construction cost for Renovation/Modernization ($): 7742000
Assisted Living: FF&E costs for Additions ($): 6870
Assisted Living: FF&E costs for Renovation/Modernization ($): 680130
Assisted Living: Site development costs Additions ($): 18320
Assisted Living: Site development costs for Renovation/Modernization ($): 897680
Assisted Living: Soft costs for Additions ($): 22000
Assisted Living: Soft costs for Renovation/Modernization ($): 2178000
Assisted Living Dementia/Memory Support: Total Construction cost for Renovation/Modernization ($): 1600000
Assisted Living Dementia/Memory Support: FF&E costs for Renovation/Modernization ($): 126000
Assisted Living Dementia/Memory Support: Site development costs for Renovation/Modernization ($): 276000
Assisted Living Dementia/Memory Support: Soft costs for Renovation/Modernization ($): 663000

Project Funding Sources

Conventional/Private Funding %: 100

Gender breakdown of the residents

Men %: 27
Women %: 73

Status of the residents

Married/domestic partner (%): 6
Single (%): 94

Source of resident payments

Government subsidy payment (%): 1
Private payment (%): 99

Average age of residents

Assisted Living: Average age designed to support: 86
Assisted Living: Average entry age: 86
Assisted Living: Average current age: 86
Assisted Living Dementia/Memory Support: Average age designed to support: 86
Assisted Living Dementia/Memory Support: Average entry age: 86
Assisted Living Dementia/Memory Support: Average current age: 86

Occupancy

Assisted Living Dementia/Memory Support occupancy date: 06 2010
Assisted Living Dementia/Memory Support current occupancy (%): 100
Assisted Living occupancy date: 11 1979
Assisted Living occupancy at opening (%): 95
Assisted Living current occupancy (%): 92

Blanche Robertson Garden Cottage at Penick Village

Client/Owner: Penick Village

Architect: CJMW Architecture

Architectural design, Interior Design, MEP/FP engineering design: CJMW Architecture

Structural Engineering: Arrowood & Arrowood, PC

Landscape Architecture: Lappas + Havener, PA

Civil Engineering: Mulkey Engineers & Consultants

General Contractor: Pinnacle Development

LEED for Homes Coordination: NC Solar Center

Energy Rater: Commission WorCx

Building Data

Assisted Living: Total Building GSF: 6997
Assisted Living: Total NSF of Common Spaces: 3927
Assisted Living: Total NSF of Residential Spaces: 3070

Assisted Living			
Unit type	Number of units	Size range (NSF)	Typical size (NSF)
Studio	10	303–337	307
Total (all units)	10		

Accessible Assisted Living Units (%): 100

Project costs, actual (or estimated, if the project has yet to be built)

Assisted Living: Total cost for New Construction ($): 1450000

Project Funding Sources

Conventional/Private Funding %: 100

Gender breakdown of the residents

Women %: 100

Status of the residents

Single (%): 100

Source of resident payments

Private payment (%): 80
Other payment source (%): 20
Organization financial assistance support.

Average age of residents

Assisted Living: Average age designed to support: 80
Assisted Living: Average entry age: 89
Assisted Living: Average current age: 90

Occupancy

Assisted Living occupancy date: 05 2010
Assisted Living occupancy at opening (%): 100
Assisted Living current occupancy (%): 100

Foulkeways Community Center

Client/Owner: Foulkeways at Gwynedd

Architect & Interiors: RLPS Architects

Contractor: C. Raymond Davis & Sons, Inc.

Civil Engineer: Woodrow & Associates, Inc.

MEP Engineer: Reese Engineering, Inc.

Structural Engineer: MacIntosh Engineering

Food Service: Culinary Design Service, Inc.

Photography: Larry Lefever Photography

Building Data

Independent Living: Total NSF of Common Spaces: 24773
Independent Living: Total Building GSF: 36683

Project costs, actual (or estimated, if the project has yet to be built)

Senior Community Center: Total Construction cost for Renovation/Modernization ($): 9777235
Senior Community Center: FF&E costs for Renovation/Modernization ($): 649220
Senior Community Center: Site development costs for Renovation/Modernization ($): 120505
Senior Community Center: Soft costs for Renovation/Modernization ($): 1595882

Project Funding Sources

Non-Taxable Bond Offering Funding %: 100

Gender breakdown of the residents

Men %: 30
Women %: 70

Status of the residents

Married/domestic partner (%): 42
Single (%): 58

Source of resident payments

Private payment (%): 99
Medicaid/Medicare payment (%): 1

Average age of residents

Independent Living: Average age designed to support: 84
Independent Living: Average entry age: 75
Independent Living: Average current age: 84

Occupancy

Senior Community Center occupancy date: 05 2010

Franciscan Sisters of St. Joseph

Client/Owner: Franciscan Sisters of St. Joseph

Architect: Perkins Eastman

Contractor: Lecesse Construction

Interior designer: Perkins Eastman

Landscape architect: RGR Landscape Architecture

Structural engineer: Jensen BRV Engineering, PLLC

Mechanical engineer: Turner Engineering, PC

Electrical engineer: Turner Engineering, PC

Civil engineer: Wm. Schutt & Associates Engineering and Land Surveying, PC

Building Data

Independent Living: Total Building GSF: 67000

Long-Term Skilled Nursing: Total Building GSF: 47000

Independent Living			
Unit type	Number of units	Size range (NSF)	Typical size (NSF)
Studio	32	300	300
Total (all units)	32		

Accessible Independent Living Units (%): 100

Long-Term Skilled Nursing			
Unit type	Number of units	Size range (NSF)	Typical size (NSF)
Private room*	40	300	300
Total (all units)	40		

*Single occupant

Project costs, actual (or estimated, if the project has yet to be built)

Independent Living: Total cost for New Construction ($): 6500000

Independent Living: FF&E costs for New Construction ($): 398000

Independent Living: Site development costs for New Construction ($): 1566438

Independent Living: Soft costs for New Construction ($): 2500000

Long-Term Skilled Nursing: Total cost for New Construction ($): 6500000

Long-Term Skilled Nursing: FF&E costs for New Construction ($): 155000

Long-Term Skilled Nursing: Site development costs for New Construction ($): 1566438

Long-Term Skilled Nursing: Soft costs for New Construction ($): 2500000

Wellness/Fitness Center: Total cost for New Construction ($): 500000

Wellness/Fitness Center: Site development costs for New Construction ($): 1566438

Wellness/Fitness Center: Soft costs for New Construction ($): 2500000

Project Funding Sources

Conventional/Private Funding %: 100

Gender breakdown of the residents

Women %: 100

Status of the residents

Single (%): 100

Source of resident payments

Other payment source (%): 100

Project was self-financed by the client from long-term investment funds.

Average age of residents

Independent Living: Average age designed to support: 70

Independent Living: Average entry age: 70

Independent Living: Average current age: 70

Long-Term Skilled Nursing: Average age designed to support: 85

Long-Term Skilled Nursing: Average entry age: 85

Long-Term Skilled Nursing: Average current age: 85

Occupancy

Independent Living occupancy date: 07 2010

Independent Living occupancy at opening (%): 80

Independent Living current occupancy (%): 80

Long-Term Skilled Nursing occupancy date: 07 2010

Long-Term Skilled Nursing occupancy at opening (%): 90

Long-Term Skilled Nursing current occupancy (%): 95

Wellness/Fitness Center occupancy date: 07 2010

Gilchrist Center for Hospice Care

Architect: Marks, Thomas Architects

Client/Owner: Greater Baltimore Medical Center

GC: Whiting Turner

MEP: EBL Engineers

Interior Designer: Marks, Thomas Architects

Civil: DMW

Landscape Architect: Site Resources

Kitchen Designer: Savoy Brown

Furniture Dealer: Price Modern

Building Data

Hospice: Total Building GSF: 35000

Hospice: Total NSF of Common Spaces: 14000

Hospice: Total NSF of Residential Spaces: 17000

Hospice			
Unit type	Number of units	Size range (NSF)	Typical size (NSF)
Private room*	34	360–380	375
Total (all units)	34		

*Single occupant

Project costs, actual (or estimated, if the project has yet to be built)

Hospice: Total Construction cost for Renovation/Modernization ($): 3000000

Hospice: FF&E costs for Renovation/Modernization ($): 400000

Hospice: Site development costs for Renovation/Modernization ($): 500000

Hospice: Soft costs for Renovation/Modernization ($): 300000

Project Funding Sources

Other Funding Source %: 100

Occupancy

Hospice occupancy date: 10 2009

Hospice occupancy at opening (%): 100

Hospice current occupancy (%): 100

Landis Homes: Hybrid Homes

Client/Owner: Landis Homes Retirement Community

Architect & Interiors: RLPS Architects

Contractor: Benchmark Construction

Civil Engineer: RGS Associates

MEP Engineer: Reese Engineering

Structural Engineer: Zug Associates

Photography: Larry Lefever Photography

Building Data
Independent Living: Total Building GSF: 72682
Independent Living: Total NSF of Common Spaces: 3288
Independent Living: Total NSF of Residential Spaces: 34440

Independent Living			
Unit type	Number of units	Size range (NSF)	Typical size (NSF)
One-bedroom	1	875	875
One-bedroom plus den	8	1315	1315
Two-bedroom	8	1370	1370
Two-bedroom plus den	8	1620	1620
Total (all units)	25		

Accessible Independent Living Units (%): 100

Project costs, actual (or estimated, if the project has yet to be built)
Independent Living: FF&E costs for New Construction ($): 90000
Independent Living: Site development costs for New Construction ($): 1550000
Independent Living: Soft costs for New Construction ($): 1147000

Project Funding Sources
Non-Taxable Bond Offering Funding %: 100

Gender breakdown of the residents
Men %: 27
Women %: 73

Status of the residents
Living with family/friend (%): 13
Married/domestic partner (%): 54
Single (%): 33

Source of resident payments
Private payment (%): 100

Average age
Independent Living: Average age designed to support: 75
Independent Living: Average entry age: 76
Independent Living: Average current age: 77

Occupancy
Independent Living occupancy date: 10 2010
Independent Living occupancy at opening (%): 33
Independent Living current occupancy (%): 45

Leonard Florence Center for Living:
New 100-bed Skilled Nursing Green House ®

Client/Owner: Chelsea Jewish Foundation

Architect: DiMella Shaffer

Contractor: Erland Construction

MEP/FP Engineering: R.W. Sullivan

Structural Engineering: L.A. Fuess

Civil Engineering: Nitsch Engineering

Landscape Architects: Leonard Design

Communications, Security, Nurse Call and Audio Visual: CCR Pyramid

Food Service: Crabtree McGrath

Lighting: Conceptual Lighting

Building Data
Hospice: Total NSF of Residential Spaces: 6000
Long-Term Skilled Nursing: Total Building GSF: 94442
Long-Term Skilled Nursing: Total NSF of Common Spaces: 19500
Long-Term Skilled Nursing: Total NSF of Residential Spaces: 36000
Short-Term Rehab: Total NSF of Residential Spaces: 18000

Long-Term Skilled Nursing			
Unit type	Number of units	Size range (NSF)	Typical size (NSF)
Private room*	60	232–341	253
Total (all units)	60		

*Single occupant

Short-Term Rehab			
Unit type	Number of units	Size range (NSF)	Typical size (NSF)
Private room*	30	232–288	245
Total (all units)	30		

*Single occupant

Hospice			
Unit type	Number of units	Size range (NSF)	Typical size (NSF)
Private room*	10	232–288	245
Total (all units)	10		

*Single occupant

Project costs, actual (or estimated, if the project has yet to be built)
Long-Term Skilled Nursing: Total cost for New Construction ($): 23064000
Long-Term Skilled Nursing: FF&E costs for New Construction ($): 1400000
Long-Term Skilled Nursing: Site development costs for New Construction ($): 1950000
Long-Term Skilled Nursing: Soft costs for New Construction ($): 6500000

Project Funding Sources
Conventional/Private Funding %: 30
Public-Private Sector Funding %: 70

Gender breakdown of the residents
Men %: 35
Women %: 65

Status of the residents

Married/domestic partner (%): 28
Single (%): 72

Source of resident payments

Medicaid/Medicare payment (%): 62
Private payment (%): 38

Average age of residents

Hospice: Average age designed to support: 85
Hospice: Average entry age: 79
Hospice: Average current age: 77
Long-Term Skilled Nursing: Average age designed to support: 65
Long-Term Skilled Nursing: Average entry age: 78
Long-Term Skilled Nursing: Average current age: 75
Short-Term Rehab: Average age designed to support: 73
Short-Term Rehab: Average entry age: 80
Short-Term Rehab: Average current age: 79

Occupancy

Short-Term Rehab occupancy date: 03 2010
Short-Term Rehab current occupancy (%): 100
Hospice occupancy date: 09 2010
Hospice current occupancy (%): 100
Long-Term Skilled Nursing occupancy date: 02 2010
Long-Term Skilled Nursing occupancy at opening (%): 8
Long-Term Skilled Nursing current occupancy (%): 100

Longwood at Oakmont: Hanna Healthcare Center

Client/Owner: Presbyterian SeniorCare
Architect & Interiors: RLPS Architects
Contractor: Mistick Construction Company
Civil Engineer: The Gateway Engineers, Inc.
MEP Engineer: Reese Engineering, Inc.
Structural Engineer: Zug & Associates, Ltd.
Landscape: Victor-Wetzel Associates
Food Service: CURA Hospitality, Inc.
Construction Manager: BF Consulting
Photography: Larry Lefever Photography

Building Data

Skilled Nursing Dementia/Memory Support: Total NSF of Residential Spaces: 4985
Long-Term Skilled Nursing: Total Building GSF: 31706
Long-Term Skilled Nursing: Total NSF of Common Spaces: 6117
Long-Term Skilled Nursing: Total NSF of Residential Spaces: 8854
Short-Term Rehab: Total Building GSF: 10653
Short-Term Rehab: Total NSF of Common Spaces: 2657
Short-Term Rehab: Total NSF of Residential Spaces: 3950
Skilled Nursing Dementia/Memory Support: Total Building GSF: 15980
Skilled Nursing Dementia/Memory Support: Total NSF of Common Spaces: 2048

Long-Term Skilled Nursing			
Unit type	Number of units	Size range (NSF)	Typical size (NSF)
Private room*	24	323	323
Shared room**	4	551	551
Total (all units)	28		

*Single occupant
**Two occupants with separate bed areas but a shared bathroom

Short-Term Rehab			
Unit type	Number of units	Size range (NSF)	Typical size (NSF)
Private room*	10	242–427	242
Shared room**	2	545	545
Total (all units)	12		

*Single occupant
**Two occupants with separate bed areas but a shared bathroom

Skilled Nursing Dementia/Memory Support			
Unit type	Number of units	Size range (NSF)	Typical size (NSF)
Private room*	16	305–340	305
Total (all units)	16		

*Single occupant

Project costs, actual (or estimated, if the project has yet to be built)

Long-Term Skilled Nursing: Total Construction cost for Additions ($): 5072160
Long-Term Skilled Nursing: FF&E costs for Additions ($): 342058
Long-Term Skilled Nursing: Site development costs Additions ($): 539111
Long-Term Skilled Nursing: Soft costs for Additions ($): 1014500
Short-Term Rehab: Total Construction cost for Renovation/Modernization ($): 2113400
Short-Term Rehab: FF&E costs for Renovation/Modernization ($): 97731
Short-Term Rehab: Soft costs for Renovation/Modernization ($): 507250
Skilled Nursing Dementia/Memory Support: Total Construction cost for Renovation/Modernization ($): 1268040
Skilled Nursing Dementia/Memory Support: FF&E costs for Renovation/Modernization ($): 48866
Skilled Nursing Dementia/Memory Support: Soft costs for Renovation/Modernization ($): 507250

Project Funding Sources

Non-Taxable Bond Offering Funding %: 77
Other Funding Source %: 23

Gender breakdown of the residents

Men %: 21
Women %: 79

Status of the residents

Married/domestic partner (%): 18
Single (%): 82

Source of resident payments

Medicaid/Medicare payment (%): 14
Private payment (%): 14
Other payment source (%): 72
Life Care Contract

Average age of residents

Long-Term Skilled Nursing: Average age designed to support: 85
Long-Term Skilled Nursing: Average entry age: 90
Long-Term Skilled Nursing: Average current age: 90
Short-Term Rehab: Average age designed to support: 75
Short-Term Rehab: Average entry age: 85
Short-Term Rehab: Average current age: 87
Skilled Nursing Dementia/Memory Support: Average age designed to support: 85
Skilled Nursing Dementia/Memory Support: Average entry age: 88
Skilled Nursing Dementia/Memory Support: Average current age: 91

Occupancy

Long-Term Skilled Nursing occupancy date: 01 2009
Long-Term Skilled Nursing occupancy at opening (%): 100
Long-Term Skilled Nursing current occupancy (%): 100
Short-Term Rehab occupancy date: 09 2009
Short-Term Rehab occupancy at opening (%): 50
Short-Term Rehab current occupancy (%): 83
Skilled Nursing Dementia/Memory Support occupancy date: 10 2009
Skilled Nursing Dementia/Memory Support occupancy at opening (%): 93
Skilled Nursing Dementia/Memory Support current occupancy (%): 100

Mary's Meadow at Providence Place

Client/Owner: Sisters of Providence
Architect: EGA PC
Civil Engineer/Landscape: Berkshire Design Group
Specialty Landscape: Steve Roberts Landscape Architecture and Construction
Structural Engineer: Shelley Engineering Inc.
Mechanical/Plumbing Engineer: McGill Engineering
Electrical Engineer: Reno Engineering
Interior Design: Carangelo Commercial Interiors

Building Data

Long-Term Skilled Nursing: Total Building GSF: 22950
Long-Term Skilled Nursing: Total NSF of Common Spaces: 3850
Long-Term Skilled Nursing: Total NSF of Residential Spaces: 9000
Short-Term Rehab: Total Building GSF: 7650
Short-Term Rehab: Total NSF of Common Spaces: 1280
Short-Term Rehab: Total NSF of Residential Spaces: 3000

Long-Term Skilled Nursing			
Unit type	Number of units	Size range (NSF)	Typical size (NSF)
Private room*	30	300	300
Total (all units)	30		

*Single occupant

Short-Term Rehab			
Unit type	Number of units	Size range (NSF)	Typical size (NSF)
Private room*	10	300	300
Total (all units)	10		

*Single occupant

Project costs, actual (or estimated, if the project has yet to be built)

Long-Term Skilled Nursing: Total cost for New Construction ($): 8250000
Long-Term Skilled Nursing: FF&E costs for New Construction ($): 450000
Long-Term Skilled Nursing: Site development costs for New Construction ($): 1125000
Long-Term Skilled Nursing: Soft costs for New Construction ($): 1050000
Short-Term Rehab: Total cost for New Construction ($): 2750000
Short-Term Rehab: FF&E costs for New Construction ($): 150000
Short-Term Rehab: Site development costs for New Construction ($): 375000
Short-Term Rehab: Soft costs for New Construction ($): 350000

Project Funding Sources

Conventional/Private Funding %: 100

Gender breakdown of the residents

Men %: 20
Women %: 80

Status of the residents

Married/domestic partner (%): 25
Single (%): 75

Source of resident payments

Medicaid/Medicare payment (%): 72
Private payment (%): 26
Other payment source (%): 2
Religious order endowment.

Average age of residents

Long-Term Skilled Nursing: Average age designed to support: 90
Long-Term Skilled Nursing: Average entry age: 87
Long-Term Skilled Nursing: Average current age: 88
Short-Term Rehab: Average age designed to support: 75
Short-Term Rehab: Average entry age: 70
Short-Term Rehab: Average current age: 70

Occupancy

Long-Term Skilled Nursing occupancy date: 08 2009
Long-Term Skilled Nursing occupancy at opening (%): 33
Long-Term Skilled Nursing current occupancy (%): 96
Short-Term Rehab occupancy date: 10 2009
Short-Term Rehab occupancy at opening (%): 100
Short-Term Rehab current occupancy (%): 95

Moldaw Family Residences, at the Taube-Koret Campus for Jewish Life

Client/Owner: Moldaw Family Residences, at the Taube-Koret Campus for Jewish Life

Architect: Steinberg Architects

Planning Research Design for Aging: Innovage

Project Manager: Sares Regis Development

General Contractor: Webcor Builders

Structural Engineering: Forell/Elsesser Engineers

Civil Engineer: BKF Engineers, Surveyors, Planners

Mechanical/Plumbing Engineer: ACCO Engineered Systems

Electrical Engineer: Cupertino Electric, Inc.

Landscape Architecture: Conger Moss Guillard

Building Data

Independent Living: Total NSF of Common Spaces: 54486

Independent Living: Total NSF of Residential Spaces: 164812

Assisted Living: Total NSF of Common Spaces: 1424

Assisted Living: Total NSF of Residential Spaces: 7800

Assisted Living Dementia/Memory Support: Total NSF of Common Spaces: 707

Assisted Living Dementia/Memory Support: Total NSF of Residential Spaces: 3388

Independent Living			
Unit type	Number of units	Size range (NSF)	Typical size (NSF)
One-bedroom	42	568–861	733
One-bedroom plus den	32	894–900	897
Two-bedroom	84	835–1056	1004
Three-bedroom+	12	1509	1509
Total (all units)	170		

Accessible Independent Living Units (%): 100

Assisted Living			
Unit type	Number of units	Size range (NSF)	Typical size (NSF)
Private room*	12	621–679	650
Total (all units)	12		

*Single occupant

Accessible Assisted Living Units (%): 100

Assisted Living Dementia/Memory Support			
Unit type	Number of units	Size range (NSF)	Typical size (NSF)
Private room*	11	310	310
Total (all units)	11		

*Single occupant

Project costs, actual (or estimated, if the project has yet to be built)

Other Medical Services Care Facility: Total Construction cost for Renovation/Modernization ($): 178000000

Other Medical Services Care Facility: Total cost for New Construction ($): 178000000

Other Medical Services Care Facility: FF&E costs for New Construction ($): 9000000

Other Medical Services Care Facility: FF&E costs for Renovation/Modernization ($): 9000000

Other Medical Services Care Facility: Site development costs for New Construction ($): 178000000

Other Medical Services Care Facility: Site development costs for Renovation/Modernization ($): 178000000

Other Medical Services Care Facility: Soft costs for New Construction ($): 30000000

Other Medical Services Care Facility: Soft costs for Renovation/Modernization ($): 30000000

Project Funding Sources

Non-Taxable Bond Offering Funding %: 100

Gender breakdown of the residents

Men %: 15

Women %: 85

Status of the residents

Married/domestic partner (%): 22

Single (%): 78

Source of resident payments

Private payment (%): 87

Other payment source (%): 13

Below market rate = 24 units = 13%

Average age of residents

Assisted Living: Average age designed to support: 90

Assisted Living: Average entry age: 86

Assisted Living: Average current age: 87

Independent Living: Average age designed to support: 90

Independent Living: Average entry age: 80

Independent Living: Average current age: 83

Occupancy

Independent Living occupancy date: 12 2009

Independent Living current occupancy (%): 95

Assisted Living current occupancy (%): 90

Assisted Living Dementia/Memory Support current occupancy (%): 80

Read Cloister Nursing Community Transformations

Client/Owner: Bishop Gadsden Retirement Community

Architect: Cummings & McCrady, Inc.

Interior designers: GMK Associates, Inc.

Food equipment designers: FRS

Mechanical and plumbing engineers: MECA

Electrical engineers: Epic Engineering, Inc.

Contractors: Liberty Construction Co.

Building Data
Long-Term Skilled Nursing: Total Building GSF: 35409
Long-Term Skilled Nursing: Total NSF of Common Spaces: 6650
Long-Term Skilled Nursing: Total NSF of Residential Spaces: 13782

Project costs, actual (or estimated, if the project has yet to be built)
Long-Term Skilled Nursing: Total Construction cost for Renovation/Modernization ($): 516936
Long-Term Skilled Nursing: FF&E costs for Renovation/Modernization ($): 257756
Long-Term Skilled Nursing: Soft costs for Renovation/Modernization ($): 48802

Project Funding Sources
Conventional/Private Funding %: 100

Gender breakdown of the residents
Men %: 26
Women %: 74

Status of the residents
Married/domestic partner (%): 21
Single (%): 79

Source of resident payments
Private payment (%): 100

Average Age of Residents
Long-Term Skilled Nursing: Average age designed to support: 89
Long-Term Skilled Nursing: Average current age: 90

Occupancy
Long-Term Skilled Nursing occupancy date: 01 1992
Long-Term Skilled Nursing current occupancy (%): 95

Saint John's on the Lake

Client/Owner: Saint John's Communities

Architect: Perkins Eastman

Associate Architect: Continuum Architects + Planners, S.C.

Civil: Graef

Structural: Graef

MEP: IBC Engineering Services, Inc.

Landscape Architect: Hitchcock Design Group

Food Service Consultant: Scopos Hospitality Group

Pool Consultant: Water Technologies, Inc.

Low Voltage Consultant: Arnold and O'Sheridan, Inc.

Surveying Consultant: National Surveying and Engineering

Owner's Representative: Witz Company

General Contractor: VJS Construction Services

Marketing Consultant: Spectrum

Building Data
Independent Living: Total Building GSF: 289588
Independent Living: Total NSF of Common Spaces: 85698
Independent Living: Total NSF of Residential Spaces: 146777

Independent Living			
Unit type	Number of units	Size range (NSF)	Typical size (NSF)
One-bedroom	1	1092	1092
One-bedroom plus den	13	1135-2430	1140
Two-bedroom	41	1325	1325
Two-bedroom plus den	31	1395-2460	1630
Three-bedroom+	1	2285	2285
Total (all units)	87		

Accessible Independent Living Units (%): 1
Adaptable Independent Living Units (%): 99

Project costs, actual (or estimated, if the project has yet to be built)
Independent Living: Total cost for New Construction ($): 41247000
Independent Living: FF&E costs for New Construction ($): 720000
Independent Living: Site development costs for New Construction ($): 1750000
Wellness/Fitness Center: Total cost for New Construction ($): 1640000
Wellness/Fitness Center: FF&E costs for New Construction ($): 70000

Project Funding Sources
Non-Taxable Bond Offering Funding %: 100

Gender breakdown of the residents
Men %: 43
Women %: 57

Status of the residents
Married/domestic partner (%): 69
Single (%): 31

Source of resident payments

Private payment (%): 100

Age of residents

Independent Living: Average age designed to support: 80

Independent Living: Average entry age: 78

Independent Living: Average current age: 78

Occupancy

Independent Living occupancy date: 07 2011

Independent Living current occupancy (%): 80

South Franklin Circle

Client/Owner: Judson Services, Inc.

Architect: GUND Partnership

Contractor: The Albert M. Higley Company

MEP Engineer: Karpinski Engineering

Civil Engineer: BSC Group, Inc.

Structural Engineer: Barber & Hoffman, Inc.

Interior Design Consultant: Stefura Associates

Lighting Consultant: Ripman Lighting Consultants

Acoustical Consultant: Acentech Incorporated

Landscape Architect: Oehme, van Sweden & Associates

Building Data

Assisted Living Dementia/Memory Support: Total Building GSF: 44180

Independent Living: Total Building GSF: 358272

Independent Living			
Unit type	Number of units	Size range (NSF)	Typical size (NSF)
One-bedroom	12	927-1202	927
One-bedroom plus den	31	1079	1079
Two-bedroom plus den	89	1433-2015	1433
Three-bedroom+	11	2021-2660	2985
Townhome	13	2604-2985	2771
Cottage/Duplex	43	2159-2250	2159
Total (all units)	199		

Adaptable Independent Living Units (%): 100

Assisted Living Dementia/Memory Support			
Unit type	Number of units	Size range (NSF)	Typical size (NSF)
Private room*	40	369–531	517
Total (all units)	40		

*Single occupant

Project costs, actual (or estimated, if the project has yet to be built)

Independent Living: Total cost for New Construction ($): 105000

Independent Living: FF&E costs for New Construction ($): 29000

Independent Living: Site development costs for New Construction ($): 9000000

Independent Living: Soft costs for New Construction ($): 6000000

Project Funding Sources

Conventional/Private Funding %: 100

Occupancy

Assisted Living Dementia/Memory Support occupancy date: 01 2010

Assisted Living Dementia/Memory Support current occupancy (%): 15

Independent Living occupancy date: 10 2009

Independent Living occupancy at opening (%): 50

Independent Living current occupancy (%): 50

Senior Community Center occupancy date: 10 2009

Wellness/Fitness Center occupancy date: 10 2009

The Boulders and The Ridge at RiverWoods

Client/Owner: RiverWoods at Exeter

Architect: JSA Inc

Structural Engineers: JSN Associates

MEP: RDK Engineers

Civil: Altus Engineering

Landscape Architecture: Stantec

Interior Design: Bridget Bohacz & Associates

Food Service: Crabtree McGrath Associates, Inc.

Contractor: LeCesse Construction (Construction Managers)

Building Data

Assisted Living: Total Building GSF: 71000

Assisted Living: Total NSF of Common Spaces: 18500

Assisted Living: Total NSF of Residential Spaces: 28000

Independent Living: Total Building GSF: 457250

Independent Living: Total NSF of Common Spaces: 67000

Independent Living: Total NSF of Residential Spaces: 256000

Long-Term Skilled Nursing: Total Building GSF: 23300

Long-Term Skilled Nursing: Total NSF of Common Spaces: 9000

Long-Term Skilled Nursing: Total NSF of Residential Spaces: 8500

Skilled Nursing Dementia/Memory Support: 6800

Skilled Nursing Dementia/Memory Support: 1000

Skilled Nursing Dementia/Memory Support: 2100

Independent Living

Unit type	Number of units	Size range (NSF)	Typical size (NSF)
One-bedroom	36	800–930	850
Two-bedroom plus den	15	1050–1050	1050
Two-bedroom	106	1210–1440	1350
Total (all units)	157		

Accessible Independent Living Units %: 2
Adaptable Independent Living Units %: 98

Assisted Living

Unit type	Number of units	Size range (NSF)	Typical size (NSF)
One-bedroom	47	525–530	530
Two-bedroom	4	768–837	795
Total (all units)	51		

Accessible Assisted Living Units %: 26
Adaptable Assisted Living Units %: 74

Long-Term Skilled Nursing

Unit type	Number of units	Size range (NSF)	Typical size (NSF)
Private room*	31	260–290	275
Total (all units)	31		

*Single occupant

Skilled Nursing Dementia/Memory Support

Unit type	Number of units	Size range (NSF)	Typical size (NSF)
Private room*	8	260	260
Total (all units)	8		

*Single occupant

Project costs, actual (or estimated, if the project has yet to be built)
Assisted Living: Total cost for New Construction ($): 10030000
Assisted Living: FF&E costs for New Construction ($): 254000
Assisted Living: Site development costs for New Construction ($): 1689100
Assisted Living: Soft costs for New Construction ($): 4076700
Independent Living: Total cost for New Construction ($): 63200000
Independent Living: FF&E costs for New Construction ($): 1600000
Independent Living: Site development costs for New Construction ($): 10640000
Independent Living: Soft costs for New Construction ($): 25660000
Long-Term Skilled Nursing: Total cost for New Construction ($): 3318000
Long-Term Skilled Nursing: FF&E costs for New Construction ($): 84000
Long-Term Skilled Nursing: Site development costs for New Construction ($): 558600
Long-Term Skilled Nursing: Soft costs for New Construction ($): 1348200
Skilled Nursing Dementia/Memory Support: Total cost for New Construction ($): 948000
Skilled Nursing Dementia/Memory Support: FF&E costs for New Construction ($): 24000
Skilled Nursing Dementia/Memory Support: Site development costs for New Construction ($): 159600
Skilled Nursing Dementia/Memory Support: Soft costs for New Construction ($): 385200
Wellness/Fitness Center: Total cost for New Construction ($): 1501000
Wellness/Fitness Center: FF&E costs for New Construction ($): 38000
Wellness/Fitness Center: Site development costs for New Construction ($): 252700
Wellness/Fitness Center: Soft costs for New Construction ($): 609900

Project Funding Sources
Non-Taxable Bond Offering Funding %: 100

Gender breakdown of the residents
Men %: 39
Women %: 61

Status of the residents
Married/domestic partner (%): 30
Single (%): 70

Source of resident payments
Medicaid/Medicare payment (%): 3
Private payment (%): 97

Average age of residents
Assisted Living: Average age designed to support: 80
Assisted Living: Average entry age: 84
Assisted Living: Average current age: 86
Independent Living: Average age designed to support: 70
Independent Living: Average entry age: 80
Independent Living: Average current age: 82
Long-Term Skilled Nursing: Average age designed to support: 80
Long-Term Skilled Nursing: Average entry age: 84
Long-Term Skilled Nursing: Average current age: 86
Skilled Nursing Dementia/Memory Support: Average age designed to support: 80
Skilled Nursing Dementia/Memory Support: Average entry age: 84
Skilled Nursing Dementia/Memory Support: Average current age: 86

Occupancy
Assisted Living occupancy date: 06 2010
Assisted Living current occupancy (%): 70
Independent Living occupancy date: 03 2010
Independent Living current occupancy (%): 93
Long-Term Skilled Nursing occupancy date: 06 2010
Long-Term Skilled Nursing current occupancy (%): 62
Wellness/Fitness Center occupancy date: 03 2010

The Houses on Bayberry: Arbor Acres United Methodist Retirement Community

Client/Owner: Arbor Acres United Methodist Retirement Community
Architect: RLPS Architects
General Contractor: I.L Long Construction Co.
MEP Engineer: Reese Engineering, Inc.
Civil Engineer: Allied Civil Engineering
Landscape Architect: Weyker & Associates
Photography: Larry Lefever Photography

Building Data
Independent Living: Total Building GSF: 18992
Independent Living: Total NSF of Residential Spaces: 9076

Independent Living

Unit type	Number of units	Size range (NSF)	Typical size (NSF)
One-bedroom plus den	4	1082	1082
Two-bedroom	4	1187	1187
Total (all units)	8		

Adaptable Independent Living Units (%): 100

Project costs, actual (or estimated, if the project has yet to be built)
Independent Living: Total cost for New Construction ($): 1302284
Independent Living: FF&E costs for New Construction ($): 31176
Independent Living: Site development costs for New Construction ($): 185403
Independent Living: Soft costs for New Construction ($): 195343

Project Funding Source
Conventional/Private Funding %: 100

Gender breakdown of the residents
Men %: 28
Women %: 72

Status of the residents
Married/domestic partner (%): 41
Single (%): 59

Source of resident payments
Private payment (%): 100

Average age of residents
Independent Living: Average age designed to support: 65
Independent Living: Average entry age: 72
Independent Living: Average current age: 73

Occupancy
Independent Living occupancy date: 01 2010
Independent Living occupancy at opening (%): 88
Independent Living current occupancy (%): 100

Jewish Home Lifecare

Client/Owner: Jewish Home Lifecare
Architect: Perkins Eastman
Contractor: TBD
Interior designer: Perkins Eastman
Landscape architect: Dirtworks, Inc.
Structural engineer: GACE Consulting Engineers
Mechanical engineer: Laszlo Bodak Engineer, PC
Electrical engineer: Laszlo Bodak Engineer, PC
Civil engineer: Stantec Inc.
Food Service: Food Facilities Concepts, Inc.

Low Voltage: ART Engineering Corporation
Exterior Envelope: Israel Berger & Associates, LLC
Elevator Consultant: Lerch, Bates & Associates, Inc.

Building Data
Long-Term Skilled Nursing: Total Building GSF: 224916
Long-Term Skilled Nursing: Total NSF of Common Spaces: 83534
Long-Term Skilled Nursing: Total NSF of Residential Spaces: 76344
Short-Term Rehab: Total Building GSF: 77168
Short-Term Rehab: Total NSF of Common Spaces: 43033
Short-Term Rehab: Total NSF of Residential Spaces: 31296

Long-Term Skilled Nursing

Unit type	Number of units	Size range (NSF)	Typical size (NSF)
Private room*	288	251–272	251
Total (all units)	288		

*Single occupant

Short-Term Rehab

Unit type	Number of units	Size range (NSF)	Typical size (NSF)
Private room*	80	251–255	251
Semi-private room**	40	435–471	471
Total (all units)	120		

*Single occupant
**Two occupants with separate bed areas but a shared bathroom

Project costs, actual (or estimated, if the project has yet to be built)
Long-Term Skilled Nursing: Total cost for New Construction ($): 123000000
Long-Term Skilled Nursing: FF&E costs for New Construction ($): 6600000
Long-Term Skilled Nursing: Site development costs for New Construction ($): 2000000
Long-Term Skilled Nursing: Soft costs for New Construction ($): 8600000
Short-Term Rehab: Total cost for New Construction ($): 64000000
Short-Term Rehab: FF&E costs for New Construction ($): 3300000
Short-Term Rehab: Site development costs for New Construction ($): 1000000
Short-Term Rehab: Soft costs for New Construction ($): 5400000

Project Funding Sources
Conventional/Private Funding %: 15
Non-Taxable Bond Offering Funding %: 85

Occupancy
Long-Term Skilled Nursing occupancy date: 01 2015
Short-Term Rehab occupancy date: 01 2015

Willson Hospice House

Client/Owner: Phoebe Putney Memorial Hospital / Albany Community Hospice

Architect: Perkins+Will

Planning, Architecture, Interior Design, & Landscape Architecture: Perkins+Will Atlanta

Structural Engineering: Uzun & Case

Civil Engineering: Lanier Engineering, Inc.

Mechanical Engineering: Cornelius Engineering

Electrical Engineering: Spencer Bristol Engineering

Plumbing & Life Safety Engineering: Covalent Consulting, LLC

LEED Commissioning: Energy Ace, Inc.

Program Management: KLMK Group, Inc.

Building Data
Hospice: Total Building GSF: 34000
Hospice: Total NSF of Common Spaces: 5887
Hospice: Total NSF of Residential Spaces: 5805

Hospice			
Unit type	Number of units	Size range (NSF)	Typical size (NSF)
Private room*	18	318 - 345	318
Total (all units)	18		

*Single occupant

Project costs, actual (or estimated, if the project has yet to be built)
Hospice: Total cost for New Construction ($): 8860000
Hospice: FF&E costs for New Construction ($): 1366250
Hospice: Site development costs for New Construction ($): 1365000
Hospice: Soft costs for New Construction ($): 1957500

Project Funding Sources
Conventional/Private Funding %: 44
Other Funding Source %: 56

Gender breakdown of the residents
Men %: 40
Women %: 60

Status of the residents
Single (%): 100

Source of resident payments
Medicaid/Medicare payment (%): 95
Private payment (%): 5

Average age of residents
Hospice: Average age designed to support: 75
Hospice: Average entry age: 77
Hospice: Average current age: 77

Occupancy
Hospice occupancy date: 07 2010
Hospice occupancy at opening (%): 22
Hospice current occupancy (%): 67

Sun City Palace Showa Kinen Koen

Owner / Administrator: Half Century More (Tokyo, Japan)

Design Architect: BAR Architects (San Francisco, CA)

Architect of Record: Ken Asai Architectural Research (Tokyo, Japan)

Landscape Architect: SWA Group (Sausalito, CA)

Interior Designer for Independent Living: BAMO (San Francisco, CA)

Interior Designer for Nursing Care: Yokomizo Associates (San Francisco, CA)

Structural, Mechanical, Electrical, Civil Engineer: Ken Asai Architectural Research

Building Data
Independent Living: Total Building GSF: 550000
Independent Living: Total NSF of Common Spaces: 81000
Independent Living: Total NSF of Residential Spaces: 330000
Short-Term Rehab: Total NSF of Residential Spaces: 139000

Independent Living			
Unit type	Number of units	Size range (NSF)	Typical size (NSF)
One-bedroom	405	450–600	530
Two-bedroom	113	600–890	750
Three-bedroom+	19	890–990	930
Total (all units)	537		

Accessible Independent Living Units (%): 100

Short-Term Rehab			
Unit type	Number of units	Size range (NSF)	Typical size (NSF)
Private room*	108	200–240	215
Total (all units)	108		

*Single occupant

Project costs, actual (or estimated, if the project has yet to be built)
Independent Living: Total cost for New Construction ($): 123000000
Independent Living: FF&E costs for New Construction ($): 6500000
Independent Living: Site development costs for New Construction ($): 6300000
Independent Living: Soft costs for New Construction ($): 13000000
Long-Term Skilled Nursing: FF&E costs for New Construction ($): 1500000
Short-Term Rehab: FF&E costs for New Construction ($): 38000

Project Funding Sources
Conventional/Private Funding %: 100

Gender breakdown of the residents
Men %: 34
Women %: 66

Status of the residents
Married/domestic partner (%): 40
Single (%): 60

Source of resident payments
Private payment (%): 100

Average age of residents
Independent Living: Average age designed to support: 72
Independent Living: Average entry age: 70
Short-Term Rehab: Average age designed to support: 80
Short-Term Rehab: Average entry age: 78

The Mather South

Client/Owner: Mather LifeWays
Architect: Solomon Cordwell Buenz
MEP: Affiliated Engineers (AEI)
Civil: Spaceco
Structural: Halvorson
Landscape: Dan Weinbach
Interior Design: IDA
Food Service: Robert Pacifico
Acoustics: Shiner
Pool: Innovative Aquatic Design (IAD)
LEED Consultant: Sieben Energy

Building Data
Independent Living: Total Building GSF: 204068
Independent Living: Total NSF of Common Spaces: 38796
Independent Living: Total NSF of Residential Spaces: 130975

Independent Living			
Unit type	Number of units	Size range (NSF)	Typical size (NSF)
One-bedroom	28	890-1152	986
One-bedroom plus den	8	1190	1190
Two-bedroom	27	1188-1309	1256
Two-bedroom plus den	36	1458-1989	1669
Total (all units)	99		

Adaptable Independent Living Units (%): 100

Project costs, actual (or estimated, if the project has yet to be built)
Independent Living: Total cost for New Construction ($): 56366080
Independent Living: FF&E costs for New Construction ($): 195000
Independent Living: Site development costs for New Construction ($): 684767
Independent Living: Soft costs for New Construction ($): 17000000
Wellness/Fitness Center: Soft costs for New Construction ($): 1000000

Project Funding Sources
Conventional/Private Funding %: 97
Other Funding Source %: 3

The Townhomes on Hendricks Place

Client/Owner: Moravian Manor
Architect: RLPS Architects
Contractor: Simeral Construction Company
Civil Engineer: RGS Associates
Structural Engineer: Zug Associates
Mechanical: Reese Engineering
Electrical: Reese Engineering

Building Data
Independent Living: Total Building GSF: 42584
Independent Living: Total NSF of Residential Spaces: 36445

Independent Living			
Unit type	Number of units	Size range (NSF)	Typical size (NSF)
Two-bedroom plus den	12	2609–2833	2833
Total (all units)	12		

Adaptable Independent Living Units (%): 100

Project costs, actual (or estimated, if the project has yet to be built)
Independent Living: Total cost for New Construction ($): 4700000
Independent Living: Site development costs for New Construction ($): 750000
Independent Living: Soft costs for New Construction ($): 570000

Project Funding Sources
Conventional/Private Funding %: 100

Average age of residents
Independent Living: Average age designed to support: 65

Occupancy
Independent Living occupancy date: 06 2012

Project Data
IAHSA Projects

Belong Wigan Care Village

Project Capacity and Numbers of Units

	Units, Beds, Clients, or Daily Visits
Independent living apartments (units)	54
Special care for persons with dementia	66
Skilled nursing care (beds)	66 (same beds)
Kitchen (daily meals served)	66 meals from 6 household kitchens. Main kitchen serves the main bistro 7 days per week.
Elder day care (clients)	3
Elder outreach (clients)	7
Fitness/rehab/wellness (daily visits)	12
Other	All 6 household units (66 rooms) are designed to accommodate for the needs of the person with dementia. The registration category enables us to support up to 67 people with dementia and nursing care to include a guest room.

Breakdown of Independent Living Units

Unit type	Number of Units	Typical Size per Unit
One bedroom units	35	50–53 square meters
Two bedroom units	19	61–71 square meters

Breakdown of Dementia Special Care Units

Unit type	Number of Units	Typical Size per Unit
Studio/bed-sit units	66 plus 1 guest room	18–23 square meters

Breakdown of Skilled Nursing Care Units

Unit type	Number of Units	Typical Size per Unit
One bed/single occupancy rooms	66 as above	

The Pines Lodge

Project Capacity and Numbers of Units

	Units, Beds, Clients, or Daily Visits
Assisted living/hostel care (units)	80
Special care for persons with dementia	64
Kitchen (daily meals served)	432

Breakdown of Assisted Living/Hostel Care Units

Unit type	Number of Units	Typical Size per Unit
One bedroom units	80	31 square meters

Breakdown of Dementia Special Care Units

Unit type	Number of Units	Typical Size per Unit
One bedroom units	64	27 square meters

The Royal Star & Garter Home, Solihull

Project Capacity and Numbers of Units

	Units, Beds, Clients, or Daily Visits
Special care for persons with dementia	15
Skilled nursing care (beds)	45
Kitchen (daily meals served)	60
Other	activity room, therapy suite, library/IT room, bar & cafe

Breakdown of Dementia Special Care Units

Unit type	Number of Units	Typical Size per Unit
Studio/bed-sit units	15	26.5 square meters

Breakdown of Skilled Nursing Care Units

Unit type	Number of Units	Typical Size per Unit
One bed/single occupancy rooms	45	26.5 square meters

Sandford Station Care Village

Project Capacity and Numbers of Units

	Units, Beds, Clients, or Daily Visits
Independent living apartments (units)	101
Independent living cottages/villas (units)	7
Special care for persons with dementia	71
Kitchen (daily meals served)	yes
Elder outreach (clients)	potentially
Fitness/rehab/wellness (daily visits)	physio on site
Pool(s) and related areas (daily visits)	pool and gym

Breakdown of Independent Living Units

Unit type	Number of Units	Typical Size per Unit
One bedroom units	31	49.8 square meters
Two bedroom units	47	64.4 square meters
Two bedroom plus units	30	97.6 square meters

Sunrise of Chorleywood

Project Capacity and Numbers of Units

	Units, Beds, Clients, or Daily Visits
Assisted living/hostel care (units)	65
Special care for persons with dementia	22
Kitchen (daily meals served)	yes
Fitness/rehab/wellness (daily visits)	yes
Pool(s) and related areas (daily visits)	yes
Other	The emphasis is on independence. However, there is a provision of activity areas and well landscaped gardens, including sensory gardens and resident gardens.

Breakdown of Assisted Living Units

Unit type	Number of Units	Typical Size per Unit
Studio/bed-sit units	11	40 square meters
One bedroom units	38	28 square meters
Two bedroom units	15	49 square meters

Breakdown of Dementia Special Care Units

Unit type	Number of Units	Typical Size per Unit
One bedroom units	13	28 square meters
Two bedroom units	9	49 square meters

The Wohl Building

Project Capacity and Numbers of Units

	Units, Beds, Clients, or Daily Visits
Special care for persons with dementia	40
Kitchen (daily meals served)	40

Breakdown of Dementia Special Care Units

Unit type	Number of Units	Typical Size per Unit
Studio/bed-sit units	40	20.7 square meters

Index of Architects

Index of Projects